ADAM LIAW

TONIGHT'S DINNER 2

Hardie Grant

BOOKS

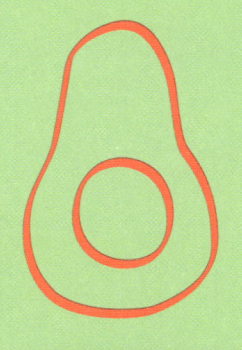

INTRODUCTION
6–9

INGENIOUS BREAKFASTS
10–31

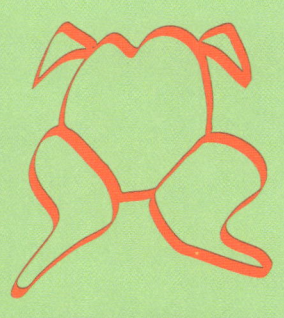

LIGHT FANTASTIC
32–55

FAMILY FAVOURITES
56–95

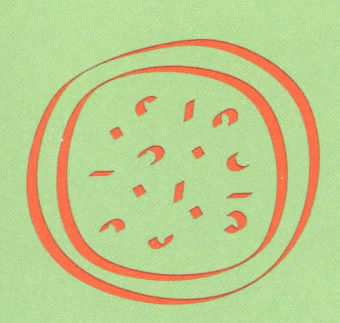

MEAT FREE
96–121

PIZZA & PASTA
122–151

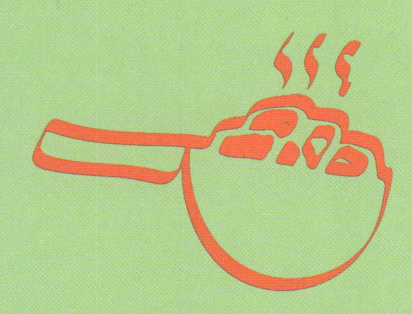

WOK
152–177

SWEET
178–203

A Day in the Life of *The Cook Up*	204
The Secret to Seasoning	208
Menu Planner	216
Index	218
About Adam	222
Thank You	223

Learning to cook a recipe from a book isn't a bad way to do it, but it can be a little easier if you have someone to cook along with. For *Tonight's Dinner 2*, I'm very proud that every recipe in this book has a video guide from *The Cook Up* you can consult to take you through the process.

You might see that some of the recipes are a little different to how they were cooked on the show. In those cases, I've made minor tweaks to make them tastier, healthier, or easier for you to cook at home.

Just scan the QR code or head to the URL below to watch, read and cook along with me.

sbs.com.au/ tonightsdinner

Cooking is important.

That's a simple statement, but one that I think is worth considering closely.

The way we live today, you could almost say that it isn't even true. After all, we can eat without cooking quite easily. Your phone probably has a few apps that get someone to bring you any of a thousand dishes within an hour, if your budget allows it.

Over the years, the proportion of our supermarkets devoted to ingredients has reduced to a fraction of what it once was. The aisles containing already-cooked food are more numerous than ever before, a trend that probably won't change anytime soon. Supermarkets and food manufacturers can make a lot more money by selling you a value-added product.

For much of human existence, cooking has been a necessity. If you're reading this book and have watched *The Cook Up*, you're likely in that relative minority of people in the world for whom many kinds of foods are readily available, and cooking could perhaps be considered optional. But if cooking is optional, there must be a reason for us to decide to do it at all.

That reason might be that you enjoy it. It might be that it's cheaper for you to do it yourself than to have that need met by a restaurant, supermarket or food corporation. It might be that the quality you can produce at home is higher than what that corporation would serve you in a packet. It might be that you want greater control over what and how you eat. Or it might be a combination of all the above plus more.

Your reasons for cooking are all your own. I cook, quite simply, because I think cooking is important. And I'm only now starting to understand just how important it truly is.

—

Cooking was a hobby of mine for many years, but I no longer consider it one. That's not to say that I don't enjoy cooking, because I really do (most of the time at least). It's just that now, the enjoyment I get from cooking sits far lower in the hierarchy of reasons for why I choose to do it.

I have always believed that the food we eat contains within it a great deal of information that we might otherwise struggle to understand.

The dish that will be tonight's dinner on your family's table took a very long route to get there, and I don't mean how long it took to make. It will get to your table as a result of tens of thousands of years of human decisions – some of those decisions were yours, some were your forebears, and many of them were made by total strangers who contributed to what is now a body of human wisdom.

Those decisions affected what crops to grow and how to grow them. They affected how we understand how our bodies work and what we need to eat to survive first, and thrive second. They affected how we structure our economies and societies.

If you want to be a nerd about it, a plate of Spaghetti bolognese (page 136) started its journey to your table even before the beginnings of agriculture, when our tastes guided what foods we foraged or hunted. It adapted over millennia of trial and error as humans had to learn what foods were good for us and what might kill us. (Even as recently as the 15th century, many people in Italy thought the tomatoes we use in bolognese were poisonous, with tomatoes only arriving around that time from the Americas.)

It would have adapted as we learned to domesticate and farm both plants and animals. It would have travelled from Italy around the world with waves of migration after the Second World War, and it would have only landed on your table after we developed the industries and systems that made those ingredients available to you at a reasonable price and at minimal effort, plucked easily from the shelves of your local supermarket.

My writing a recipe for it and you perhaps cooking it are just the very last steps in an extraordinarily long journey.

The thing is, while the story of any dish might contain within it the grandest story of all of human existence itself, it also contains something much more personal to you. It contains your own story, and it is being written every time you sit down at your table.

I've always believed this, but it's only recently that I've understood that our individual stories are told through food in ways that go to the very heart of human nature.

Our tastes define who we are, by our biology but also by the way we put context around the food we eat. As omnivores, humans need to learn about food to survive, and this ability to learn through food has become instinctive for us.

We learn about tastes even before we're born. Tastes from what a mother is eating can be passed to an unborn child, priming them with a knowledge of what to eat once they are born into any given environment. More tastes are passed in the mother's milk as that child begins to grow. And it doesn't stop there. As we go through life, we pick up the context and clues of the foods around us and it shapes our relationship with food the same way it shapes our relationship with people. Our relationships with food and people are often one and the same.

As just one example, none of us like coffee as children. If a child tastes coffee, its bitterness is immediately repulsive – a biological mechanism to warn children off something that might be poisonous. But over time, we see our parents drink it and we see that it's not poisonous. Perhaps we come to associate the aroma in the morning with our parents themselves. Then we try it socially, mixing it with the milk we've already come to love as kids. It becomes something we do with friends. Maybe we feel energised after drinking it. And after years of adding these little increments of context and experience to something we might have first hated, we've learnt to like it to a point where an espresso along with a slice of Single-malt cheesecake (page 203) is the stuff of dreams.

The same goes for vegetables. Children are highly sensitive to the bitterness that can be found in almost all vegetables, and biologically that's actually a good thing. If we were still hunter-gatherer nomads, we'd count on that sensitivity to keep us alive as we foraged all manner of fruits and vegetables.

When a child says they don't like their vegetables, it's firstly because their taste for bitterness is far more sensitive than ours as adults, and secondly it is because they just haven't had enough of those little increments of context needed to go from disliking vegetables to liking them. So next time your child won't eat the brussels sprouts in their Tempered roast vegetables (page 112), the best thing you can do is enjoy them yourself. Just like the coffee, after years of watching your positive experiences cooking, eating and enjoying the vegetable, your kids find themselves loving them, too.

I'm sure that like me, you can think of plenty of foods you hated as a kid but can't pinpoint the exact time you changed your mind about them. We learn about food every single day of our lives.

—

This is why I think cooking is important.

It gives us a chance to tell our own story, and that's as much a story about people as it is food.

I often think about the dishes that I grew up with, such as Chicken and leek (page 171) or Spring onion omelette (page 166) that my grandmother used to cook for me, or the Vietnamese 'pizzas' (page 52) that my dad showed me how to make, or the butter cookies my mum would share with me and that I've turned into cupcakes (page 198). While they're incredibly personal to me, I consider it a privilege that I get to share them with you.

But then I think about the dishes that my own children are growing up with, such as Japanese-style dry curry (page 68), the Perfect pancakes (page 30) we often make on a Sunday morning (quite honestly, you have to try these – they are truly perfect), or the Fireworks (page 159) or pizza nights (page 126) we have that they love, and I realise that the food I cook really isn't about me. Their experiences with food are very different to mine, and it's shaping their future, and improving the life we live together every day in a way that takeaway food dropped at our door every night or cooked at a supermarket and reheated at home never could.

I do want to stress, though, that I'm not judgemental about takeaway or convenience foods at all. Their convenience plays an important part in giving us control over our lives, and I have plenty of fond memories of eating fast food with my brothers and sisters. I just remind myself to be aware of the balance.

As fast and processed foods become more commoditised and more convenient, they will inevitably start to take up a bigger proportion of our lives than they once did. Do you get takeaway more often now than your family did when you were young?

We need to be aware that giving away the responsibility for our food in favour of convenience directly reduces the role we have in the food we eat. After all, we still only eat three meals a day.

The thing is, I want to be responsible for the food my family and I eat. I think it's important and I'm willing to work for it. I think that's far more important than staying at the office an extra hour.

—

That's part of why *The Cook Up* has been so popular. I always hoped it would be well received, but the level of affinity and affection people have shown for it is something that has gone well beyond what I ever could have imagined.

We celebrate every part of how we love food – from home cooks who come in for a chat to great chefs who take us out of our comfort zone – and yes, even processed foods and the shortcuts they can provide (such as putting potato gems on top of a shepherd's pie, page 81).

We try to show food as a conversation. A story. Not just a list of ingredients or a mechanical process to be followed.

Food is wonderful in the same way life is wonderful, and our experiences of food and people are inextricably linked. Through cooking we learn about life.

I hope you enjoy reading the recipes in this book, just as you've enjoyed watching them on *The Cook Up*. But more than that I hope you get up to your elbows actually making them in your kitchen because, as I said at the beginning …

Cooking is important.

NOTE This book uses 250 ml (8½ fl oz) cup measures and 20 ml (¾ fl oz) tablespoons. Oven temperatures are for conventional or fan-forced settings depending on the recipe. Fan-forced ovens are typically 20°C (70°F) hotter than conventional ovens.

Introduction // 9

/ˈbrɛkfəst/
noun
1. a meal eaten in the morning (but not always!)
2. the best way to start both your day and this book

INGENIOUS BREAKFASTS

Breakfast might well be the most important meal of the day. I don't necessarily mean that from a health perspective, but in terms of the role it plays in our lives.

Every food culture around the world has developed some kind of breakfast, to be eaten shortly after rising to prepare for the day ahead.

We eat breakfast together as a family every morning. It's a valuable time when we get to plan the day and spend time with each other.

But breakfast can also be an occasion. We're certainly not making Perfect pancakes (page 30) or Bloody Mary bacon & egg sandwiches (page 19) every Tuesday morning, but when we do it's often the start of a beautiful day.

Yemeni banana porridge

—

Serves 4
Prep 10 minutes
Cook 5 minutes

This simple breakfast porridge, called masoub in Yemen, is an excellent way to make use of both bananas past their best and any pieces of stale bread you have lying around.

6 ripe bananas

4 wholemeal pita, naan or stale bread slices (see Tip)

3 tablespoons butter

2 tablespoons honey, plus extra to serve

100 ml (3½ fl oz) pouring (single/light) cream, plus extra to serve

1 cup (180 g/6½ oz) pitted dates, chopped

¼ cup (30 g/1 oz) slivered almonds

Mash four of the bananas to a smooth mash. Using a food processor, grind the bread into fine breadcrumbs.

Combine the banana and breadcrumbs in a small saucepan with 2 tablespoons of the butter, and the honey and cream. Place over a medium heat and gently warm, stirring regularly, for about 5 minutes until the mixture forms a thick, warm pudding.

Slice the remaining bananas into 1 cm (½ in) rounds. Heat a small frying pan over a medium heat and add the remaining butter. Fry the banana slices for just a few minutes until golden brown.

Serve the porridge warm or at room temperature, topped with the fried bananas, dates, almonds and a little extra honey and cream.

TIP While usually made from stale pita from the night before, you can use any bread you like for this, or even a mix of different kinds. Blend whatever crusts or bits and pieces you have into the crumbs.

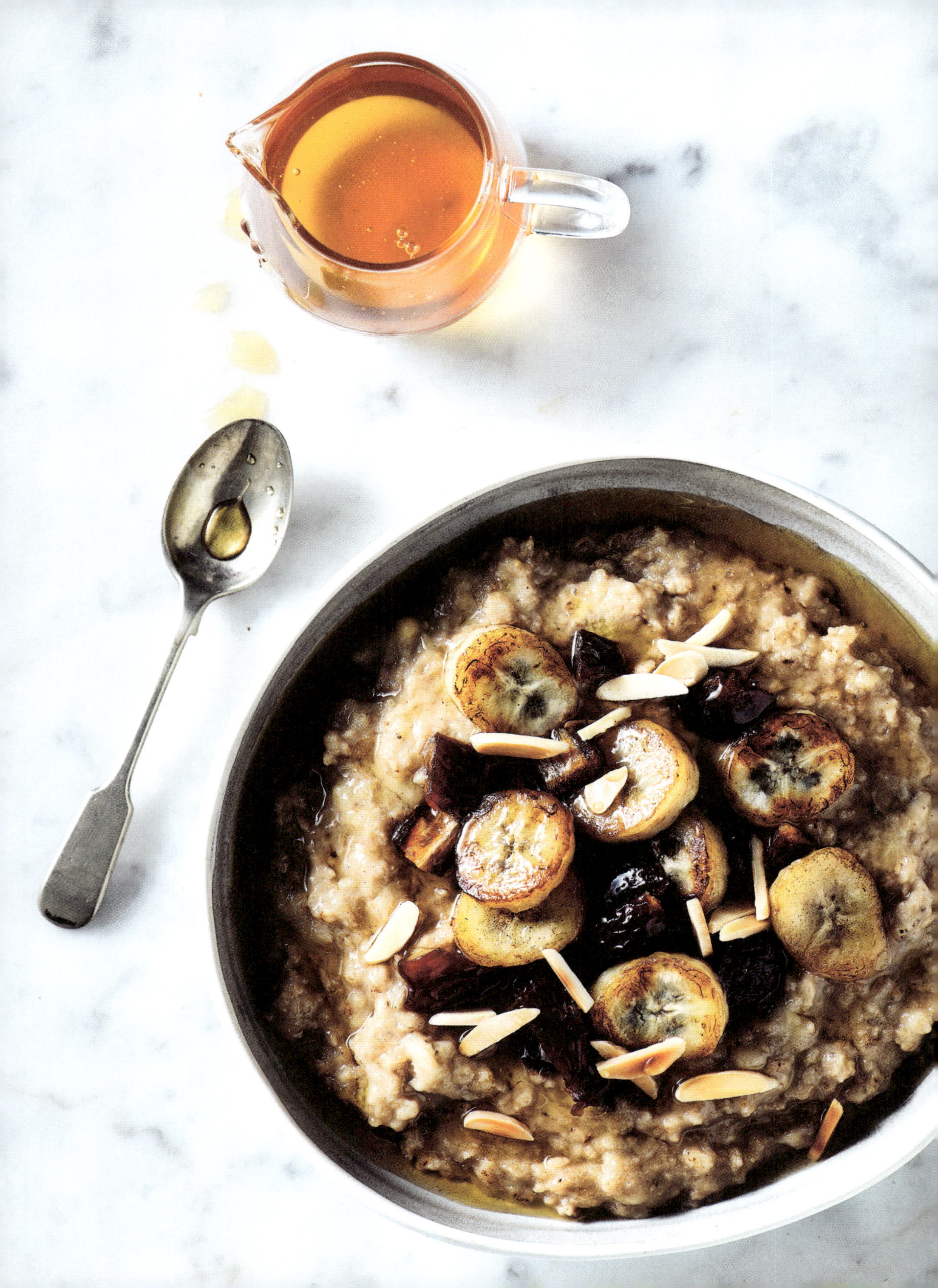

Chocolate peanut butter

—

Makes 1 cup
Prep 10 minutes

Peanut butter might not immediately jump to mind as something you should make at home, but it's very, very easy — and when you make it yourself, you know exactly what goes into it. Plus, you get to make variations, like this one.

2 cups (320 g/11½ oz) roasted unsalted peanuts, shelled and de-skinned

¼ teaspoon salt

1 tablespoon Dutch-process cocoa powder (see Tips)

1 tablespoon caster (superfine) sugar or honey

2 teaspoons vegetable oil (see Tips)

Place the peanuts and salt in a high-speed blender and blend for 5 minutes until you have a smooth paste. It will start off as peanuts, then become fine crumbs, then a dough — and then if you keep blending, the dough will break down to a 'butter'.

Add the cocoa, sugar and vegetable oil and blend to a very smooth butter.

Store your peanut butter in an airtight container at room temperature. It should keep in the pantry for months.

TIPS Dutch-process cocoa powder provides a richer, darker colour than ordinary cocoa powder, but you can use any cocoa powder you like.

I like to add a little vegetable oil to keep the peanut butter quite liquid, but if you prefer a chunkier and thicker peanut butter, just leave it out.

If you can afford one, a high-speed blender is a worthwhile investment. It will allow you to produce perfectly smooth soups, sauces, pastes and butters just like this one. You can still make this peanut butter in a regular blender or food processor, but it might not be quite as smooth.

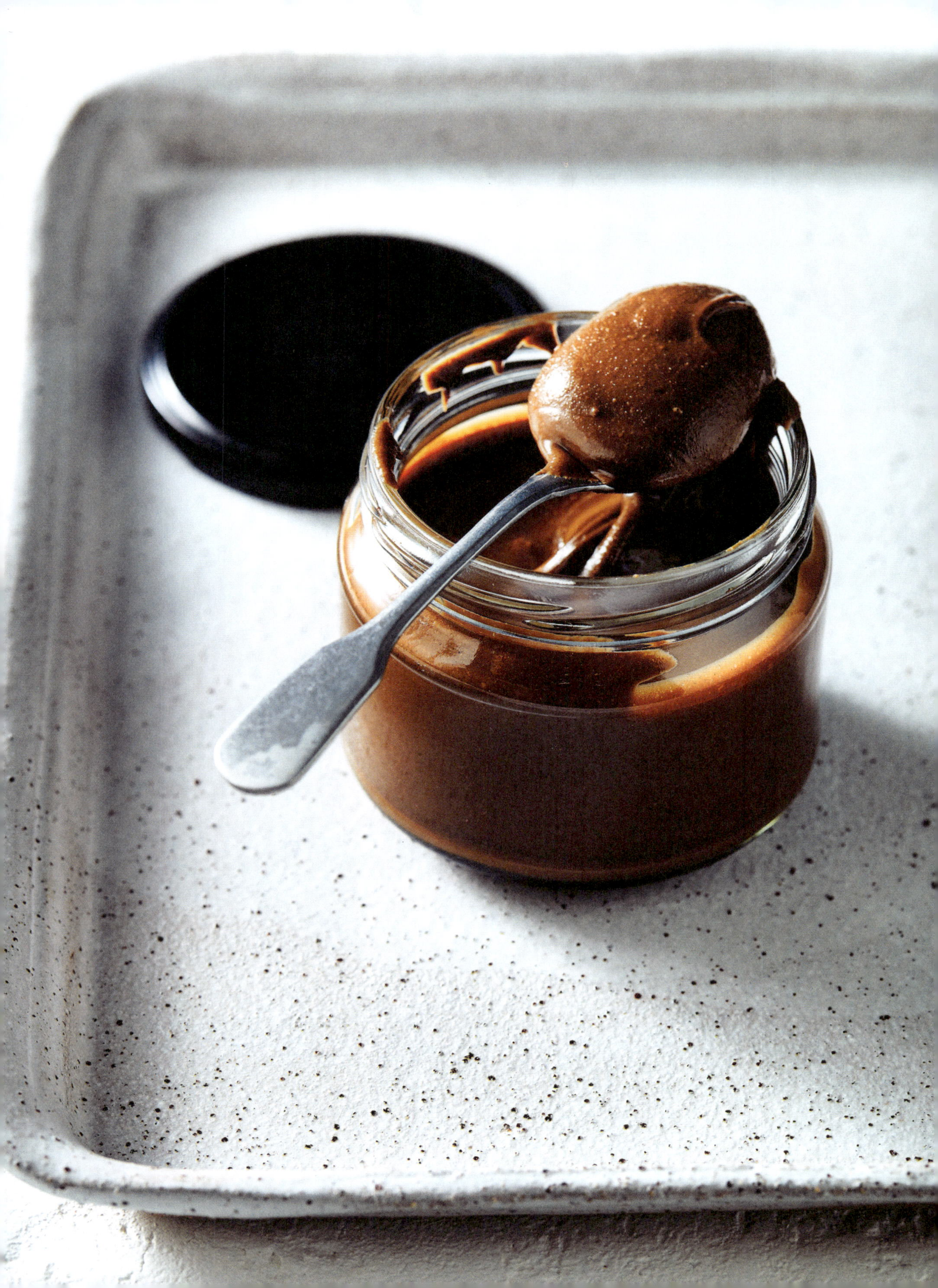

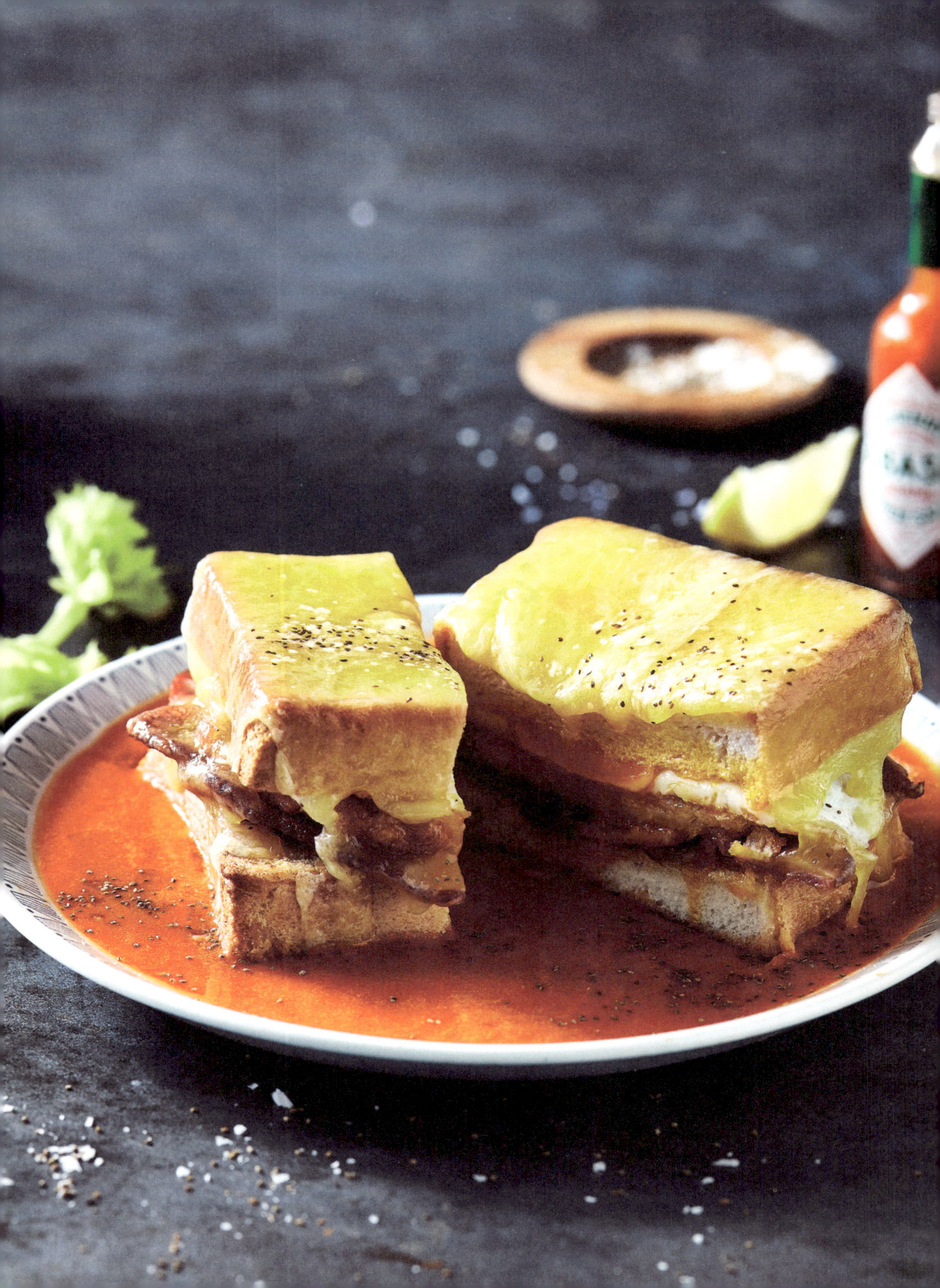

Bloody Mary bacon & egg sandwich

—

Serves 2
Prep 15 minutes
Cook 25 minutes

Inspired by Portugal's famous Francesinha, this frankly ill-advised sandwich is a Sunday morning in search of a Saturday night. That said, the addition of a hash brown to a bacon and egg breakfast roll is something that should be done more often in Australia.

2 frozen hash browns
4 slices thick white bread
2 tablespoons vegetable oil
8 bacon rashers
2 eggs
salt and black pepper, to season
butter
4 slices tasty or cheddar cheese
celery salt, to serve (see Tips)
celery sticks, to serve
lemon wedges, to serve

BLOODY MARY SAUCE

2 tablespoons olive oil
1 small onion, diced
4 garlic cloves, roughly chopped
200 ml (7 fl oz) tomato passata (puréed tomatoes)
2 cups (500 ml/17 fl oz) beef, chicken or vegetable stock
juice of ½ lemon
2 tablespoons vodka
2 teaspoons worcestershire sauce
½ teaspoon Tabasco sauce, plus extra to serve
½ teaspoon sugar

Start with the Bloody Mary sauce. Heat a small saucepan over a medium heat and add the olive oil, onion and garlic. Fry for about 4 minutes until fragrant, then add the remaining ingredients and bring to a simmer. Cover and simmer for about 20 minutes, then blend to a smooth sauce with a stick blender; the consistency should be similar to a light tomato soup. Keep warm.

Cook the hash browns according to the packet directions and lightly toast the bread. Heat an overhead grill (broiler) to high.

Meanwhile, heat a medium frying pan over a medium heat and add half the oil. Fry the bacon for about 3 minutes until browned, then remove from the pan and crack in the eggs. Fry for a minute or two until the whites are set but the yolks are still runny. Season with salt and pepper.

Butter the toast, then assemble the sandwiches with bacon on the bottom, hash brown in the middle and egg on top.

Place the cheese on top (hanging over the edge of the toast so that it wraps the sandwich as it melts). Grill (broil) for about 2 minutes until the cheese has melted.

Transfer to a plate, then pour the sauce over. Sprinkle with the celery salt and serve with celery sticks, lemon wedges and extra Tabasco.

TIPS A Francesinha is a deliciously decadent sandwich from Porto in Portugal, filled with meats, covered with melted cheese (and often topped with an egg), smothered in a tomato and beer-based sauce, and served with fries. If you ever get the chance to try one, go for it, but perhaps consult your cardiologist first.

I often make my own celery salt by dehydrating celery leaves in the oven and grinding them with a few celery seeds and salt. It's great on potatoes, chicken wings and even silken tofu.

Ingenious Breakfasts // 19

Falafel pancakes
—

Serves 4
Prep 20 minutes
Stand 10 minutes
Cook 15 minutes

1 cup (110 g/4 oz) besan (chickpea flour)

2 tablespoons olive oil, plus extra for pan-frying

400 g (14 oz) tinned chickpeas, drained

1 onion, roughly chopped

½ cup roughly chopped parsley

½ cup roughly chopped coriander (cilantro)

1 large green chilli, chopped

2 teaspoons baking powder

1 teaspoon ground cumin

salt and black pepper, to season

TARATOR SAUCE

½ cup (140 g/5 oz) tahini

1 garlic clove, crushed

juice of ½ lemon

¼ teaspoon salt

TO SERVE

2 cups (70 g/2½ oz) rocket (arugula) leaves, lightly dressed with olive oil

assorted Lebanese pickles

lemon wedges

Just when you think the perfect brunch dish doesn't exist, along come these falafel pancakes. They look hugely impressive, but the reality is that your food processor or blender does all the work.

For the tarator sauce, whisk or blend the ingredients with ½ cup (125 ml/4 fl oz) water to a smooth consistency.

Combine the besan, olive oil and 1 cup (250 ml/8½ fl oz) water in a bowl and set aside for 10 minutes to hydrate. Place the chickpeas, onion, herbs, chilli, baking powder and cumin in a blender or small food processor. Season with salt and pepper and whiz to a coarse consistency. Add to the besan mixture and mix into a thick batter.

Heat a large frying pan over a medium heat and add an extra 2–3 tablespoons olive oil. Ladle in about ½ cup (125 ml/4 fl oz) of batter for each pancake and fry for about 3 minutes until golden brown, then flip and fry for a further 2 minutes until cooked through. Depending on the size of your pan, you should be able to fry a few pancakes at a time. Remove from the pan and repeat with the remaining batter.

Serve the pancakes with the tarator sauce, rocket, pickles and lemon wedges.

TIP Tarator sauce will keep in the fridge for a week, and you can also drizzle it over vegetables, or serve it with fish or grilled meats.

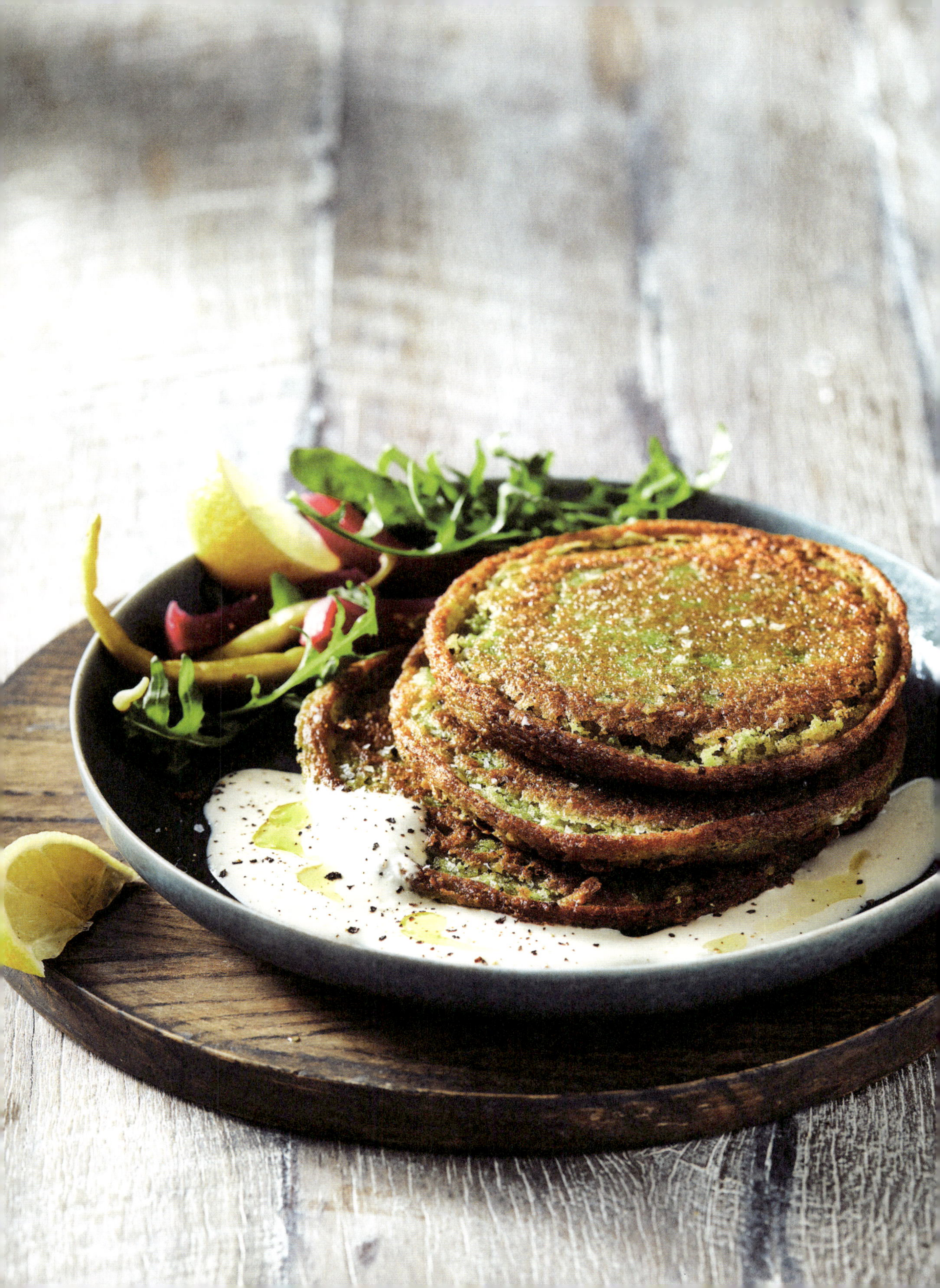

Green eggs & ham breakfast roll

Serves 4
Prep 15 minutes
Cook 5 minutes

2 cups (90 g/3 oz) baby English spinach leaves

1 teaspoon ground turmeric

1 teaspoon vegetable oil

8 eggs

75 g (2¾ oz) butter, plus extra for the buns

salt and black pepper, to season

4 large soft bread rolls, split

2 tablespoons mayonnaise

400 g (14 oz) very thinly shaved ham

I reckon Dr Seuss was on to something. This simple breakfast roll is essentially just ham and scrambled eggs, fortified here with a bit of spinach.

Combine the spinach, turmeric, vegetable oil and two of the eggs (see Tips) in a blender and blend to a smooth purée. Add the remaining eggs and blend slowly until just combined.

Heat a non-stick frying pan over a medium heat and add the butter. Swirl to coat the pan with a layer of butter; you don't need to wait for the butter to melt. Pour in the egg mixture and scrape slowly with a spatula from the outside to the centre until just set into soft folds of egg. Season with salt and remove from the pan.

While the eggs are cooking, toast the buns under an overhead grill (broiler), then spread them with a little butter, mayonnaise and black pepper and heap with a generous amount of shaved ham.

Top the buns with the eggs, put the lids on and serve.

TIPS I add the vegetable oil and two of the eggs first so the eggs don't foam too much while puréeing the spinach. Mixing the remaining eggs on lower speed will avoid incorporating too much air.

When making scrambled eggs, it's important to stop cooking them before they look like they're ready. Whole eggs set at about 65°C (150°F), so they will continue to cook from their own warmth after you've removed the pan from the heat.

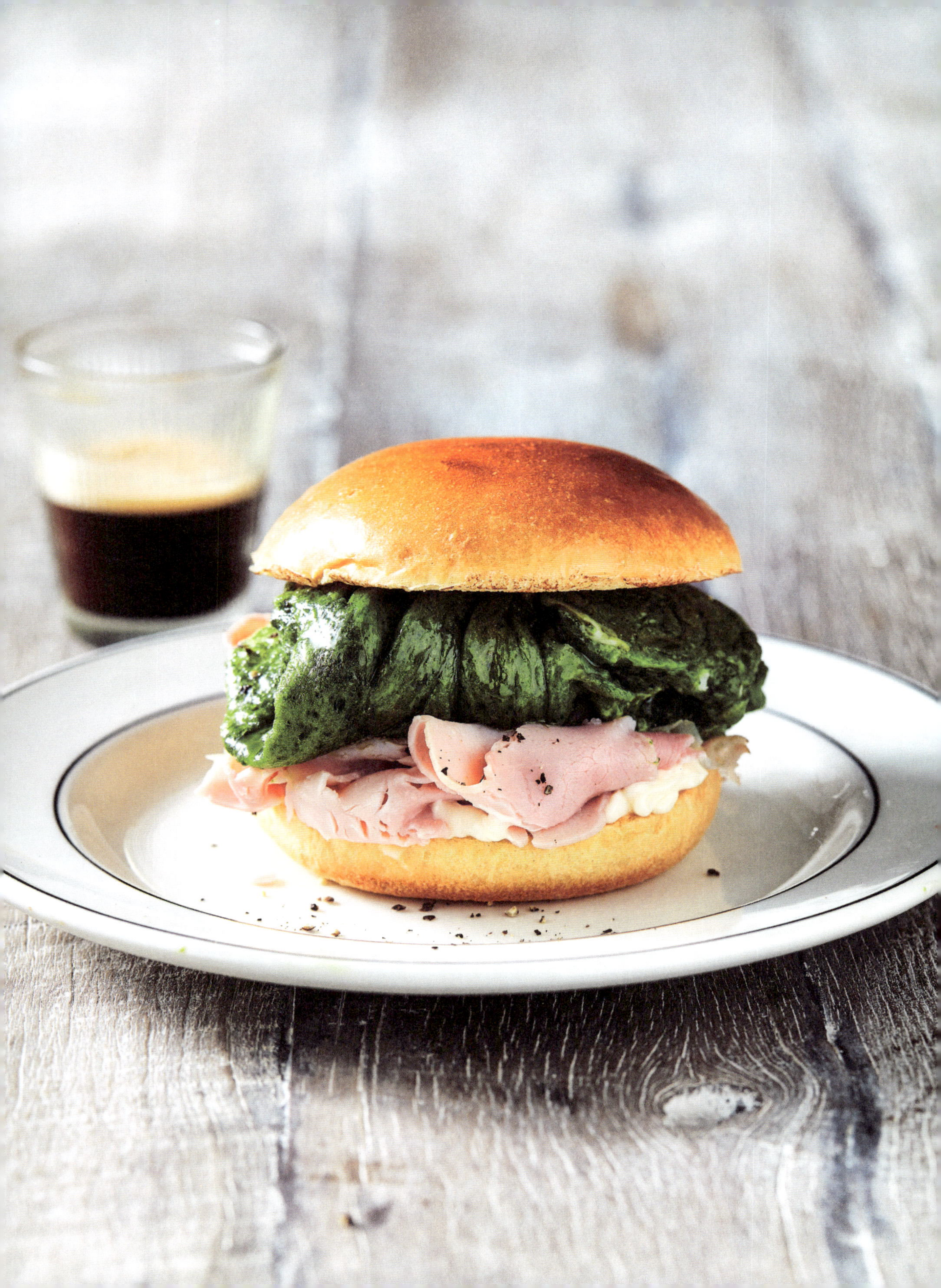

Hot smoked salmon kedgeree

—

Serves 4
Prep 15 minutes
Cool 5 minutes
Cook 15 minutes

Kedgeree is a dish from colonial India that combines smoked fish, rice and eggs. It's another one of those dishes so common around the world that combines leftover carbs from the night before with eggs to make a convenient and nutritious breakfast. Think of it as a curried fried rice.

3 tablespoons ghee

1 red onion, finely sliced

2 garlic cloves, roughly chopped

2 teaspoons grated fresh ginger

2 bay leaves

1 tablespoon mustard seeds

2 tablespoons curry powder of your choice

2 tomatoes, seeds removed, finely diced

juice of 1 lemon

3 cups (555 g/1 lb 4 oz) leftover (cooked and cooled) basmati rice (see Tips)

salt and black pepper, to season

200 g (7 oz) hot smoked salmon, broken into chunks

¼ cup finely shredded dill

lemon wedges, to serve

thick yoghurt, to serve

TURMERIC EGGS

4 eggs

2 tablespoons ghee

1 teaspoon ground turmeric

¼ teaspoon chilli powder

salt, to season

For the turmeric eggs, bring a saucepan of water to the boil. Using a metal skewer or pin, prick a hole in the base of each egg (see Tips), then boil for 6½ minutes. Refresh in iced water for about 5 minutes until completely cool, then peel. Heat a small frying pan over a medium heat and add the ghee, turmeric and chilli powder. Add the eggs, season with salt and spoon the ghee over them, rolling them around the pan for about 3 minutes until they are vibrantly yellow and lightly fried on the outside. Remove from the pan.

Heat a large frying pan over a medium heat and add the ghee and onion. Fry the onion for about 5 minutes until fragrant and golden. Add the garlic, ginger, bay leaves, mustard seeds and curry powder and fry for a further minute.

Add the tomato and cook for 1 minute, then add the lemon juice and rice. Stir to coat the rice evenly in the ghee and spices, then add the salmon. Fry for a further minute or two to warm the salmon and rice, then transfer to a serving plate.

Top the rice with the eggs and dill and serve with lemon wedges and yoghurt.

TIPS To cook basmati rice, bring a large pot of water to the boil and salt it as you would for pasta. Add the rice and boil for 10 minutes, then drain in a colander and rinse with cold water. You can make this with any leftover rice; it doesn't have to be basmati. Or just order extra rice with your next Indian takeaway and freeze it for dishes like this.

Pricking a hole in the base of the eggs helps them to peel more easily after boiling. Trust me, it really works.

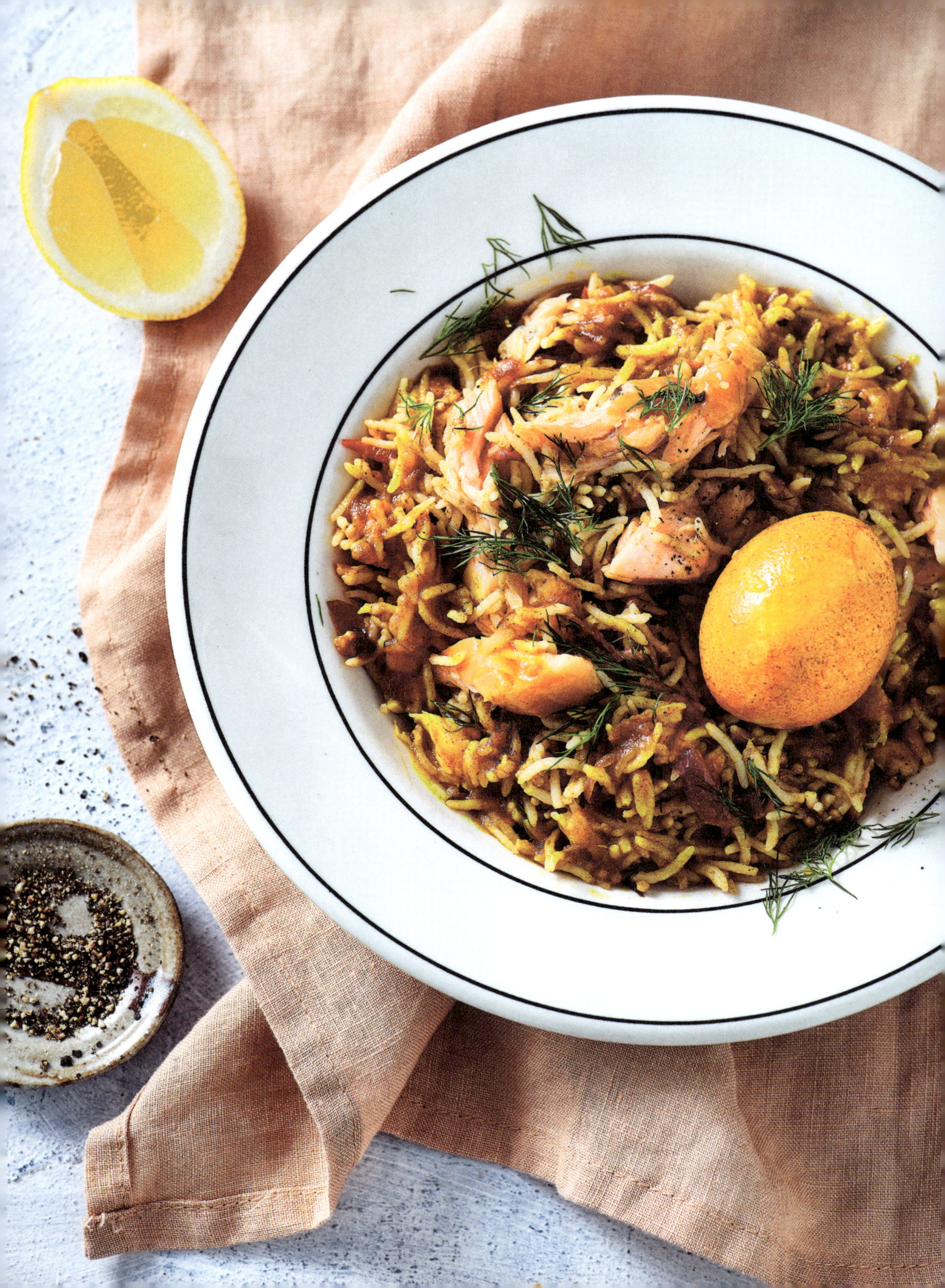

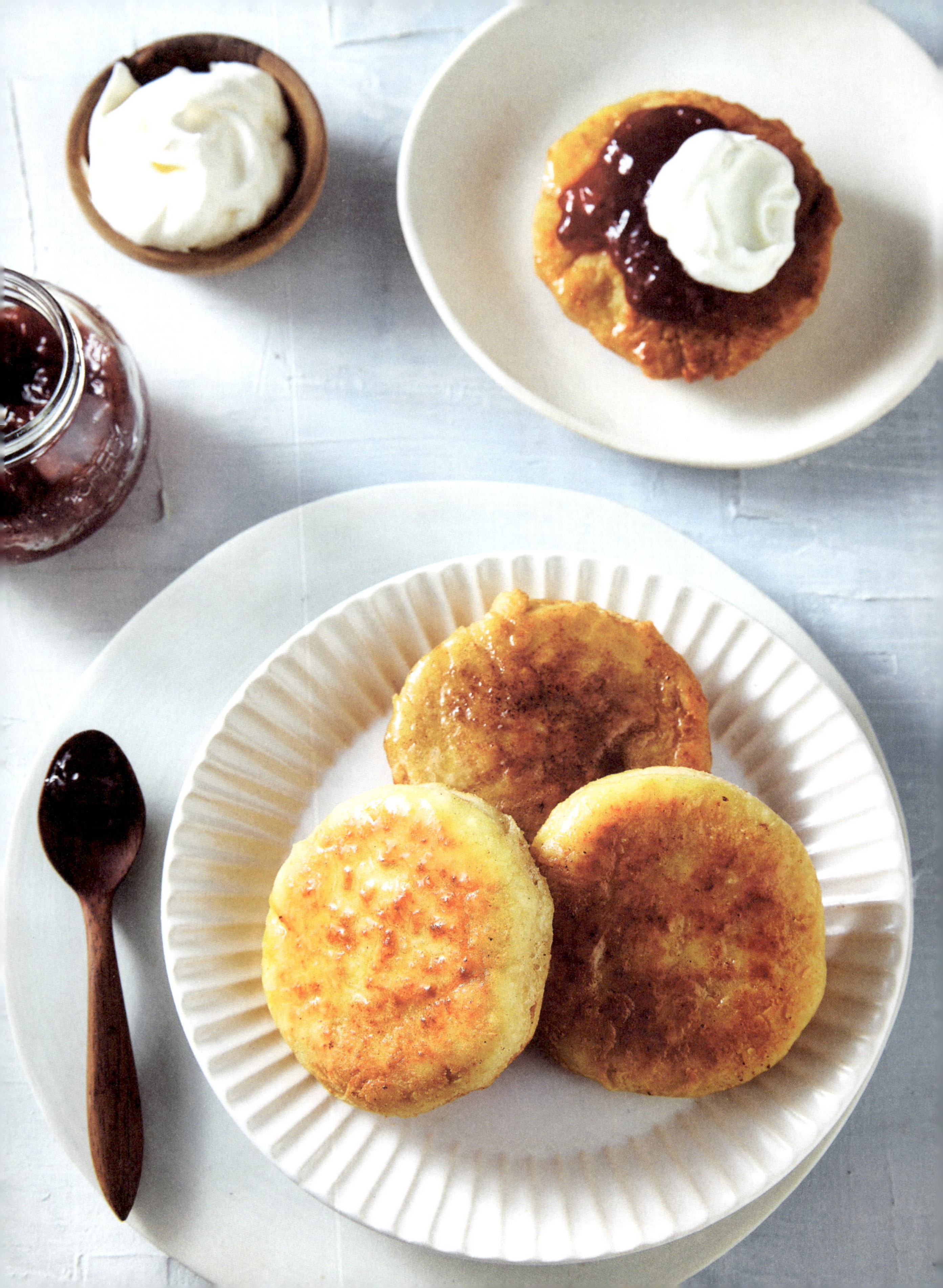

Puftaloons

—

Makes 8
Prep 15 minutes
Cook 15 minutes

These pan-fried scones make a great breakfast, but can also be a simple afternoon tea. The key is frying the scones slowly in plenty of butter. And when I say 'plenty of butter', I mean I want you to look at the amount of butter in the pan and then check the recipe again because you're worried.

2 cups (300 g/10½ oz) self-raising flour

½ teaspoon salt

1 cup (250 ml/8½ fl oz) milk

90 g (3 oz) butter, for frying (see Tip)

strawberry jam, to serve

300 ml (10 fl oz) thickened (whipping) cream, lightly whipped

Combine the flour, salt and milk in a bowl and mix until it just barely comes together into a shaggy dough. Do not overmix the dough. I repeat, DO NOT OVERMIX THE DOUGH. It should still be lumpy and inconsistent.

Shape the dough into a rectangle about 2 cm (¾ in) thick on a cutting board, and then cut out rounds with an 8 cm (3¼ in) cutter. Gently re-form any leftover dough and cut rounds again until all the dough is cut. (You could also cut square puftaloons with a knife if you prefer.)

Heat one-third of the butter in a small frying pan over a low heat. Fry 3–4 puftaloons at a time for about 3 minutes on each side until browned.

Serve the warm puftaloons with jam and whipped cream.

TIP Look, just use plenty of butter, OK?

Welsh rarebit ham sandwich

—

Serves 2
Prep 10 minutes
Cook 10 minutes

You can make a Welsh rarebit with just a bit of toast covered in the deliciously cheesy sauce accented with mustard and dark beer, but this version puts thin ham sandwiches under the grill instead. They're absolutely delicious, and so easy to make.

½ teaspoon English mustard

½ cup (125 ml/4 fl oz) dark beer

30 g (1 oz) butter, plus extra for the bread

1½ teaspoons worcestershire sauce

200 g (7 oz) cheese, grated (see Tip)

4 thin slices sourdough

a few slices ham

2 egg yolks

black pepper, to season

finely shredded parsley, to serve

Heat your oven's overhead grill (broiler) to very high. Combine the mustard, beer, butter, worcestershire sauce and cheese in a small saucepan and whisk over a medium heat until it has melted into a cheesy sauce.

Sandwich the ham between the sourdough slices to make two sandwiches, then butter the outsides of the bread. Fry the sandwiches on one side in an ovenproof frying pan for 2 minutes until lightly browned, then flip over.

Beat the egg yolks into the warm cheese mixture and pour generously over the sandwiches in the pan. Place the entire pan under the grill for 3–4 minutes until the sauce is browned and bubbling.

Grind over a little pepper, scatter with parsley and serve straight from the pan.

TIP Any meltable, grateable, strong cheese will work for this. Cheddar is my preference, or you could try fancier cheeses, such as Caerphilly or Lancashire if you felt so inclined.

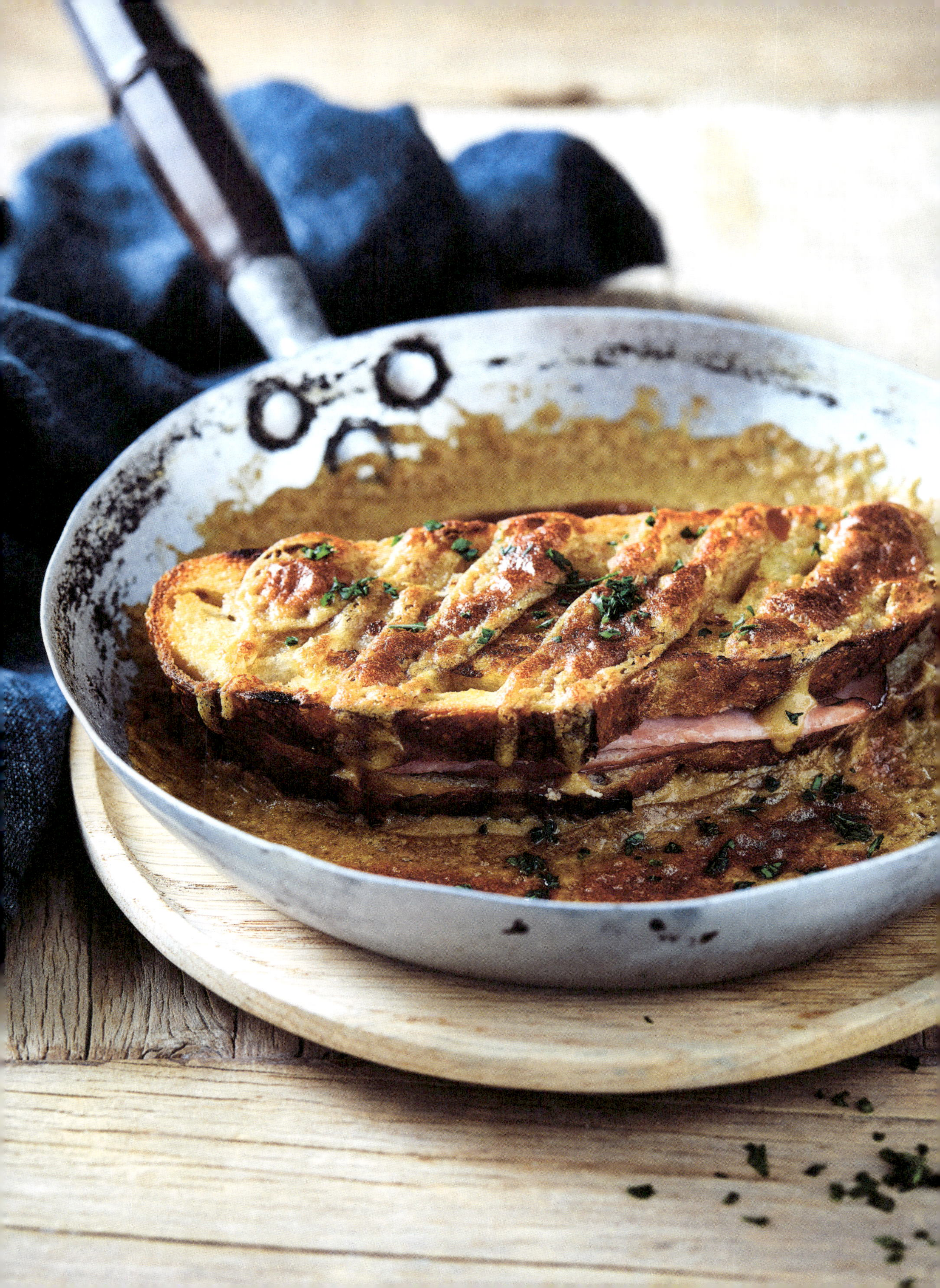

Perfect pancakes

Makes 10
Prep 10 minutes
Chill 30 minutes or overnight
Cook 5 minutes per pancake

I know it takes a bit of self-confidence to call these 'perfect pancakes' — but honestly, just look at them. I've received hundreds of messages from people who've tried these and confidently call them the best pancakes they've ever made. And now you can make them, too.

450 ml (15 fl oz) milk

2 eggs

2½ cups (375 g/13 oz) self-raising flour

50 g (1¾ oz) caster (superfine) sugar

1 teaspoon baking powder

butter, to serve

maple syrup, to serve

300 ml (10 fl oz) thickened (whipping) cream, whipped

Combine the milk, eggs, flour, sugar and baking powder in a blender (in that order) and blend until smooth. Refrigerate for at least 30 minutes, but preferably overnight.

When ready to cook, heat a non-stick frying pan over a medium–low heat. Ladle about ⅓ cup (80 ml/2½ fl oz) of batter into the pan. If you want perfectly even colour, don't add any butter or oil to the pan (you can add it to the pancakes later). Keep the mixture in the fridge between batches (see Tips).

Cook for about 3–4 minutes until the pancakes have risen and about half the surface is covered with bubbles. Flip and cook for a further 2–3 minutes until cooked through to the centre.

Serve the warm pancakes with a pat of butter and maple syrup, with some whipped cream on the side.

TIPS The key to thick pancakes that aren't rubbery is stopping too much gluten forming. Using a blender cuts the strands of gluten that develop, so the pancakes stay fluffy. Resting the batter in the fridge overnight also helps the gluten relax. Keeping the batter very cold in the fridge — even in between cooking each pancake — helps keep the batter thick, which makes for thicker pancakes.

To mix the batter by hand, beat the eggs in a bowl and whisk in the milk. Sift the flour and baking powder together and gradually add to the liquids with the sugar, stirring gently with a whisk until incorporated. Do not overwork the batter. Pass through a sieve to remove any lumps, then refrigerate for at least 30 minutes, but preferably overnight.

I use a large non-stick hotplate on an induction stovetop to cook a few pancakes at a time, but you could also use multiple frying pans if you want to speed up the process.

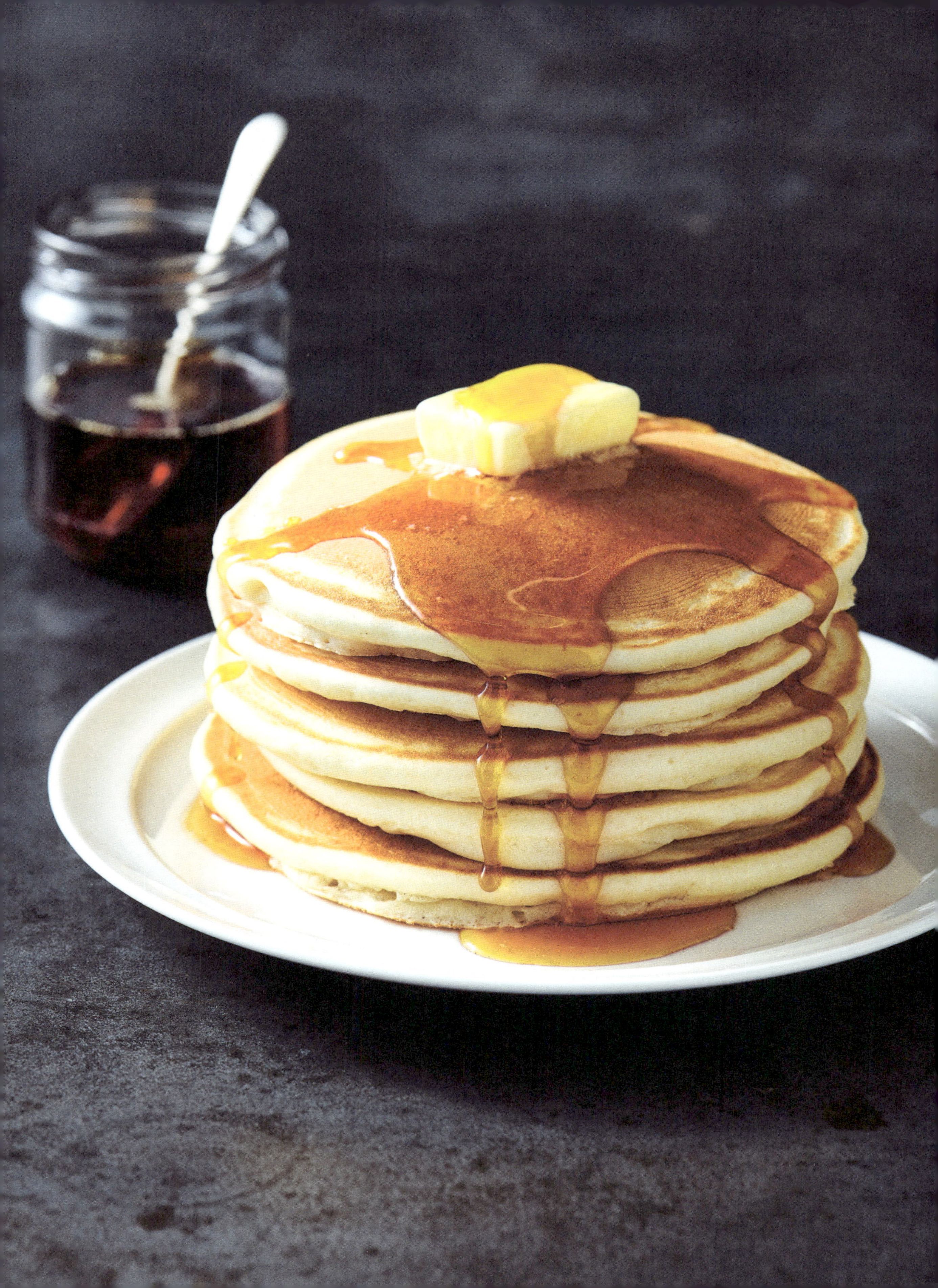

/lʌɪt/fan'tastɪk/
adjective

1. not heavy, a smaller meal or amount of food
2. extraordinarily good

LIGHT FANTASTIC

The lost art of the light meal is one we should all strive to keep alive in our kitchens.

Not every meal needs to be hearty and filling. And if you don't feel like eating much, it doesn't mean you should just skip, snack or sidestep cooking dinner.

A simple soup (page 37), a Japanese rice bowl (page 40), mushrooms on toast with a salad and a glass of wine (page 39), or a classic ratatouille with or without a piece of grilled fish (page 45) — these are all excellent meals that can satisfy the size of your appetite.

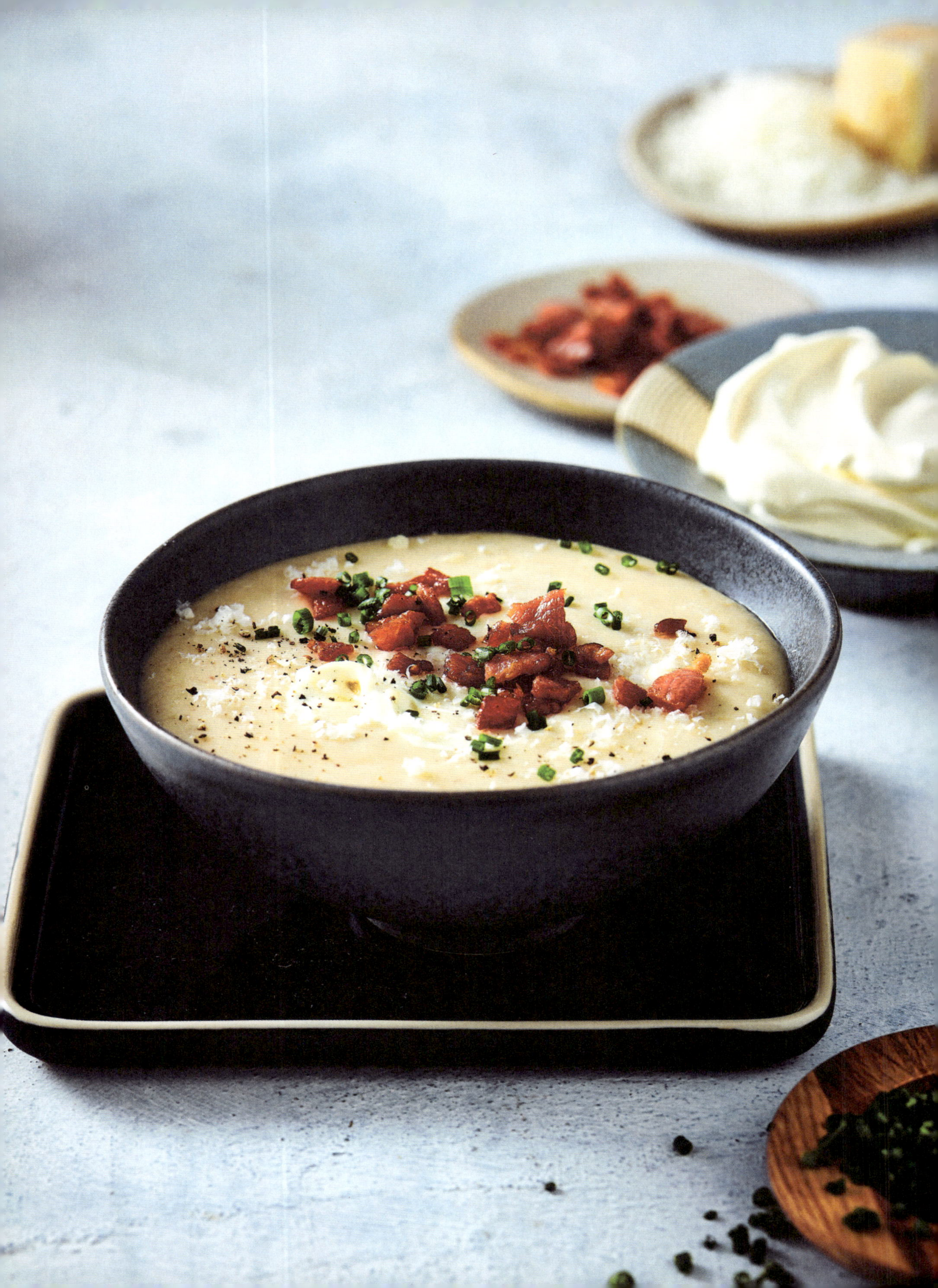

Baked potato soup

—

Serves 4
Prep 10 minutes
Cook 1 hour

Soup doesn't need to be a starter. It can be a whole meal in itself. Make a batch of this baked potato soup and put the toppings in the middle of the table so everyone can add their own.

3 large potatoes, scrubbed

25 g (1 oz) butter

100 g (3½ oz) thick-cut bacon or speck, diced

1 small onion, diced

8 cups (2 litres/68 fl oz) chicken stock, approximately

¼ cup (60 g/2 oz) sour cream

salt and black pepper, to season

TO SERVE

grated cheese, such as parmesan, tasty or cheddar

butter, cut into 2 cm (¾ in) cubes

sour cream

finely chopped chives

Heat your oven to 200°C (400°F) fan-forced. Prick the potatoes all over with a small, sharp knife and microwave, uncovered, for 10 minutes. Transfer to a lined baking tray and bake for 45 minutes (see Tip). Remove from the oven, allow to cool for a few minutes (or longer), then roughly chop and set aside.

Heat a large saucepan over a medium heat and add the butter and bacon. Fry for a few minutes until the bacon is browned. Remove the bacon from the pan and set aside.

Add the onion to the remaining oil in the pan and fry for a few minutes until the onion is translucent.

Add the chopped potatoes and enough stock to cover them. Bring to a simmer and cook for 5 minutes, then blend with a stick blender to produce a chunky soup. Stir in the sour cream and season well with salt.

Serve the soup with the toppings, the fried bacon and black pepper on the side.

TIP Microwaving is an excellent way to cook, or par-cook, potatoes, due to their natural water content.

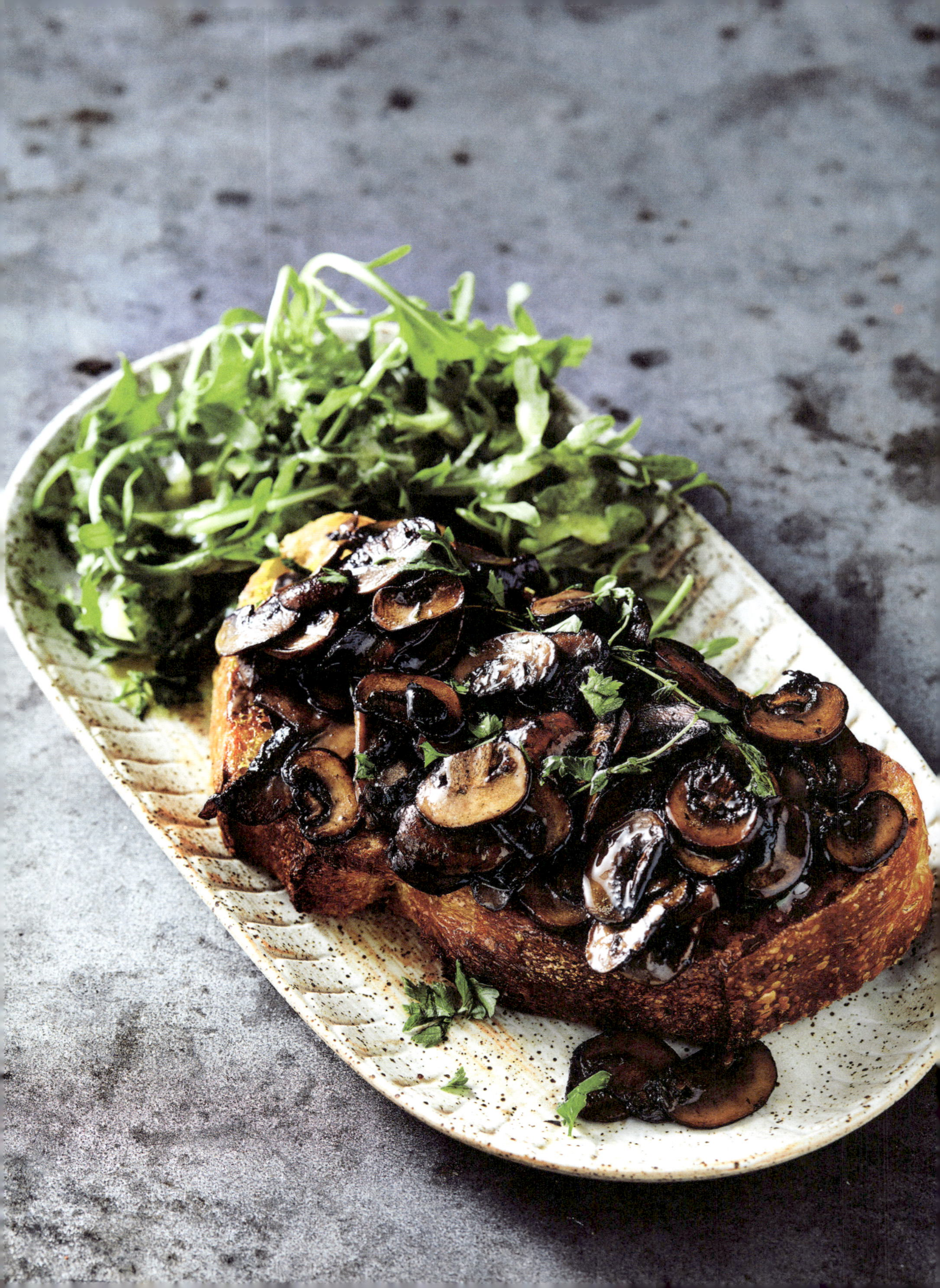

Mushrooms on parmesan toast

—

Serves 2
Prep 10 minutes
Cook 10 minutes

Cooking simply is quite often just a matter of respect. Rather than looking at mushrooms on toast as being a 'cheat' dinner, respect the elegance and economy of making a delicious meal in 10 minutes. Add a green salad and a glass of wine and you have a refined little French bistro number.

200 g (7 oz) brown button mushrooms, sliced

2 large portobello mushrooms, sliced

25 g (1 oz) butter, softened, plus extra for the bread

1 garlic clove, sliced

2 thyme sprigs

1 tablespoon brandy or cognac (optional)

2 tablespoons sour cream

2 thick slices sourdough

¼ cup (25 g/1 oz) finely grated parmesan

1 tablespoon finely shredded parsley

ROCKET SALAD

1 tablespoon olive oil

½ teaspoon dijon mustard

2 teaspoons white-wine vinegar

3 cups (35 g/5 oz) baby rocket (arugula) leaves

For the salad, mix the olive oil, mustard and vinegar together, then toss through the rocket leaves.

Microwave the mushrooms for 3 minutes (see Tip). Heat a medium frying pan over a high heat, add the butter and fry the mushrooms, garlic and thyme for about 5 minutes until well browned. Stir in the brandy, if using, and sour cream. Fry for a further minute or two until the mushrooms are coated and saucy.

Spread the sourdough slices with butter and top with the parmesan, pressing it gently onto the bread. Heat a small frying pan over a medium heat and fry the bread, parmesan side down, for about 3 minutes until the parmesan is crisp. You only need to cook one side.

Transfer the parmesan toasts to serving plates. Top with the mushroom mixture, scatter with the parsley and serve with the salad on the side.

TIP Microwaving mushrooms before frying speeds up cooking and collapses the air spaces in the mushrooms that usually suck up all the oil in the pan when you fry them raw. The cell walls of mushrooms are made from chitin, a strong polysaccharide that is similar to cellulose (fibre). It doesn't break down easily, which is why mushrooms hold their shape when cooked instead of breaking down to mush (pun intended).

Stamina-don

Serves 4
Prep 10 minutes
Cure 30 minutes
Cook 10 minutes

A 'don' (short for 'donburi') in Japanese technically means a 'bowl', but in food terms it refers to a one-bowl meal of rice and topping. While there are many different kinds of donburi, what defines a Stamina-don is the garlicky fried pork that is always served with rice and egg.

1 tablespoon vegetable oil

500 g (1 lb 2 oz) thinly sliced pork belly (see Tips)

1 small brown onion, sliced

4 garlic cloves, grated

2 cm (¾ in) piece fresh ginger, peeled and grated

2 tablespoons soy sauce

2 tablespoons mirin

2 tablespoons sake

2 teaspoons sugar

6–8 cups cooked Japanese-style rice, to serve

1 nori sheet, cut into quarters

4 spring onions (scallions), very finely sliced

SOY-CURED EGG YOLKS

½ cup (125 ml/4 fl oz) soy sauce

4 egg yolks

For the soy-cured egg yolks, place the soy sauce in a small bowl and drop in the egg yolks. Stand at room temperature for about 30 minutes, or longer if you prefer your yolks firmer (see Tips).

Heat a frying pan or wok over a medium heat and add the oil. Fry the pork for about 2 minutes until lightly browned, then add the onion, garlic, ginger, soy sauce, mirin, sake and sugar. Cook, stirring occasionally, for 5 minutes until the sauce thickens and lightly coats the pork. Remove from the heat.

To build the donburi, divide your rice among four bowls and place a square of nori on each. Top the rice with the pork mixture.

Make a nest of spring onion on top of the pork, then add an egg yolk to each. Serve immediately.

TIPS You can reuse the soy sauce from curing the eggs to fry the pork.

Thinly sliced, skinless pork belly is available fresh from Asian butchers and some supermarkets, and frozen at Asian grocers. To slice your own, freeze skinless pork belly for about 1½ hours, then slice thinly with a sharp knife. Partially freezing the meat makes it firmer and easier to slice thinly.

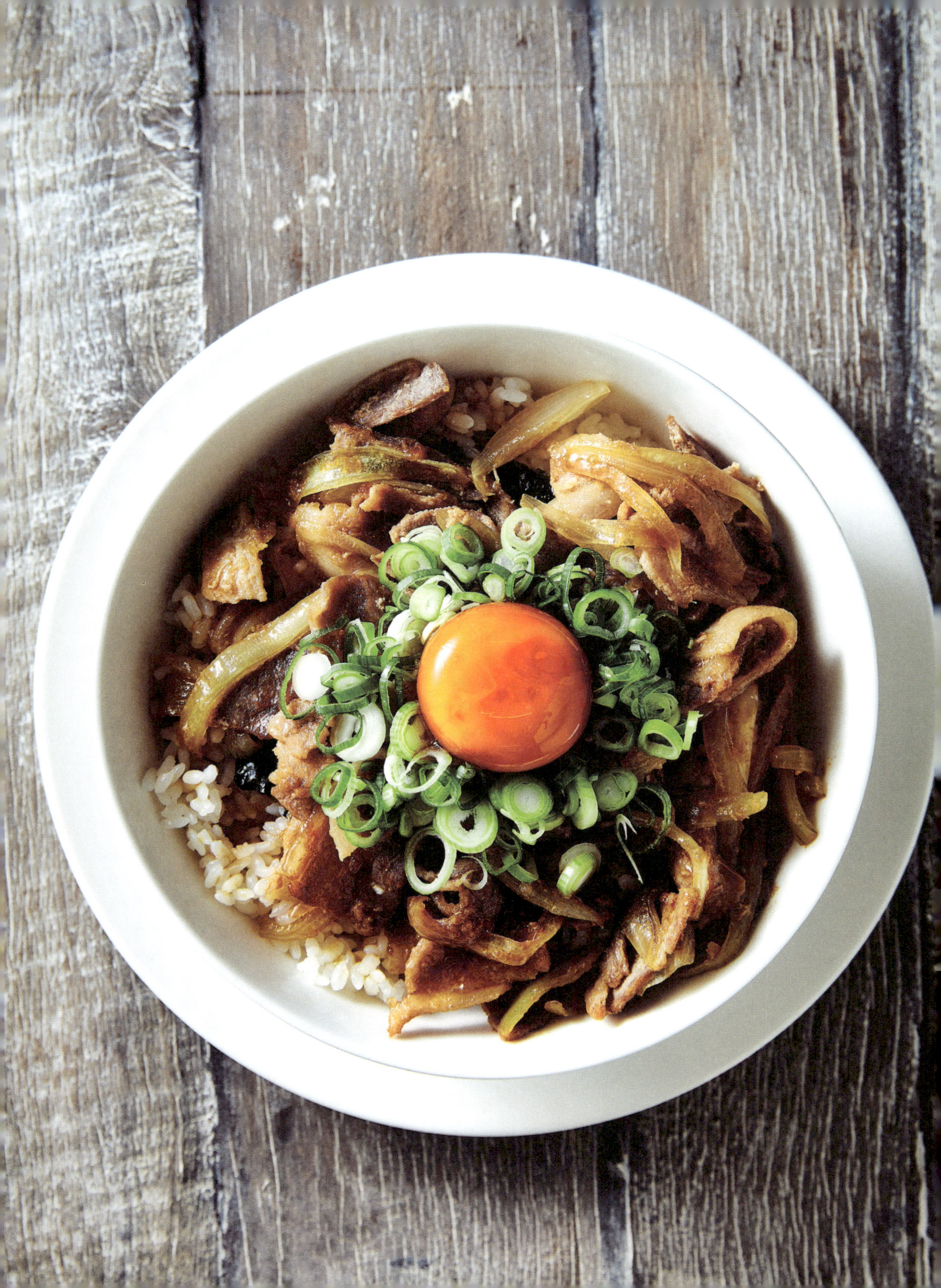

Tomato & garlic bread salad

—

Serves 2–4
Prep 10 minutes
Cook 10 minutes

You could enjoy this as a side dish to a barbecue or similar, but simply serving this salad with a bowl of olives would make a great light meal in summer when tomatoes are in season.

5 garlic cloves, grated

½ cup (125 ml/4 fl oz) olive oil, plus extra for drizzling

1 tablespoon finely shredded parsley

salt and black pepper, to season

½ small sourdough loaf

600 g (1 lb 5 oz) mixed tomatoes (such as cherry, oxheart, roma/plum; see Tip)

1 teaspoon harissa, or other chilli paste (optional)

¼ teaspoon honey

juice and grated zest of 1 lemon

1 tablespoon finely chopped chives

Heat an overhead grill (broiler) to high. Combine the garlic, olive oil and parsley in a large bowl and season with salt and pepper. Tear the bread into chunks, add to the bowl and toss to coat generously with the garlic oil. Transfer to a lined baking tray and grill for 5–10 minutes, turning once or twice until browned.

While the bread is toasting, halve the tomatoes and place in the now-empty garlicky bowl; you don't need to clean it. Season well with salt. Add the harissa, honey and lemon juice and zest, mixing well.

When the bread chunks are toasted, toss them through the tomato mixture to combine. Top with chives and serve immediately.

TIP You need great tomatoes for a dish like this. I'm not fastidious about never refrigerating tomatoes, as many tomatoes you buy will have been refrigerated at some point anyway, but you will want to bring them back to room temperature before you make this dish.

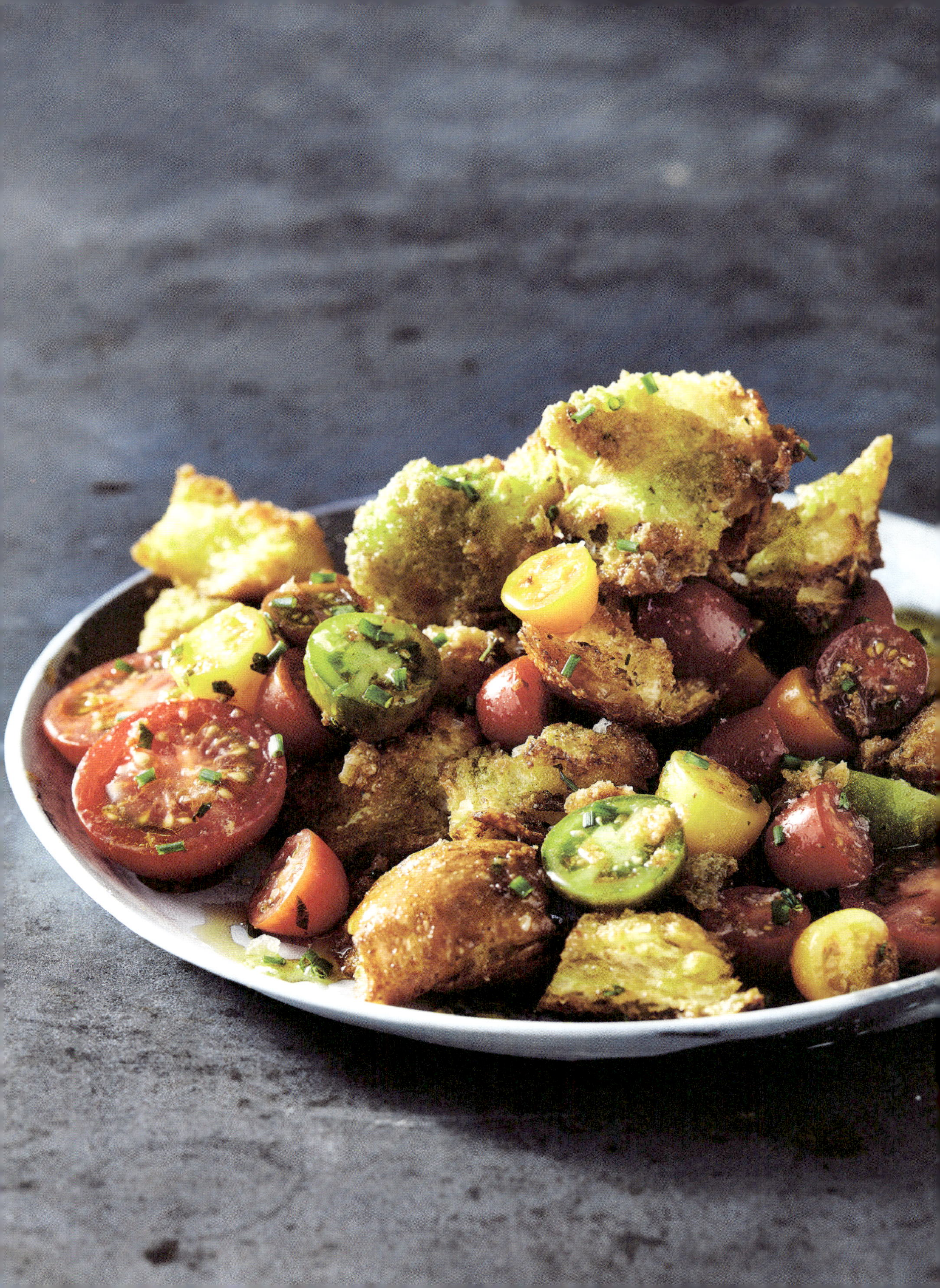

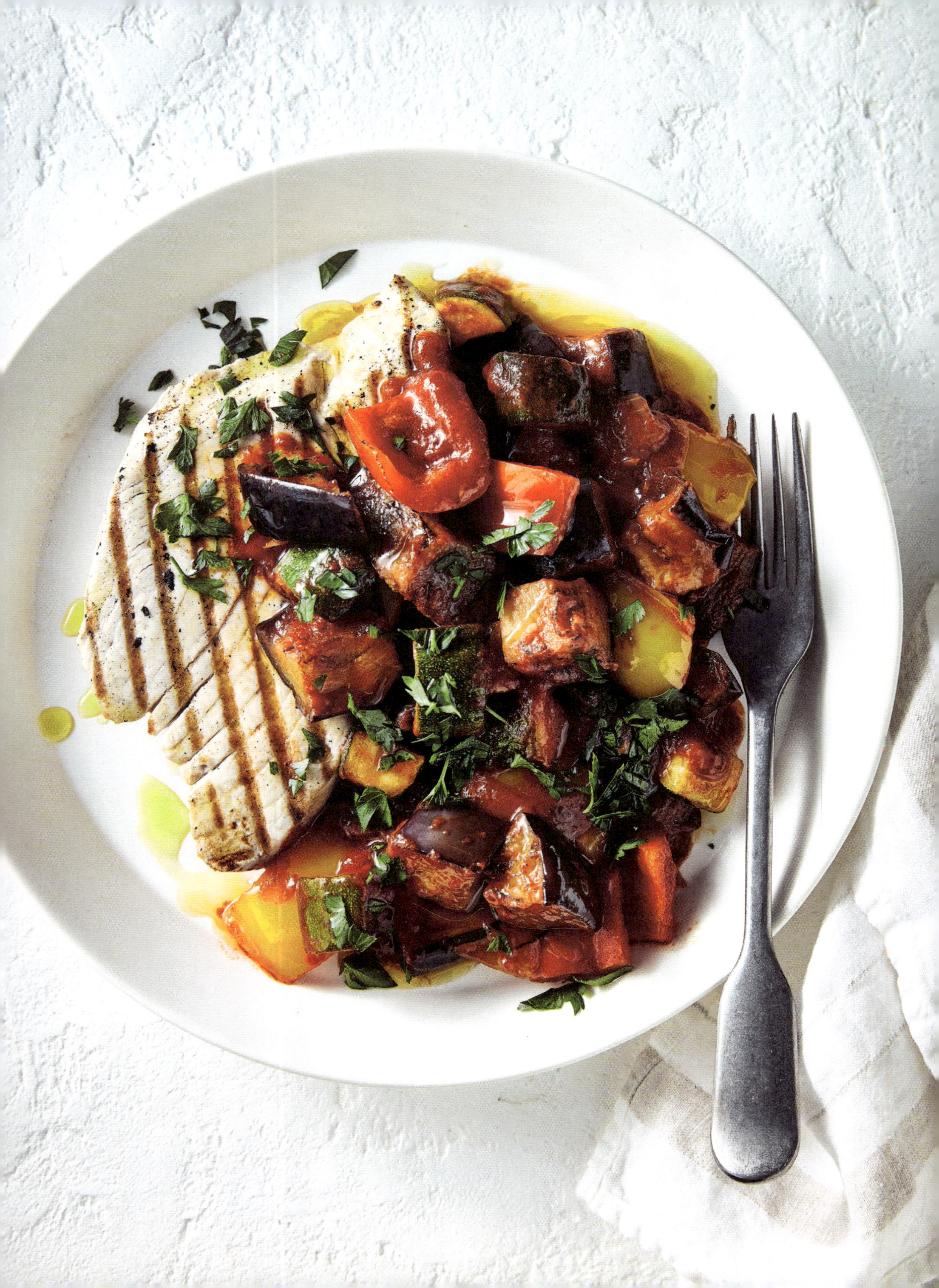

Ratatouille

—

Serves 8
Prep 20 minutes
Cook 40 minutes

Ratatouille is one of my favourite things to cook, largely because it's so incredibly versatile. You can have it at room temperature, warm or chilled. You can have it as a side dish, a main course on its own, or with bread, pasta or grilled fish or meats. In Provence, it's a classic accompaniment for tuna, whether grilled or even tinned.

700 ml (23½ fl oz) tomato passata (puréed tomatoes)

1 bouquet garni (made with sprigs of parsley, thyme, rosemary and bay leaves)

2 large eggplants (aubergines)

4 zucchini (courgettes)

1 red capsicum (bell pepper)

1 yellow capsicum (bell pepper)

2 brown onions

4 garlic cloves

¾ cup (190 ml/6½ fl oz) olive oil

salt and black pepper, to season

¼ cup finely shredded parsley

Heat a heavy-based casserole dish over a medium heat, add the passata and bouquet garni and bring to a simmer (see Tips). Partially cover with a lid and simmer for 20–30 minutes.

Meanwhile, cut the eggplant, zucchini, capsicums and onions into 3 cm (1¼ in) chunks and roughly chop the garlic. Heat a frying pan (or two) over a medium heat. Add about one-third of the olive oil and fry the eggplant for about 5 minutes until lightly browned. Remove from the pan and set aside.

Add a little more oil to the pan and fry the zucchini for about 5 minutes until lightly browned, then remove from the pan. Add the remaining oil and fry the capsicum, onion and garlic for about 10 minutes until fragrant and browned.

Mix the sautéed vegetables through the passata (see Tips), season well with salt and black pepper and cook, uncovered, for a further 10 minutes.

Stir in the parsley and serve.

TIPS A lot of photos online (and in movies about rats) will show ratatouille baked as elegant interleaved slices of vegetables. Don't do it. It might look good, but it just doesn't taste as good.

If you're not averse to it, adding a teaspoon of fish sauce or a few chopped anchovies to the tomato passata will greatly improve the flavour of your ratatouille. Trust me. See also the Ratatouille slice on page 103.

Light Fantastic // 45

Chicken & sausage poule au pot

Serves 4
Prep 10 minutes
Cook 45 minutes

Stews don't need to be heavy and beefy. There's something lovely and understated about the classic French poule au pot. Traditionally made with a whole chicken, it's a little easier (and tastier) using thigh cutlets on the bone, and good chicken sausages.

4 chicken thigh cutlets

4 good-quality chicken sausages

4 potatoes, peeled and halved

1 onion, quartered

4 carrots, cut into 5 cm (2 in) lengths

2 celery stalks, halved

¼ medium cabbage, cut into wedges

2 teaspoons salt, plus extra for seasoning

¼ cup (60 ml/2 fl oz) white wine

2 bay leaves

2 tablespoons fish sauce (optional)

½ cup (125 g/4½ oz) crème fraîche

2 tablespoons dijon mustard

2 tablespoons finely shredded parsley, to serve

Place the chicken, sausages, potato, onion, carrot, celery and cabbage in separate areas of a heavy-based saucepan or flameproof casserole dish. Pour 8 cups (2 litres/68 fl oz) boiling water over (see Tip). Add the salt, wine, bay leaves and fish sauce, if using.

Bring to a very low simmer, then cover and simmer for 45 minutes skimming off any scum that rises to the surface in the first 10 minutes or so. Check that the vegetables are softened to your liking, then taste the soup and season as needed with salt.

Mix together the crème fraîche, mustard and parsley, diluting with some of the soup broth to a sauce the consistency of pouring cream. Season with salt to taste.

Serve the chicken, sausages and vegetables with a little of the soup broth, with the sauce on the side.

TIP If you prefer a stronger flavour, you can add stock instead of water, or a mixture of stock and water — but if you season the dish appropriately, I don't think that's necessary.

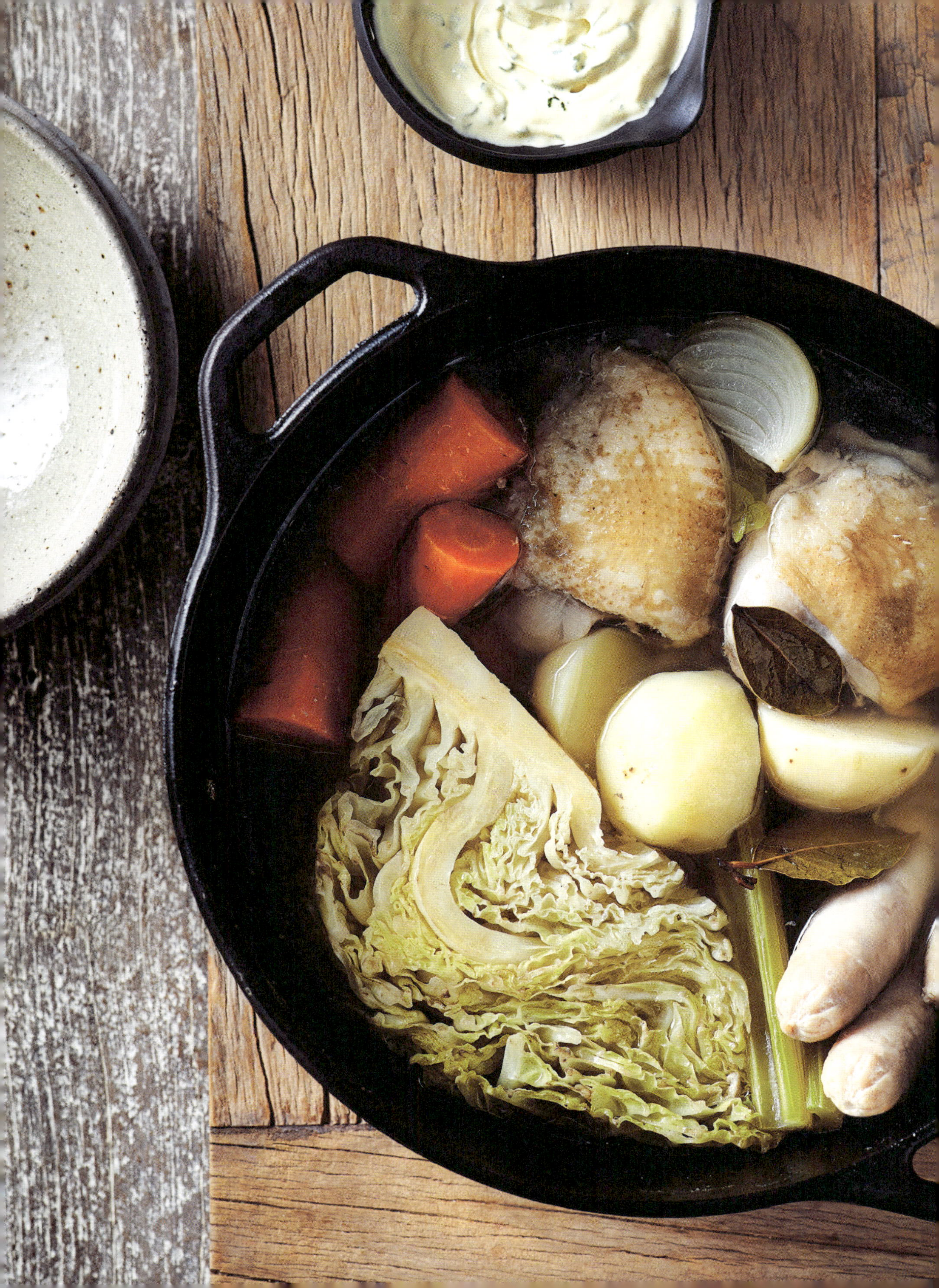

Peanut lamb salad

A bit gado gado, a bit satay, and a bit Sunday barbecue, this is one salad nobody would ever mistake for a side dish.

Serves 4
Prep 15 minutes
Cook 10 minutes

4 deep-fried tofu puffs (see Tip)

1 tablespoon vegetable oil

300 g (10½ oz) lamb leg or rump steaks

2 tablespoons kecap manis

2 Lebanese (short) cucumbers, cut into matchsticks

1 small carrot, cut into matchsticks

2 cups (180 g/6½ oz) bean sprouts

2 cups (90 g/3 oz) baby English spinach leaves

4 spring onions (scallions), finely sliced

3 tablespoons crushed roasted peanuts

3 tablespoons fried Asian shallots

1 red bird's eye chilli, sliced

PEANUT DRESSING

3 tablespoons peanut butter

1 teaspoon curry powder

1 tablespoon soy sauce

1 tablespoon fish sauce

1 teaspoon palm sugar (jaggery)

juice of 1 lemon

2 teaspoons sesame oil

Combine the dressing ingredients and mix well. If the dressing is too thick, add a few tablespoons of water; it should be about the consistency of pouring cream.

Heat a frying pan over a medium heat. Dry-fry the tofu puffs for 1–2 minutes on each side until browned and crisp, then remove to a chopping board and cut into 1 cm (½ in) slices.

Add the oil to the pan and fry the lamb steaks until cooked to your liking, drizzling with the kecap manis at the end and allowing it to caramelise on the lamb. Set aside to rest for about 5 minutes.

In a bowl, combine the cucumber, carrot, bean sprouts, spinach and spring onion and mix with the dressing, reserving a little dressing for serving. Toss together well and transfer to a serving plate.

Slice the lamb and place on top of the salad. Drizzle with the reserved dressing and serve scattered with the peanuts, fried shallots and chilli.

TIP Tofu puffs are available fresh or frozen at Asian grocers. You've probably seen them before in laksa. In fact, a bit of laksa paste added into the peanut dressing wouldn't be a bad idea at all.

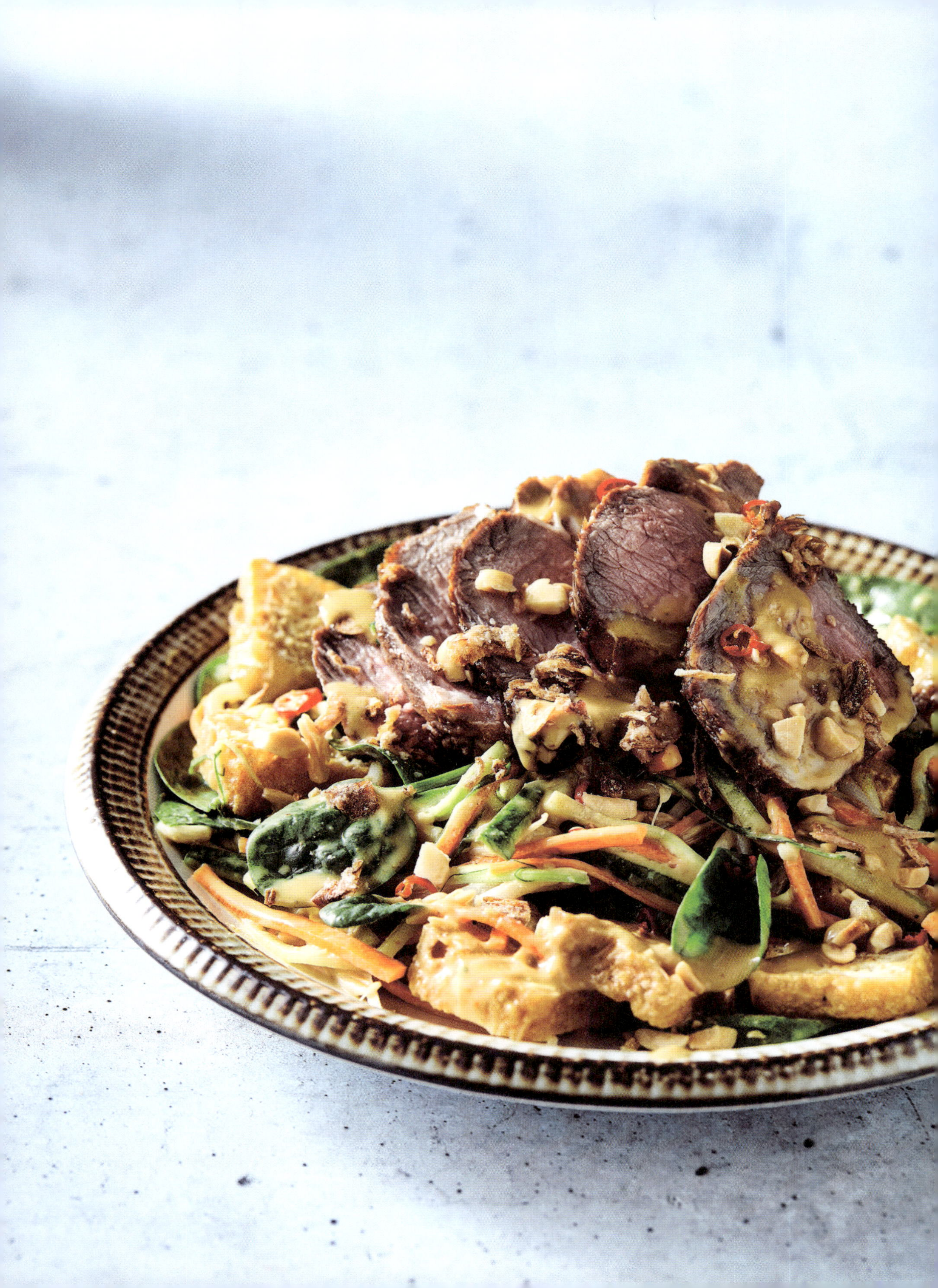

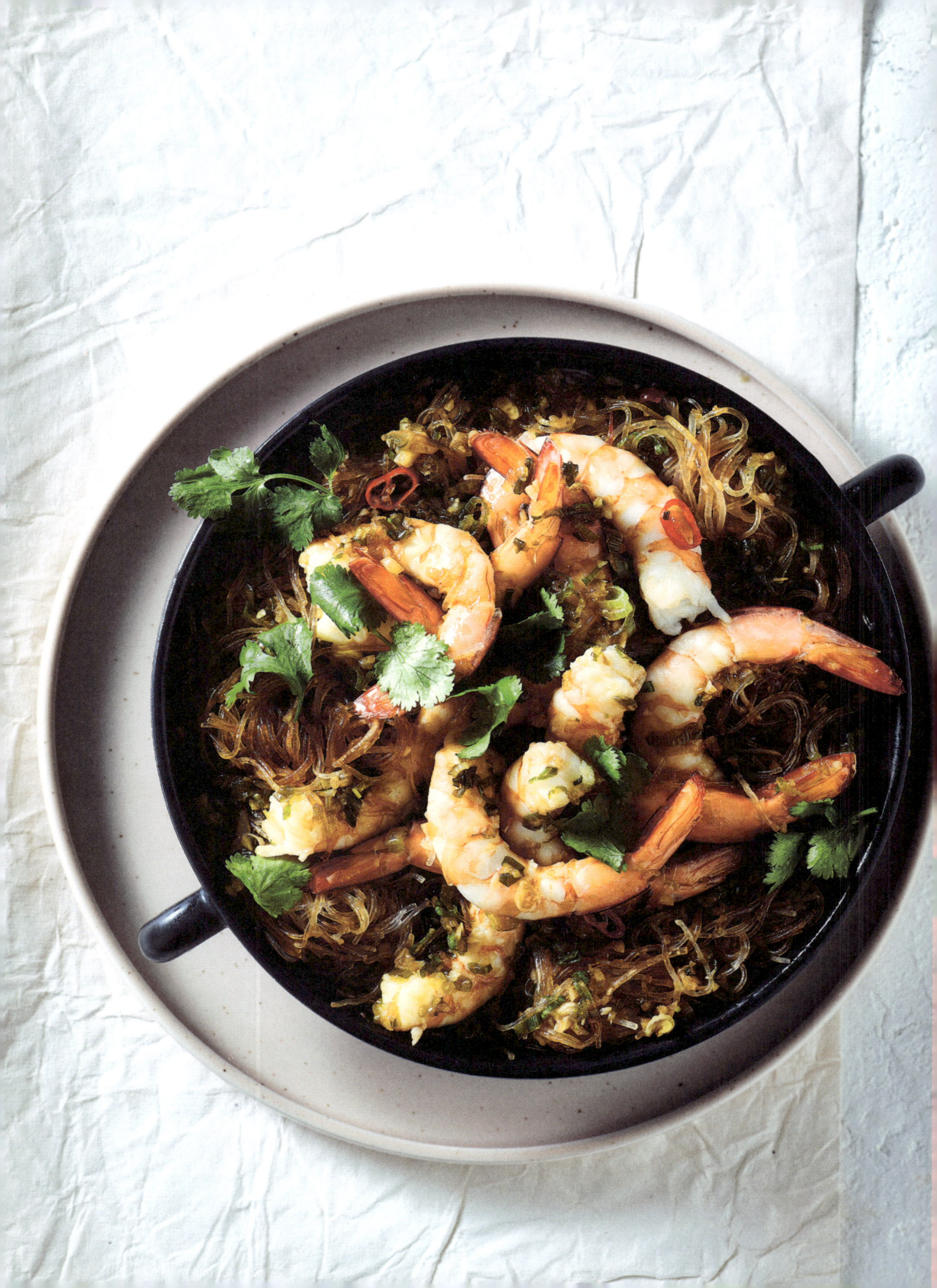

Steamed prawns with glass noodles

—

Serves 4
Prep 10 minutes
Soak 20 minutes
Cook 15 minutes

120 g (4½ oz) packet of mung bean vermicelli (see Tips)

2 tablespoons vegetable oil

4 garlic cloves, crushed

2 cm (¾ in) piece fresh ginger, peeled and finely chopped

1 red bird's eye chilli

4 spring onions (scallions), finely sliced

2 tablespoons oyster sauce

1 tablespoon soy sauce

1 tablespoon dark soy sauce

1 tablespoon Shaoxing wine

1 teaspoon sugar

12 raw prawns (shrimp), peeled and deveined, tails intact

coriander (cilantro) sprigs, to serve

If this is the kind of thing you'd order in a restaurant but feel nervous about making at home, I think you'll be pleasantly surprised. As the noodles steam, they soak up not just the sauce but the juices from the prawns (shrimp), producing something so delicious you'll be making it again and again.

Soak the vermicelli in cold water for 20 minutes.

Heat the oil in a small saucepan and fry the garlic, ginger, chilli and spring onion until the garlic is lightly browned and the spring onion fragrant. Remove from the heat. Add the oyster sauce, soy sauces, Shaoxing wine and sugar and stir through.

Drain the vermicelli and place on a lipped heatproof plate. Arrange the prawns on top, then pour the sauce mixture over. Steam for 10 minutes in a bamboo steamer or steam oven (see Tips) until the prawns are cooked and the noodles softened.

Lightly stir the noodles to ensure they're all coated with the sauce, then scatter with coriander and serve.

TIPS Rice vermicelli and mung bean vermicelli may look similar when they're dried and in the shops, but they are very different things. Read the labels closely to avoid getting the wrong ones.

Bamboo steamers are cheap and available from Asian grocers. You can place them in a wok or over a pot. If you don't have any kind of steamer, an upturned bowl in the base of a large, lidded pot will work just as well.

Vietnamese 'pizzas'

Serves 6
Prep 10 minutes
Cook 15 minutes

Bánh tráng nuong is one of my favourite Vietnamese foods ever, and it's so incredibly convenient. The dried rice papers can be kept in your cupboard for ages, and all you really need to do to make it work is fire up the barbecue or chargrill pan and pick a few toppings.

¼ cup (60 ml/2 fl oz) vegetable oil

500 g (1 lb 2 oz) pork belly, skin removed

1 small bunch spring onions (scallions), finely sliced

2 garlic cloves, roughly chopped

1 teaspoon grated fresh ginger

2 teaspoons fish sauce

1 teaspoon sugar

6 rice paper sheets

2 eggs, beaten

½ cup finely shredded coriander (cilantro)

Japanese mayonnaise, to serve

sriracha, to serve

Cut the pork belly into 1 cm (½ in) cubes. Heat a large frying pan over a medium heat and add about 1–2 tablespoons of the oil. Fry the pork belly for about 5 minutes until lightly browned. Add the spring onion, garlic and ginger and fry for a minute until fragrant. Add the fish sauce, sugar and remaining oil and cook, stirring occasionally, for 3–4 minutes until the pork has caramelised. Remove from the heat.

On a preheated barbecue grill or in a dry chargrill pan, working in batches, cook one of the rice paper sheets on one side over a medium–high heat for about a minute. Flip and spoon on some of the pork belly mixture and a generous amount of its oil, and a bit of beaten egg.

When the egg sets and the rice paper is crisp, remove the rice paper to a chopping board. Cut into pieces with scissors, scatter with the coriander and serve immediately, with mayonnaise and sriracha for drizzling over.

TIPS You don't need to reconstitute the rice paper by soaking it in water. It will grill to a crisp base for your toppings.

The pork belly topping is quick to make, but you can use sliced ham or luncheon meats if you prefer.

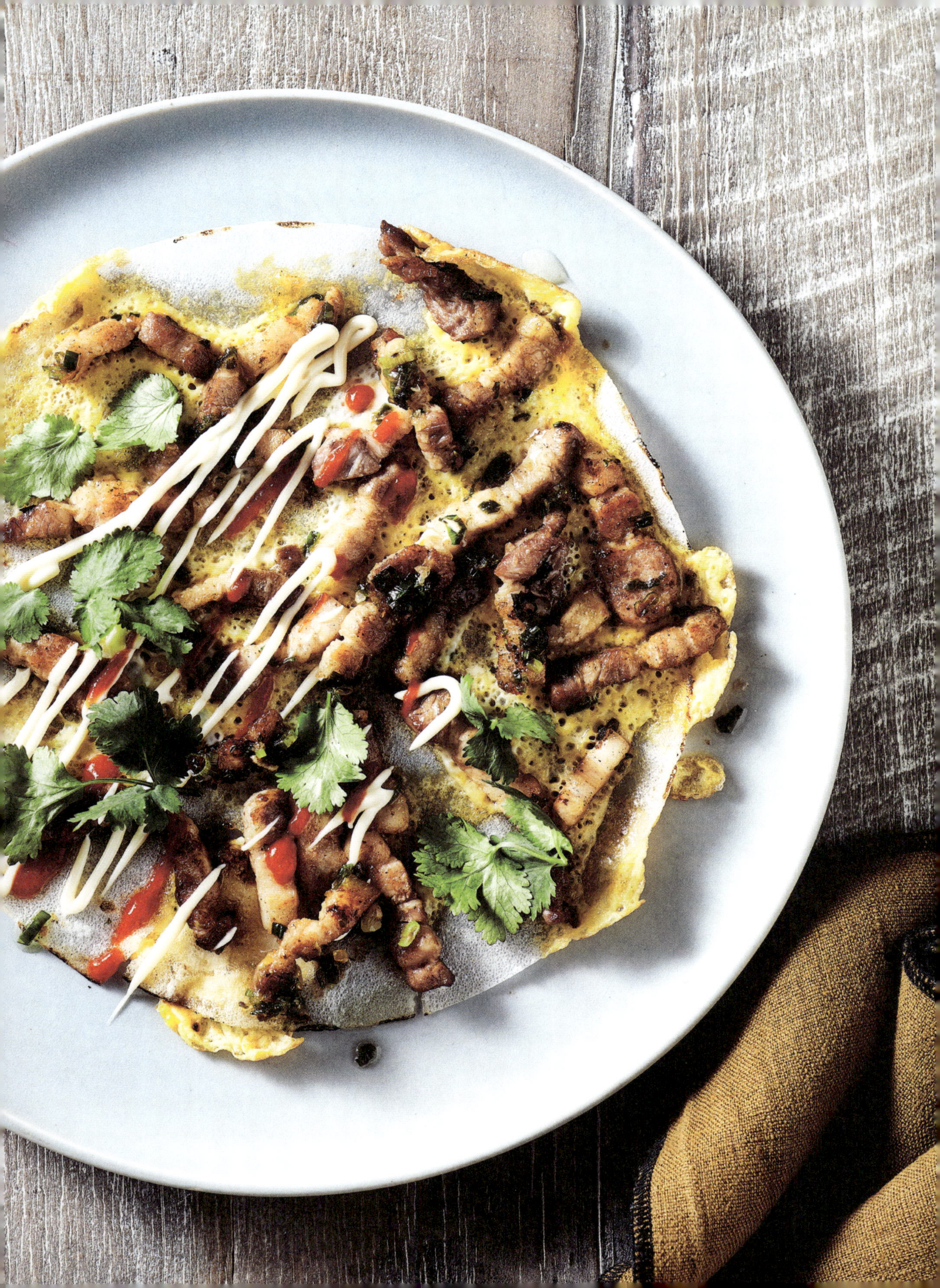

Open steak sandwich with pickle persillade

Skirt steak is a very underrated cut. It's much cheaper than primary cuts, and although it might look tough as a boot, cooked medium-rare it is incredibly tender and flavourful. The key is to rest it really, really well and slice it across the grain.

Serves 8
Prep 20 minutes
Rest 15 minutes
Cook 1 hour

1 skirt steak, about 600 g (1 lb 5 oz)
salt and black pepper, to season
olive oil, for drizzling
4 thick slices sourdough
8 radicchio leaves

CARAMELISED ONIONS
4 brown onions, thinly sliced
20 g (¾ oz) butter
salt, to season

MUSTARD & PARMESAN BUTTER
50 g (1¾ oz) butter, softened
½ cup (50 g/1¾ oz) finely grated parmesan
2 tablespoons dijon mustard

PICKLE PERSILLADE
3 dill pickles, finely chopped
1 pickled onion, finely chopped
2 garlic cloves, finely chopped
½ cup finely shredded parsley
½ cup (125 ml/4 fl oz) olive oil

Start by caramelising the onions. Place the onions and butter in a saucepan, season with salt and heat over a medium-low heat. Cook, stirring every 6 minutes or so, for about 45 minutes until the onions are caramelised.

Heat a chargrill pan or frying pan over a high heat. Season the steak with salt and pepper and drizzle with olive oil. Cook the steak to medium-rare (see Tips). Set aside to rest for 10–15 minutes while you prepare the remaining ingredients.

Mix the mustard and parmesan butter ingredients together and set aside.

In a small bowl, combine the pickle persillade ingredients, mixing in a couple drops of the liquid from the pickles and/or onions, to taste.

Toast the bread and spread generously with the mustard and parmesan butter. Place the radicchio leaves on top and cover with caramelised onion.

Reheat your chargrill or frying pan to very hot and quickly sear the steak for about 30 seconds on each side to reheat it.

Slice the steak across the grain and arrange it on top of the sandwich. Spoon the persillade over and serve.

TIPS I caramelise onions when I have an hour to kill at home. I add the onions to the pan over a low heat and set a timer for 6 minutes. Then I get a bit of work done or read a book, stirring the pot when the timer goes off. Then I set it again and repeat until the onions are done.

The easiest way to check how well your steak is cooked is to use a thermometer. Failing that, simply press it with your fingers as it cooks in the pan and imagine yourself cutting it with a knife. Take it out of the pan when it feels like you want it to feel as you're cutting it.

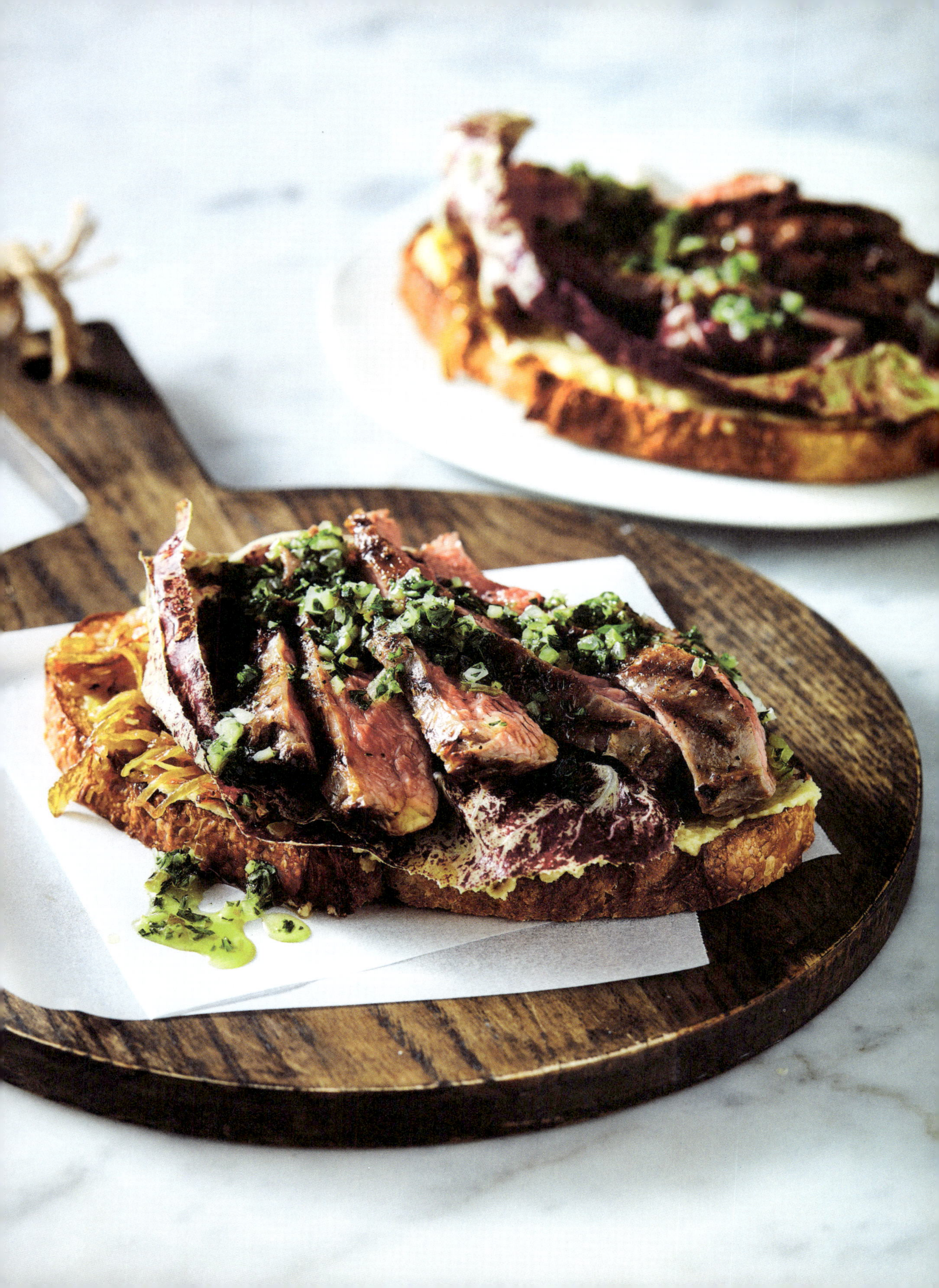

/famıli/'feıv(ə)rıt/
noun
1. designed to be suitable for all members of a family
2. especially well liked or preferred

FAMILY FAVOURITES

I have always considered a family dinner to be incredibly important. It informs our relationships with people, and with food.

It's this connection between people and food that makes me want to keep trying new things. Every time a new dish hits the table there's a new conversation to be had about it, and something as simple as that can keep a family moving forward.

The way I eat today is different to how I ate as a child. It's different to how I ate as recently as ten or even five years ago, and that change happens one dish at a time.

Who knows, some of the dishes in this chapter might change the way your family eats. Maybe you'll look back in a few years' time and see that Ten-minute cheeseburgers (page 63) have become 'mum's cheeseburgers', or Roast chicken with whole mushroom sauce (page 83) has become your go-to roast chicken a couple of times a month.

Barbecued chicken with charred greens & chimichurri

—

Serves 4
Prep 15 minutes
Stand 1 hour
Cook 1 hour
Rest 15 minutes

You're probably reading this because you're intrigued by the chicken component, but I wrote this recipe mainly for the greens. Barbecuing is a great way to cook vegetables, including leafy greens.

1 whole free-range chicken, about 1.7 kg (3 lb 12 oz)

salt and black pepper, to season

2 tablespoons white-wine vinegar

1 tablespoon dark soy sauce

¾ cup (190 ml/6½ fl oz) olive oil

200 g (7 oz) snake (yard-long) beans, or green beans

1 bunch broccolini

1 bunch English spinach

6 thick spring onions (scallions)

CHIMICHURRI

1 firmly packed cup flat-leaf parsley, roughly chopped

6 garlic cloves, roughly chopped

1 teaspoon dried oregano

½ cup (125 ml/4 fl oz) extra-virgin olive oil

2 tablespoons white-wine vinegar

salt and black pepper, to taste

1 teaspoon dried crushed chilli (optional)

Using kitchen scissors, cut the backbone out of the chicken and reserve it for making stock. Place the chicken in a large bowl and season well with salt and pepper. Pour over the vinegar, soy sauce and half the olive oil, rubbing all over the chicken. Set aside for about 1 hour.

Meanwhile, combine all the chimichurri ingredients in a bowl and stir to combine. Stand for at least 30 minutes before using.

Heat a hooded barbecue grill to 160°C (320°F). Grill the chicken, skin side down (see Tip) and with the hood pulled down, for 20 minutes, and then skin side up for a further 20 minutes. (Alternatively, if you don't have a hooded barbecue, you can roast the chicken in a preheated oven at 200°C/400°F fan-forced for 40 minutes.)

Rest the chicken for 15 minutes.

While the chicken is resting, increase the barbecue heat to high. Drizzle the vegetables liberally with the remaining olive oil and season well with salt. Grill separately in batches until cooked to your liking. The beans, broccoli and spring onion might take 5–6 minutes, but the spinach should cook in just a minute or so.

Serve the chicken on the greens, with the chimichurri spooned over the chicken, and in a bowl on the side.

TIP A weight placed on top of the chicken will help it cook more evenly. Some like to wrap a brick in foil, but honestly, any ovenproof lid from a heavy casserole dish is a better choice.

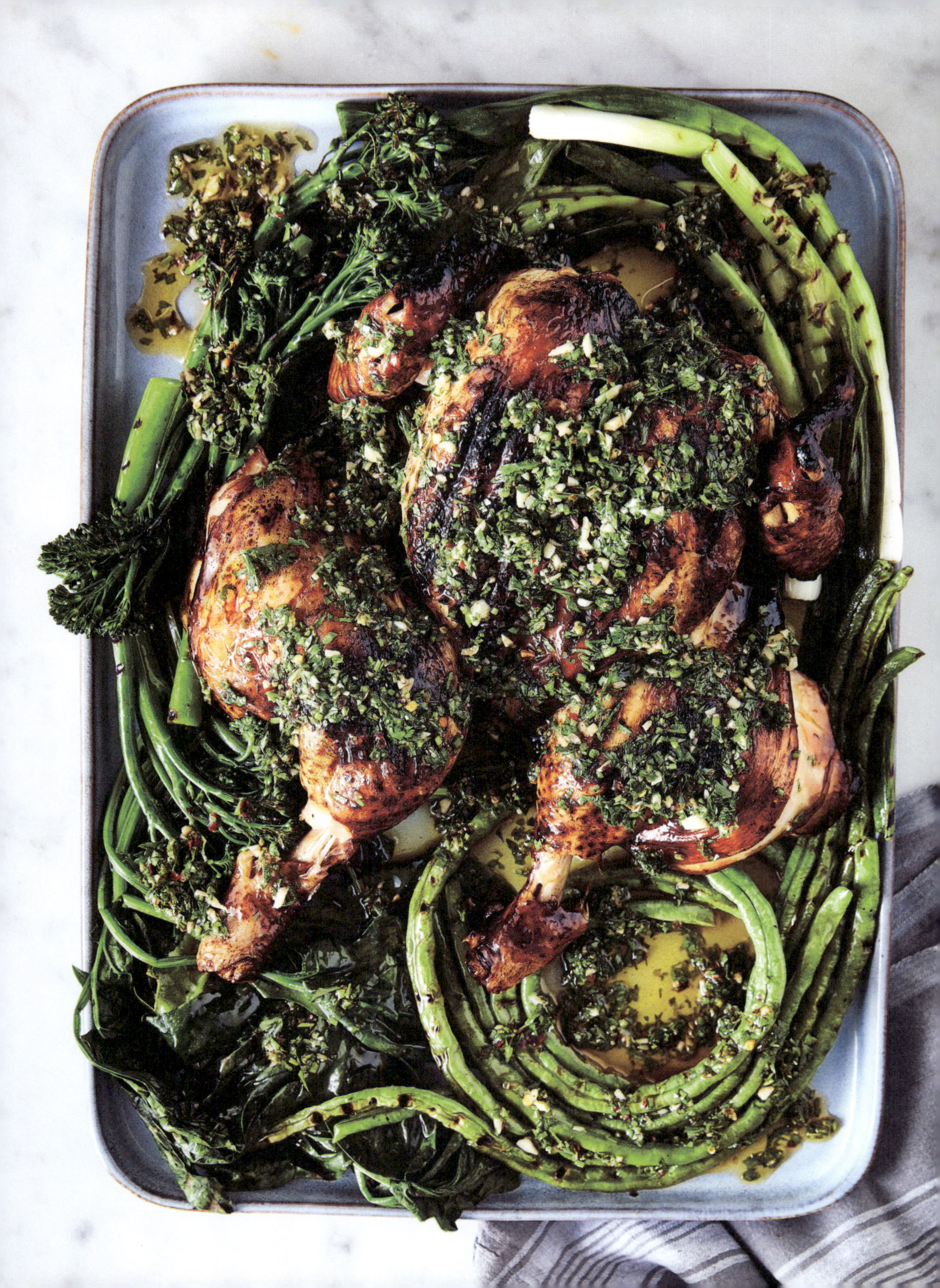

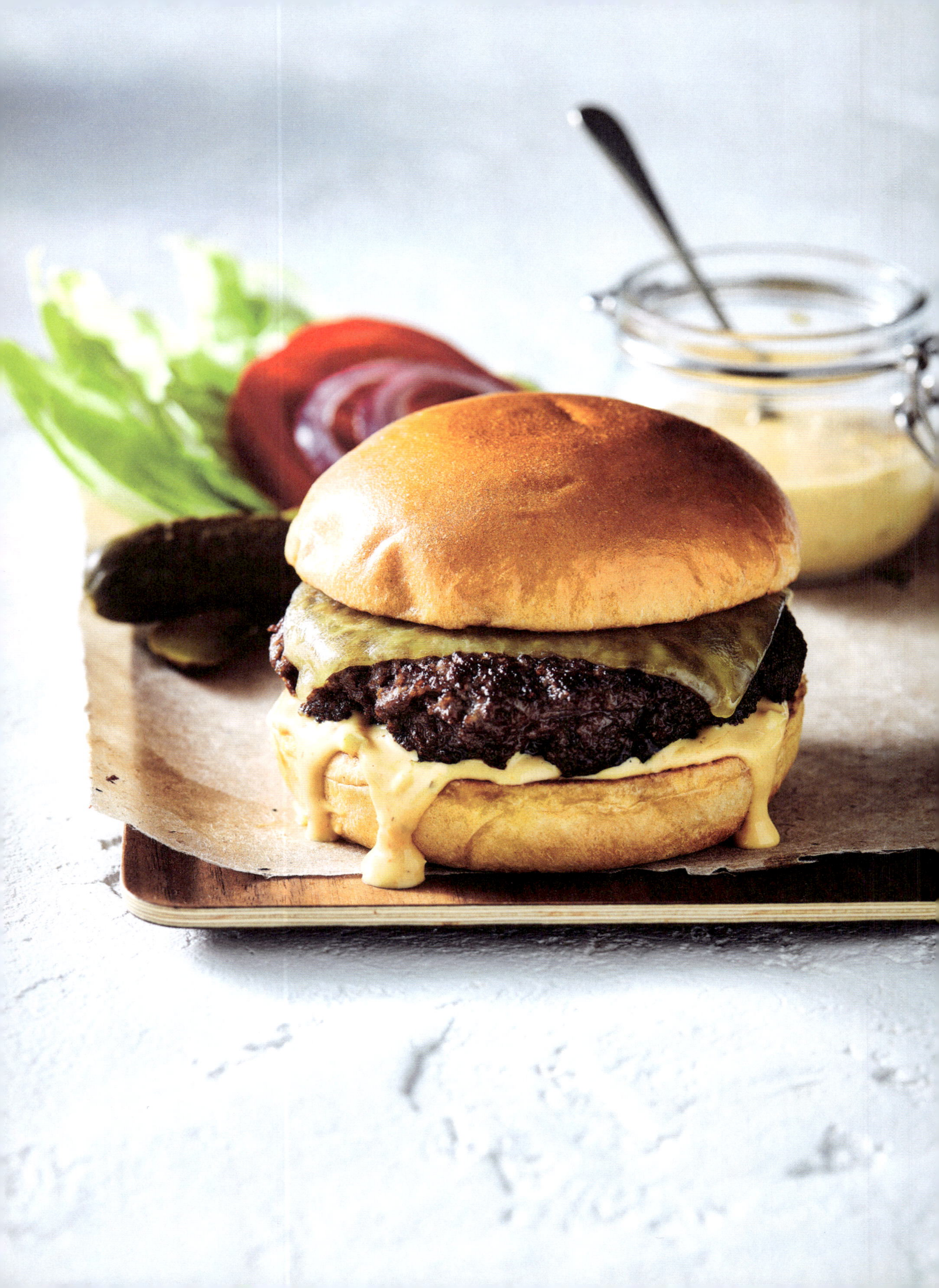

Ten-minute cheeseburgers

Serves 4
Prep 10 minutes
Cook 10 minutes

This is how we make hamburgers at home. You don't need to buy expensive patties full of fillers and flavourings. The cheapest supermarket mince produces the best bang-for-buck burgers with very little effort. Trust me.

500 g (1 lb 2 oz) cheap, fatty minced (ground) beef (see Tips)

salt and black pepper, to season

1 tablespoon vegetable oil

8 slices tasty or cheddar cheese

4 soft hamburger buns, split

4 iceberg lettuce leaves

1 red onion, thinly sliced

1 tomato, thinly sliced

AMERICAN BURGER SAUCE

¼ cup (60 g/2 oz) American yellow mustard

¼ cup (60 ml/2 fl oz) tomato sauce (ketchup)

½ cup (125 ml/4 fl oz) mayonnaise

1 tablespoon finely diced onion

2 tablespoons finely diced dill pickles

black pepper, to season

Season the beef well with salt, then shape into four balls of 125 g (4½ oz) each. Place a piece of baking paper on top of one ball, then press down firmly with the base of a heavy saucepan to flatten the ball into a patty about 20 per cent larger than your burger buns, as the patties will shrink when cooking. Repeat with the other patties.

Heat a large frying pan (or barbecue hotplate) over a medium heat. Add the oil and fry the patties on one side for about 3 minutes, then flip and place two slices of cheese on top of each. Cook for a further 2 minutes until the cheese has melted.

While the burgers are frying, place the buns cut side down on a barbecue grill or chargrill pan for just a minute until warmed and lightly toasted. Combine the burger sauce ingredients in a bowl.

Place a burger patty on the base of each bun. Add the lettuce, onion and tomato. Add a generous dollop of your burger sauce, top with bun lids and serve.

TIPS Using cheap minced meat is very important here. In Australia, mince is generally graded on fat content, with the cheapest supermarket mince being about 18 per cent fat. You need a decent fat content somewhere near 20 per cent (or even more) for a burger that is flavourful and tender.

Of course you can add cooked onion, egg, bacon or whatever else you like to your cheeseburgers, but this recipe is just for the basics.

If you like a bit of variety, change up your burger sauce. Use tonkatsu sauce, mix in a bit of gochujang for a Korean spin, or add some black garlic if you're trying to be fancy.

Roast pork belly with green mustard

—

Serves 8
Prep 15 minutes
Rest overnight, plus 20 minutes
Cook 1 hour

Pork belly is a great roasting cut. The skin is relatively flat, encouraging great crackling on every piece, and the striations of fat and meat keep the whole thing tender. The sweet and sour green mustard cuts through some of the fattiness.

2 kg (4 lb 6 oz) pork belly

1 teaspoon ground white or black pepper

3 garlic cloves, finely chopped

2 tablespoons salt

GREEN MUSTARD (MAKES EXTRA)

3 large green chillies, seeds removed

1 cup coriander (cilantro) leaves, stalks and roots

2 garlic cloves, roughly chopped

½ cup (125 g/4½ oz) smooth dijon mustard

1 tablespoon rice vinegar

2 teaspoons sugar

Cut shallow slits along the meat side of the pork. Prick many small holes into the skin of the pork with a metal skewer or sharp knife. Pour boiling water over the skin and then pat dry; you can skip this step if you like, but it does help the crackling. Rub the meat side with the pepper and garlic, then sprinkle the skin side generously with the entire 2 tablespoons of salt. Place on a rack in the fridge uncovered overnight (see Tip).

Heat your oven to 180°C (350°F) conventional. Brush the salt off the skin of the pork, then roast the pork for 45 minutes.

Turn your oven's overhead grill (broiler) to high heat and grill the pork for a further 10–15 minutes, watching carefully that the skin doesn't burn. Remove from the oven when the skin is crisp. If some parts of the skin are raised and starting to burn, you can strategically protect them with a covering of foil while the rest crisps. Once removed from the oven, rest for at least 20 minutes.

Combine all the green mustard ingredients in a small blender or food processor and blend to a smooth paste. (Alternatively, use a mortar and pestle to pound the green ingredients to a paste, then mix with the remaining ingredients.) Taste and adjust the seasoning.

Slice the rested pork and serve with the green mustard.

TIP Salting and drying the skin overnight is the never-fail secret to perfect pork crackling. It just takes a little bit of forward planning.

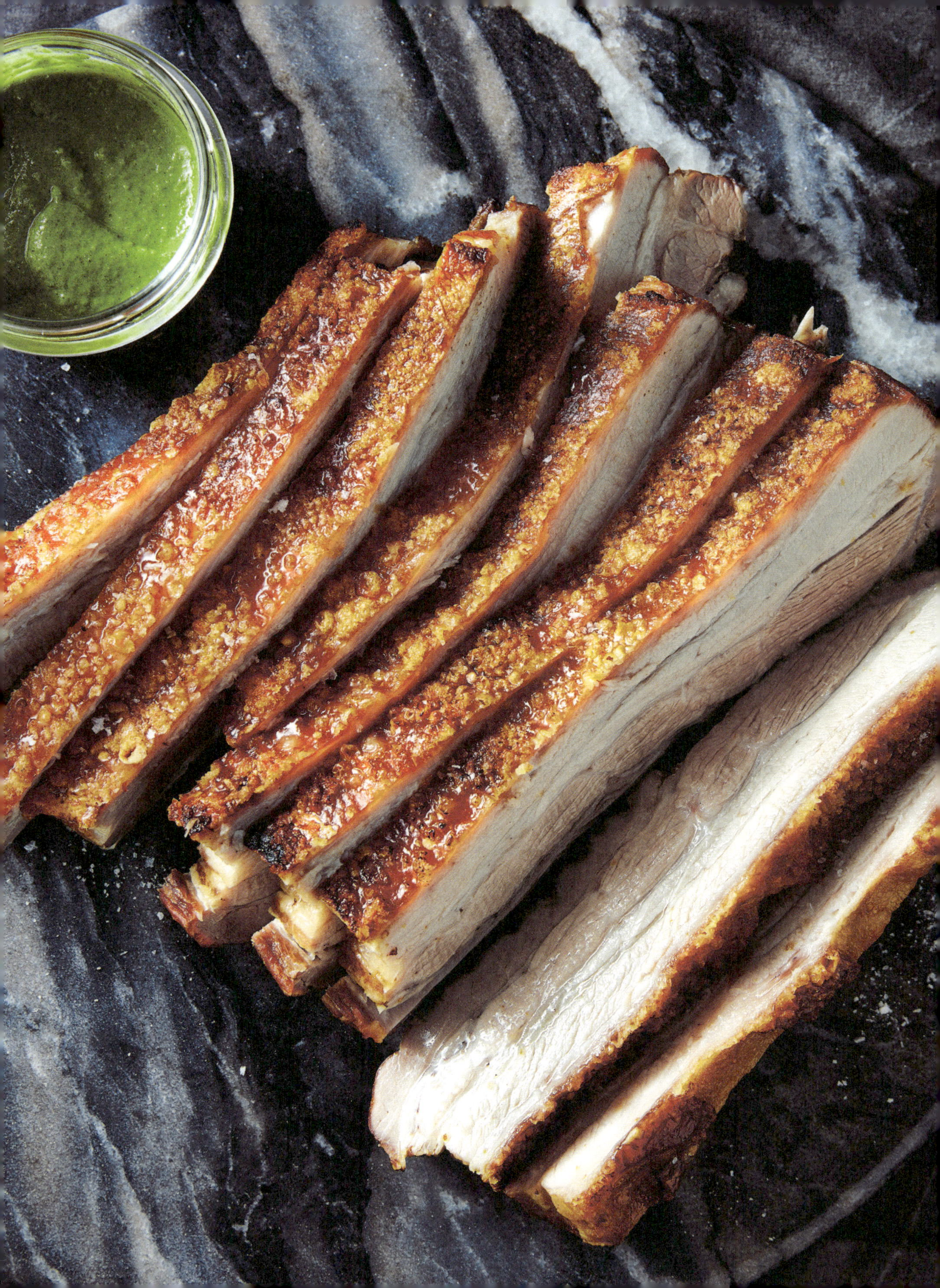

Chicken Marbella

—

Serves 6
Prep 10 minutes
Rest Overnight
Cook 1 hour

This is my version of the chicken Marbella recipe from the classic 1980s American cookbook, *The Silver Palate*. It's a great recipe that marries briny capers and olives with the sweetness of brown sugar and the sourness of red-wine vinegar. The original recipe used a whole chicken and a whole cup of sugar, but I prefer the juiciness of chicken leg quarters and a lighter hand with the sweetness.

6 chicken leg quarters, thigh and drumstick separated at the joint

1 cup (250 ml/8½ fl oz) white wine

½ cup (125 ml/4 fl oz) olive oil

½ cup (125 ml/4 fl oz) red-wine vinegar

1 cup (220 g/8 oz) pitted prunes

1 cup (175 g/6 oz) green olives

6 garlic cloves, bruised

¼ cup (45 g/1½ oz) capers

2 tablespoons brown sugar

1 teaspoon salt

2 tablespoons finely shredded parsley

Combine all the ingredients, except the parsley, in a large non-reactive bowl (see Tips) and refrigerate overnight.

Heat your oven to 180°C (350°F) fan-forced. Transfer the chicken and its marinade to a non-reactive roasting pan, leaving the chicken pieces skin side up in a single layer. Roast for 40 minutes.

Turn your oven's overhead grill (broiler) to high and grill the chicken for a further 10–15 minutes until well browned and cooked through. Remove the chicken to a plate to rest.

Place the roasting pan on the stove. Bring the marinade to a simmer and cook for about 5 minutes until the sauce is reduced and slightly thickened.

Spoon the sauce over the chicken. Serve garnished with the parsley.

TIPS Serve this dish with crusty bread, some boiled new potatoes or simply a crisp green salad.

Some bowls and cookware will react with ingredients (particularly acidic ones) to produce undesirable colours, smells and tastes. Avoid using copper, cast iron or aluminium bowls or cookware for recipes containing acids such as vinegar. Stainless steel and enamel-coated iron are fine.

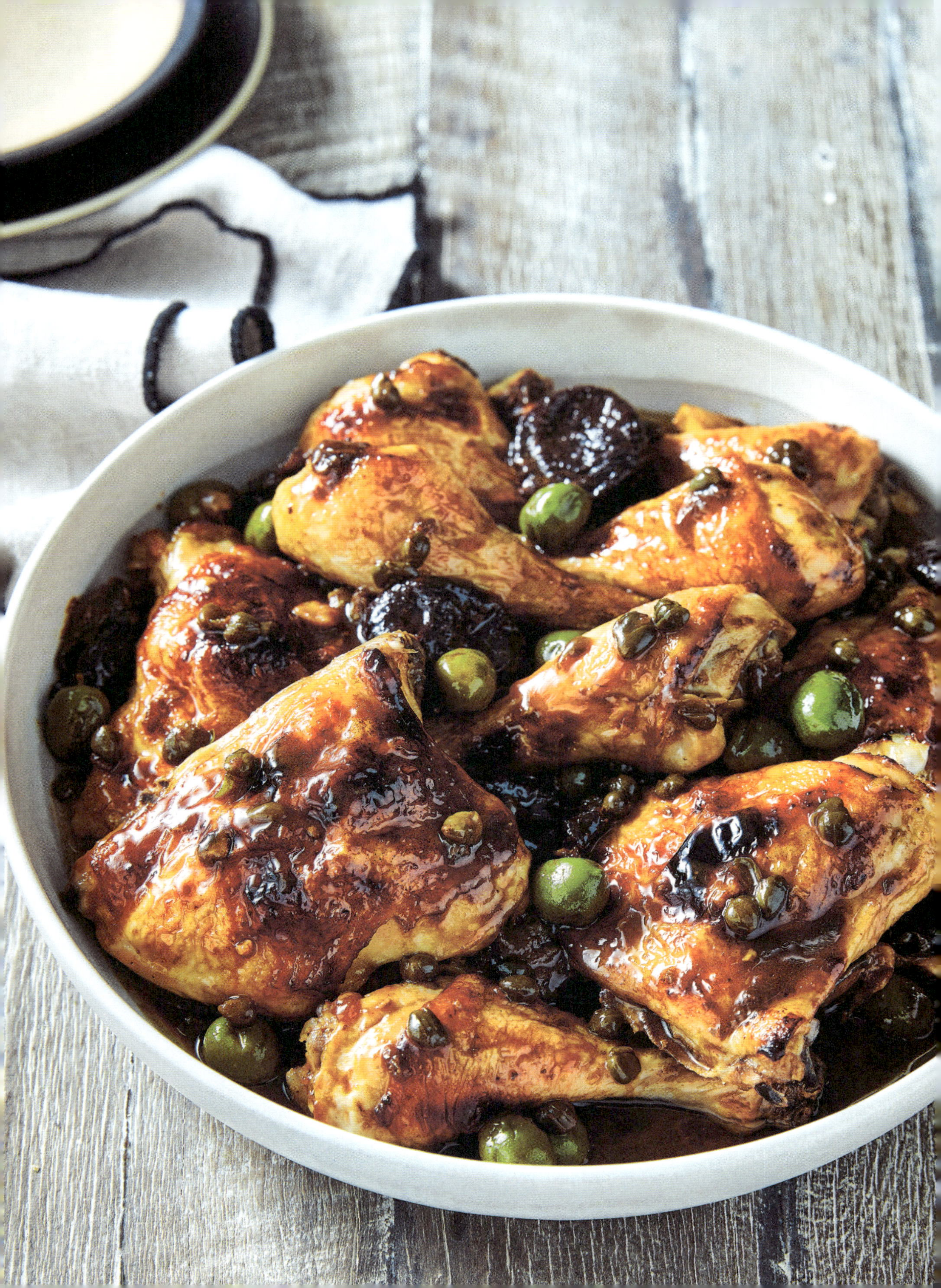

Japanese-style dry curry

Serves 10
Prep 20 minutes
Cook 40 minutes

Japanese curry roux blocks are a staple in our house, and they're more versatile than you might think. In the previous volume of *Tonight's Dinner* I showed you how to make a Japanese curry from scratch (Japanese curry sausages, page 44), but here we're using the roux blocks for a simple Japanese version of the Indian spicy minced meat dish *kheema*.

2 large brown onions

2 celery stalks

2 carrots

1 large eggplant (aubergine)

4 garlic cloves

2 tablespoons olive oil

1 kg (2 lb 3 oz) minced (ground) beef

700 ml (23½ fl oz) tomato passata (puréed tomatoes)

3 cups (465 g/1 lb) frozen peas

150–200 g (5½–7 oz) Japanese curry roux (see Tips)

8 eggs, at room temperature

cooked Japanese-style rice, to serve

finely shredded parsley, to serve

Cut the onions, celery, carrots and eggplant into 1 cm (½ in) cubes, and roughly chop the garlic.

Heat a large saucepan over a medium heat and add the oil. Fry the vegetables and garlic for about 10 minutes until fragrant and softened. Add the beef and fry, stirring and breaking up any clumps, for a few minutes until lightly browned.

Stir in the passata and about 2 cups (500 ml/17 fl oz) water, bring to a simmer and cook for 30 minutes.

Stir the peas through. Roughly chop the curry roux blocks and add them to the curry. Stir until the roux has dissolved and the curry is thick and dry.

While the curry is cooking, bring a pot of water to the boil and cook the eggs for 6½ minutes. Transfer to a bowl of iced water, cool and peel.

Serve the curry over rice, scattered with parsley, with the boiled eggs on top.

TIPS Different brands of Japanese curry roux come in slightly different sizes, but you don't need to be exact. Around 150–200 g (5½–7 oz) will be enough to flavour and thicken this amount of sauce.

Take a shortcut by adding a few cubes of Japanese curry roux and some frozen peas to leftover Bolognese sauce (page 136).

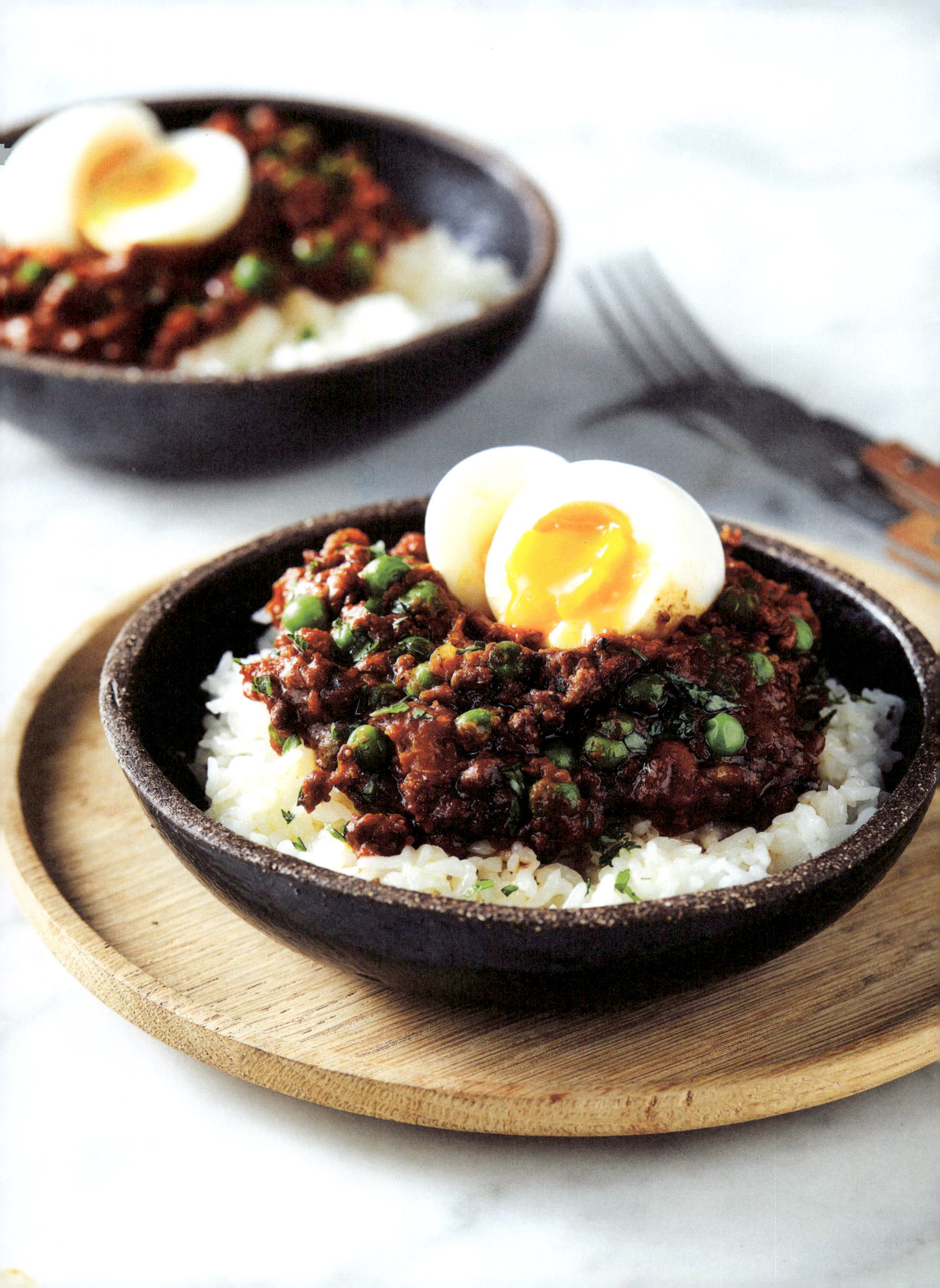

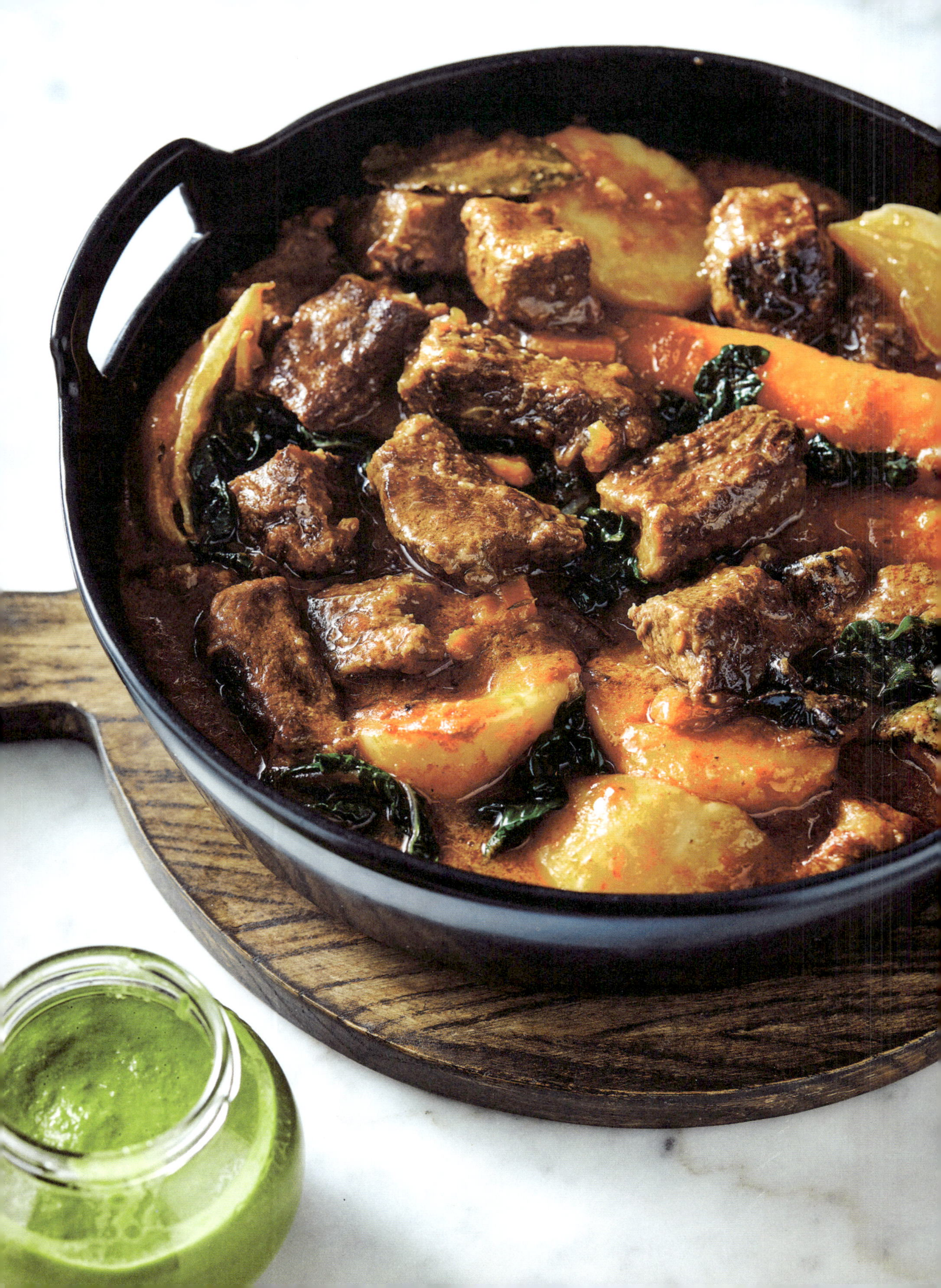

Winter beef & silverbeet stew

—

Serves 4
Prep 15 minutes
Cook 2 hours 20 minutes

A delicious stew can be improved significantly by giving it a late lift of freshness and acidity to offset the richness of the slow-cooked meat and vegetables. Just-wilted silverbeet (Swiss chard) and a tangy chutney made from the stalks make a huge difference to what would otherwise be a fairly regular stew.

2 kg (4 lb 6 oz) chuck steak

½ cup (75 g/2¾ oz) plain (all-purpose) flour

1 tablespoon sweet paprika

salt and black pepper, to season

2 tablespoons vegetable oil

3 large brown onions, peeled

1 kg (2 lb 3 oz) carrots, peeled

25 g (1 oz) butter

1 cup (250 ml/8½ fl oz) white wine

400 g (14 oz) tinned diced tomatoes

4 cups (1 litre/34 fl oz) beef stock

1 cinnamon stick

2 star anise

4 bay leaves

6 thyme sprigs

3 potatoes, peeled and halved

1 large bunch silverbeet (Swiss chard), stalks trimmed and reserved, leaves roughly torn

¼ bunch parsley, leaves picked, stalks reserved

STALK CHUTNEY

reserved parsley and silverbeet stalks

1–2 silverbeet leaves

2 tablespoons apple-cider vinegar

1 teaspoon sugar

salt, to season

2 tablespoons olive oil

For the stalk chutney, place the parsley and silverbeet stalks in a blender and blend with just enough vinegar to produce a smooth, thick paste. Season to taste with the sugar and plenty of salt. Pour into a small serving bowl, pour the olive oil on top, then set aside to rest in the fridge while the stew cooks.

Cut the steak into 5 cm (2 in) pieces, then toss with the flour, paprika and plenty of salt and pepper. Heat a large frying pan over a medium heat, add the oil and brown the meat in batches (see Tip).

While the meat is cooking, roughly chop one of the onions and a few carrots. Heat a large heavy-based flameproof casserole dish over a medium heat. Add the vegetables with the butter and fry for about 10 minutes.

Add the meat to the casserole dish. Deglaze the frying pan with the wine, stirring well to combine with the pan juices, then add the wine to the casserole dish. Stir in the tomatoes and stock and top up with enough water to cover the meat. Add the cinnamon, star anise, bay leaves and thyme, and season well with salt and pepper. Cover and simmer over a low heat for about 1 hour.

Quarter the remaining onions and add to the pot with the potatoes and whole peeled carrots. Top up with more water if needed and simmer for a further hour. About 5 minutes before serving, stir the silverbeet and parsley leaves through.

Serve the stew with the chutney on the side for drizzling over.

TIP You could brown the meat in the casserole dish, but I think browning it in a separate pan (and deglazing the pan afterwards) gives you more control, as it reduces the chances of the flour burning in the bottom of the dish as you cook multiple batches.

Oven wedges
—

Serves 4
Prep 15 minutes
Freeze 1 hour
Cook 1 hour 15 minutes

I ate a lot of wedges in the 1990s, but didn't we all. These oven-baked ones are absolutely delicious, tricked up slightly with the addition of sweet potato, and a spike of hot chilli into the classic sweet chilli sour cream combination.

2 large potatoes, washed but not peeled

1 large sweet potato, washed but not peeled

½ cup (75 g/2¾ oz) plain (all-purpose) flour

2 tablespoons salt

1 teaspoon smoked paprika

½ teaspoon onion powder

½ teaspoon garlic powder

½ teaspoon black pepper

⅔ cup (170 ml/5½ fl oz) vegetable oil

½ cup (125 g/4½ oz) sour cream

1 tablespoon sweet chilli sauce

2 teaspoons chipotle hot sauce or sriracha (optional)

Start this step well in advance to allow the potatoes to chill; you can even do it the day before. Microwave the potatoes and sweet potato together — whole and unpeeled — for 15 minutes, then allow to cool to room temperature. Cut into wedges, dust lightly with the flour (I use a pastry brush to dust them) and place on a lined baking tray in the freezer. Freeze for at least 1 hour.

Heat the salt in a dry frying pan, then transfer the hot salt to a mortar. Add the spices and grind to a fine powder.

Heat the oven to 200°C (400°F) fan-forced. Add the oil to a large baking dish and heat in the oven for about 8 minutes.

Carefully place the wedges into the hot oil in a single layer. Bake for 30 minutes, then turn the wedges over and bake for a further 20–30 minutes until crisp and browned.

Remove from the baking dish and sprinkle liberally with the seasoning. Serve with the sour cream, sweet chilli sauce and hot sauce.

TIP If you like, you can make a big batch up to the end of the freezing stage. Then, when the wedges are completely frozen, store them in a press-seal bag in the freezer, ready for roasting.

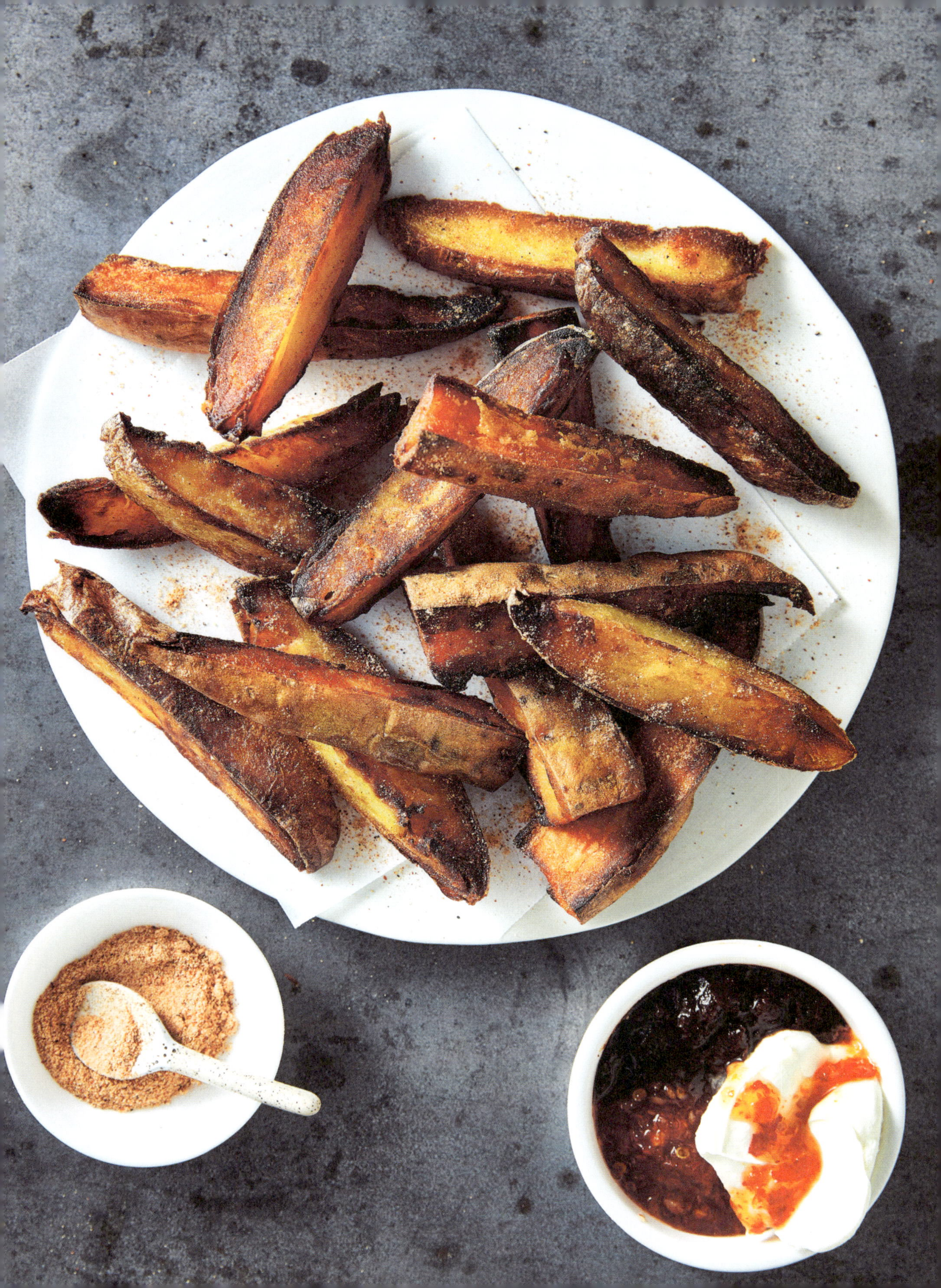

Ssamjang chicken

Serves 4
Prep 15 minutes
Cook 40 minutes
Rest 15 minutes

Consider this Shandong chicken – crispy skin chicken in sauce – via Korea. Ssamjang is a Korean sauce used for wraps and as a dipping sauce, but here I'm pouring it over a very simple butterflied roast chicken.

1 whole chicken, about 1.6 kg (3½ lb)
1 tablespoon dark soy sauce
salt, to season

SSAMJANG

¼ cup (60 ml/2 fl oz) rice vinegar
2 tablespoons gochujang (Korean red pepper paste)
1 tablespoon brown miso paste (or doenjang, Korean fermented soybean paste)
1 tablespoon sesame oil
2 teaspoons soy sauce
2 teaspoons caster (superfine) sugar
2 garlic cloves, crushed
1 red bird's eye chilli, sliced
4 spring onions (scallions), finely sliced

TO SERVE

butter lettuce leaves
Korean roasted nori sheets
steamed rice

Heat your oven to 220°C (430°F) fan-forced, and turn on the overhead grill (broiler). Cut the backbone out of the chicken using kitchen scissors, then cut the backbone into pieces and lay them in a roasting pan. Place the chicken on top. Rub both sides of the chicken with the soy sauce and season with salt. Roast for 40 minutes, then remove from the oven and rest for 15 minutes.

Combine the ssamjang ingredients in a small bowl. Add a few spoonfuls of the resting juices and oils from the chicken to produce a loose paste.

Chop the chicken into pieces, smother with the sauce and serve with lettuce leaves, nori and rice. Wrap a little chicken, nori and rice in a lettuce leaf to eat.

TIP You can buy ssamjang from Asian grocers instead of making your own. Just thin it down to a pourable consistency with a bit of vinegar, water and resting juices from the chicken.

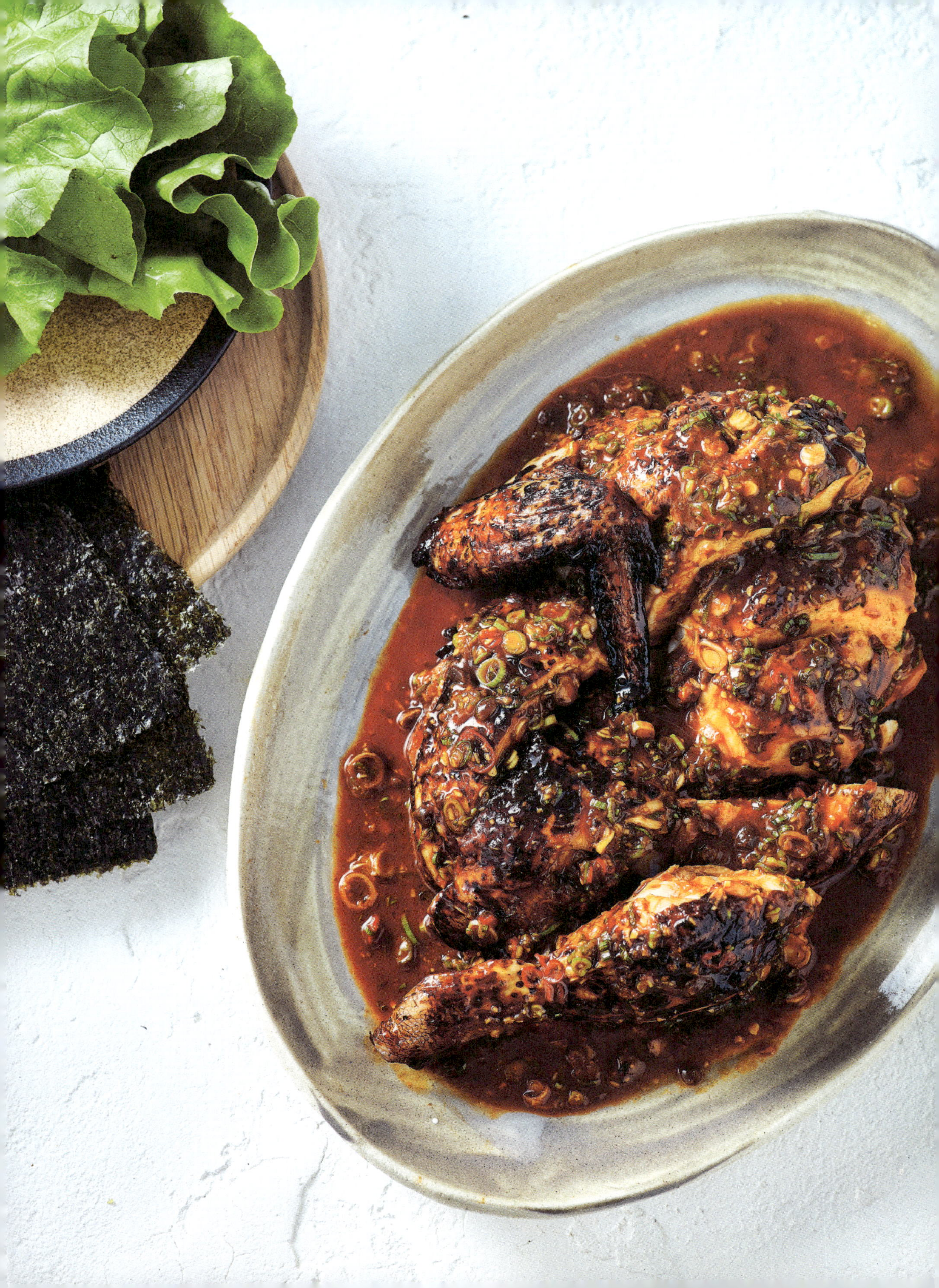

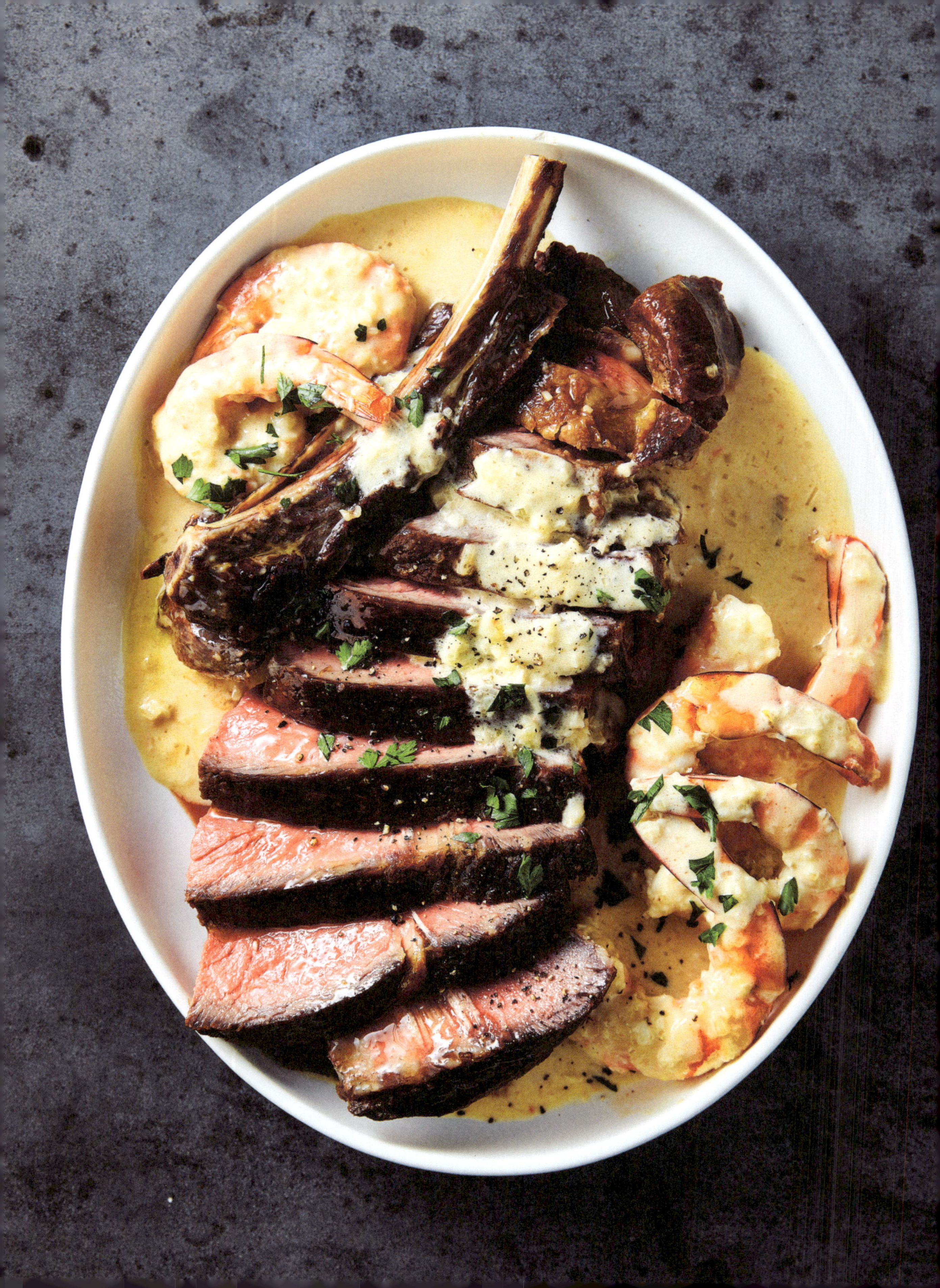

Rib-eye with creamy garlic prawns

—

Serves 4
Prep 10 minutes
Cook 20 minutes
Rest 10 minutes

2 teaspoons vegetable oil

1 thick scotch fillet steak on the bone — about 800 g (1 lb 12 oz) with bone

salt and black pepper, to season

25 g (1 oz) butter

6 garlic cloves, finely crushed

1 French shallot, very finely chopped

¾ cup (190 ml/6½ fl oz) dry white wine

1 tablespoon brandy (optional)

2 teaspoons fish sauce

200 ml (7 fl oz) thickened (whipping) cream

8 extra-large raw prawns (shrimp), peeled

1 teaspoon cornflour (cornstarch), mixed with ¼ cup (60 ml/2 fl oz) water

1 tablespoon finely chopped parsley

Surf and turf. Beef and reef. Horn and prawn. Ungulate and invertebrate. Whatever you want to call it, this is a significant indulgence, but that doesn't mean you should never do it. When we have steak at home, something like this isn't for one person. I generally plan to serve about 125 g (4½ oz) boneless uncooked meat per person — so, a 500 g (1 lb 2 oz) steak for four people. Sharing is caring.

Heat a frying pan over a medium heat and add the oil. Season the steak with salt and pepper and fry until cooked to your liking. Even with a thick steak, I like to cook it directly on lower heat for the whole time. Sear it first and then reduce the heat. A steak this size will take about 15–20 minutes on a low heat to cook to medium-rare, turning occasionally so that it cooks evenly. Alternatively, you can sear the steak in the pan, then transfer to a preheated 180°C (350°F) oven for about 8–10 minutes, depending on the thickness of your steak. Once cooked, rest the steak for about 10 minutes.

While the steak is resting, add the butter to the pan. Fry the garlic and shallot for about a minute until fragrant but not yet browned. Add the wine and brandy, if using, and simmer until the wine is reduced by half. Stir in the fish sauce and cream and bring to a simmer again until the sauce is thickened. Season to taste.

Add the prawns and simmer for about 3 minutes until the prawns are nearly cooked. If you need to, thicken the sauce with a few spoonfuls of the cornflour slurry — don't add it all — until the sauce coats a spoon (see Tip).

If you like, sear the rested steak for about 30 seconds on each side to refresh, then immediately slice the steak and arrange on a serving platter. Pour the prawns and sauce over, scatter with the parsley and serve.

TIP Thickening a sauce with a starch mixture might be a no-no in classic French cooking, but it's a definite yes-yes in Cantonese cuisine. Making sure the sauce is thick enough to coat the prawns is very important here.

Stewed spinach & mince

—

Serves 8
Prep 10 minutes
Cook 25 minutes

On *The Cook Up* I made this dish with kangaroo mince and warrigal greens, but using beef and spinach makes it an incredibly easy, affordable and delicious family meal. It's essentially a version of the classic Lebanese 'spinach and rice'.

½ cup (125 ml/4 fl oz) olive oil

1 large brown onion, finely chopped

8 garlic cloves, finely chopped

4 coriander (cilantro) plants, stalks and roots roughly chopped, leaves reserved

500 g (1 lb 2 oz) minced (ground) beef

1 kg (2 lb 3 oz) English spinach, leaves and stalks roughly chopped

1 tablespoon garam masala or baharat (Lebanese seven-spice)

1 cup (250 ml/8½ fl oz) chicken stock (or water)

salt and black pepper, to season

steamed basmati rice, to serve

¼ cup (40 g/1½ oz) toasted pine nuts, or roughly chopped macadamia nuts

lemon wedges, to serve

Heat a large frying pan over a medium heat and add the olive oil, onion, garlic and coriander stems and roots. Cook until very fragrant, then add the beef and fry for a few minutes until browned.

Add the spinach, garam masala and stock, then season well with salt and pepper. Simmer, uncovered, for about 20 minutes until the mixture is a thick stew.

Serve over rice, sprinkled with the pine nuts, with lemon wedges on the side.

TIP Fully grown English spinach is better here than baby spinach leaves, not just because it's cheaper, but because of the texture of the spinach stems. If you prefer, you can use 600 g (1 lb 5 oz) frozen spinach instead.

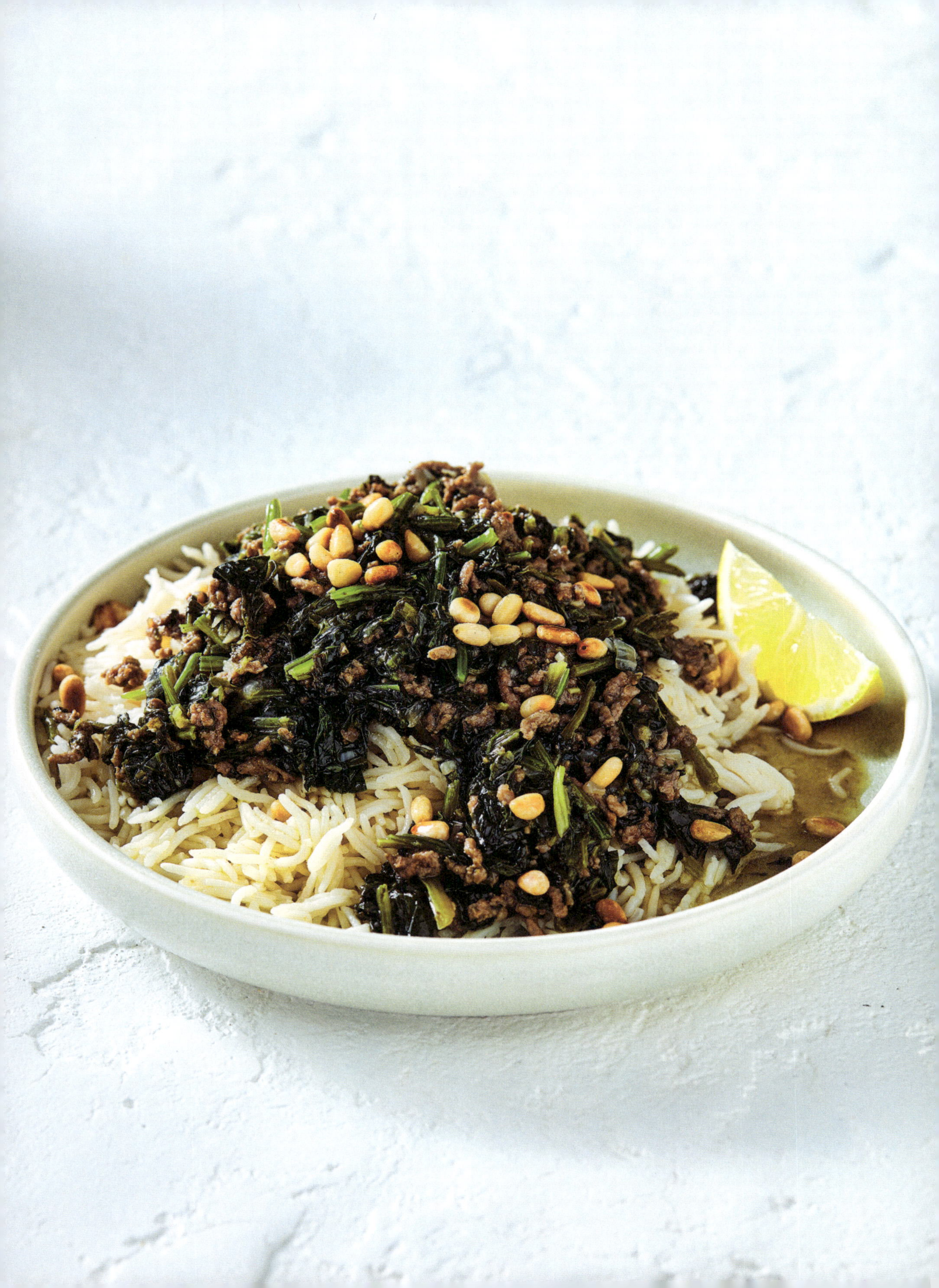

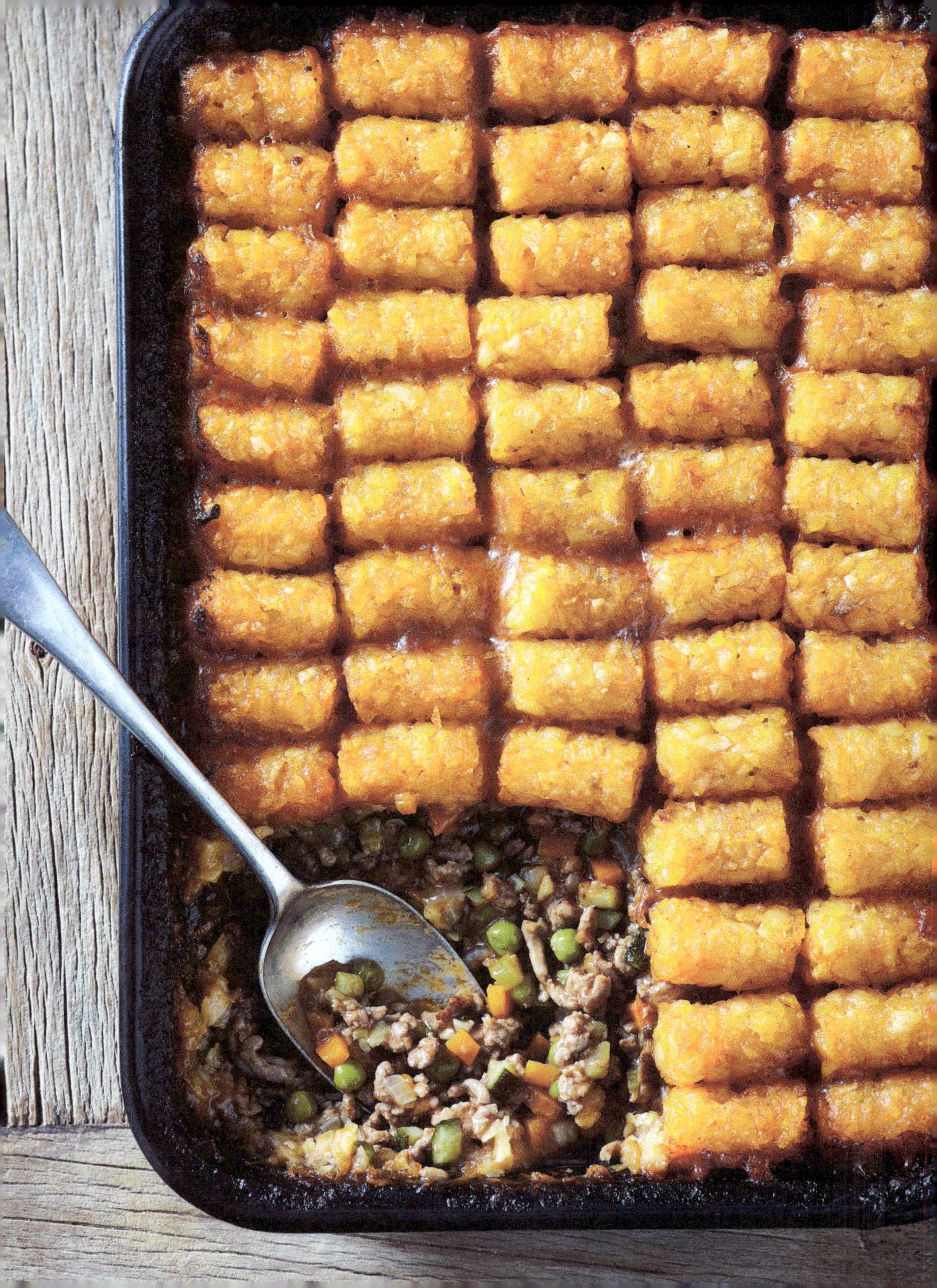

Potato gem shepherd's pie

—

Serves 8
Prep 15 minutes
Cook 2 hours 15 minutes

I love a simple shepherd's pie, but the one thing I find time consuming is making the mashed potato for the topping. This recipe skips that whole hassle by topping it with frozen potato gems instead. Don't judge it until you've tried it.

1 tablespoon olive oil

25 g (1 oz) butter

1 large brown onion, finely diced

2 garlic cloves, roughly chopped

3 carrots, finely diced

1 celery stalk, finely diced

2 zucchini (courgettes), finely diced

1 kg (2 lb 3 oz) minced (ground) lamb (or beef)

2 tablespoons tomato paste (concentrated purée)

½ cup (75 g/2¾ oz) plain (all-purpose) flour

½ cup (125 ml/4 fl oz) white wine

4 cups (1 litre/34 fl oz) beef stock

1 tablespoon worcestershire sauce

1 rosemary sprig

2 bay leaves

2 cups (310 g/11 oz) frozen peas

600 g (1 lb 5 oz) frozen potato gems, approximately

Heat a large casserole dish over a medium heat and add the olive oil and butter. Fry the onion, garlic, carrot, celery and zucchini for about 10 minutes until fragrant and lightly browned.

Add the lamb and fry for a few minutes until browned. Add the tomato paste and stir well, then add the flour and stir for about 3 minutes to combine with the lamb and vegetables. Stir in the wine, bring to a simmer and cook for 2 minutes.

Stir in the stock, worcestershire sauce and herbs. Cover and simmer for 1 hour.

Remove the lid and simmer for another 30 minutes or so until the mixture is the thickness you'd like for a shepherd's pie filling. Stir the peas into the warm mixture.

Heat your oven to 200°C (400°F) fan-forced. Transfer the filling to a large baking dish and arrange the frozen potato gems on top, covering the entire surface with as few gaps as possible.

Bake for 25 minutes until the potato gems are golden brown, then serve.

TIP For the best results, make the filling ahead of time and let it cool on the stove. Then you can top it with the potato gems and bake it when you're ready to eat.

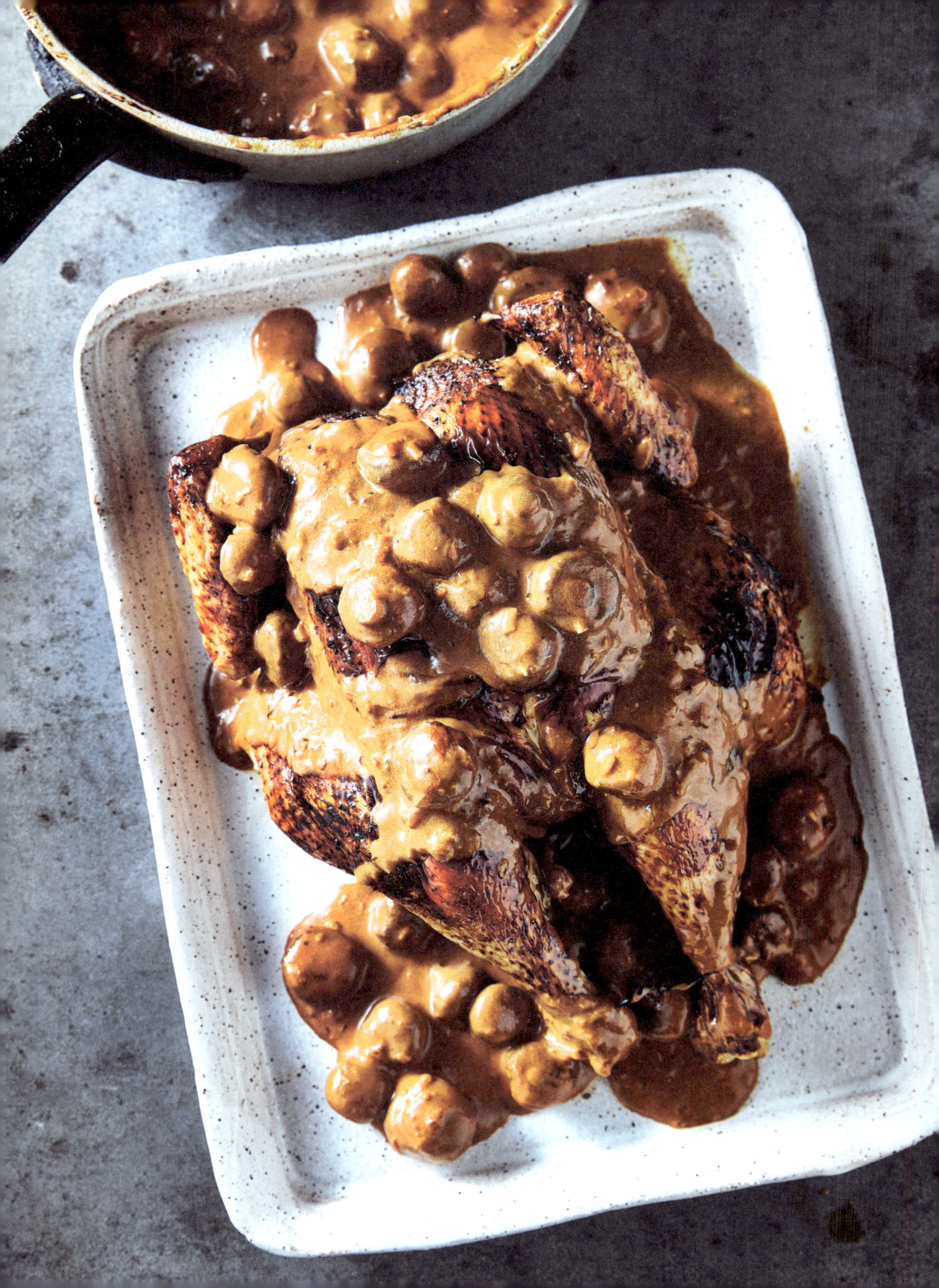

Roast chicken with whole mushroom sauce

—

Serves 8
Prep 10 minutes
Cook 1 hour
Rest 15 minutes

1 whole chicken, about 1.7 kg (3 lb 12 oz)

1 tablespoon dark soy sauce

salt and black pepper, to season

400 g (14 oz) small button mushrooms

15 g (½ oz) butter

1 onion, finely chopped

2 garlic cloves, finely chopped

2 tablespoons plain (all-purpose) flour

½ cup (125 ml/4 fl oz) white wine

1 cup (250 ml/8½ fl oz) chicken stock

150 ml (5 fl oz) thickened (whipping) cream

1 teaspoon white-wine vinegar

¼ cup finely shredded parsley

Most of the time involved in cooking is actually in the preparation. If something is in an oven or on a stove, it's often doing its thing without needing too much of our attention. I wrote this recipe to create a sauce from whole mushrooms mainly because a few friends complained that mushrooms take too long to slice.

Heat your oven to 220°C (430°F) fan-forced.

Using kitchen scissors, cut the backbone out of the chicken and reserve for making stock. Rub the chicken all over with the soy sauce and season well with salt and pepper. Spread the mushrooms in a roasting pan and set a rack over the top. Place the chicken on the rack, transfer to the oven and roast for 45 minutes.

Remove the chicken from the rack and rest on a plate in a warm place for 15 minutes.

While the chicken is resting, place the roasting pan with the mushrooms (and chicken juices) over a medium heat. Add the butter, onion and garlic and fry with the roasted mushrooms for about 3 minutes until lightly browned.

Stir in the flour and fry for a further few minutes until the flour starts to brown. Add the wine and stock a little at a time, stirring to remove any lumps, then bring to a simmer and cook for a few minutes until a thick sauce develops. Stir the cream through and season to taste with salt and pepper.

Joint the chicken and add any resting juices to the mushroom sauce. Stir the vinegar through the sauce and serve with the chicken, scattered with the parsley.

TIP Practice makes perfect if you want to improve your knife skills. Watch a few videos on YouTube and concentrate on cutting an onion, then a carrot. Then keep practising! If you can cut an onion and a carrot efficiently, you can cut anything.

Garlic butter salmon

—

Serves 4
Prep 10 minutes
Cook 10 minutes

The first thing I do when I buy salmon fillets is cut them in half. Smaller salmon fillets are easier to handle, cook more evenly and are probably about the right size for eating anyway.

2 salmon fillets, about 280 g (10 oz) each, skin on, scales and pin bones removed

2 tablespoons vegetable oil

salt, to season

50 g (1¾ oz) butter

6 garlic cloves, roughly chopped

2 tablespoons finely shredded parsley (see Tips)

lemon wedges, to serve

Cut the salmon fillets in half lengthways to produce four small fillets.

Heat a frying pan over a medium–high heat and add the oil. Season the salmon with salt and fry, skin side down, for about 3 minutes.

Roll the fillets over to cook each of the remaining sides for about 1 minute each until the salmon is cooked through. Remove the salmon to a serving plate.

Pour any rendered oil from the pan, wipe out the pan with paper towel and return to the heat. Add the butter to the pan and fry the garlic for about 2 minutes, stirring frequently, until the garlic is lightly browned and the butter is foaming and a hazelnut brown (see Tips).

Add the parsley and stir through quickly, then pour the contents of the pan over the salmon. Serve with lemon wedges.

TIPS This is delicious with a bowl of rice and some Japanese-style pickles, or a simple green salad, or boiled new potatoes and steamed vegetables. You can take this dish in all kinds of directions.

Change this up by using dill instead of parsley, or basil and chilli flakes, or even a few dried ground spices such as turmeric and cumin. It's really about getting the butter right. Too blond and it will taste oily; too dark and it will taste burnt.

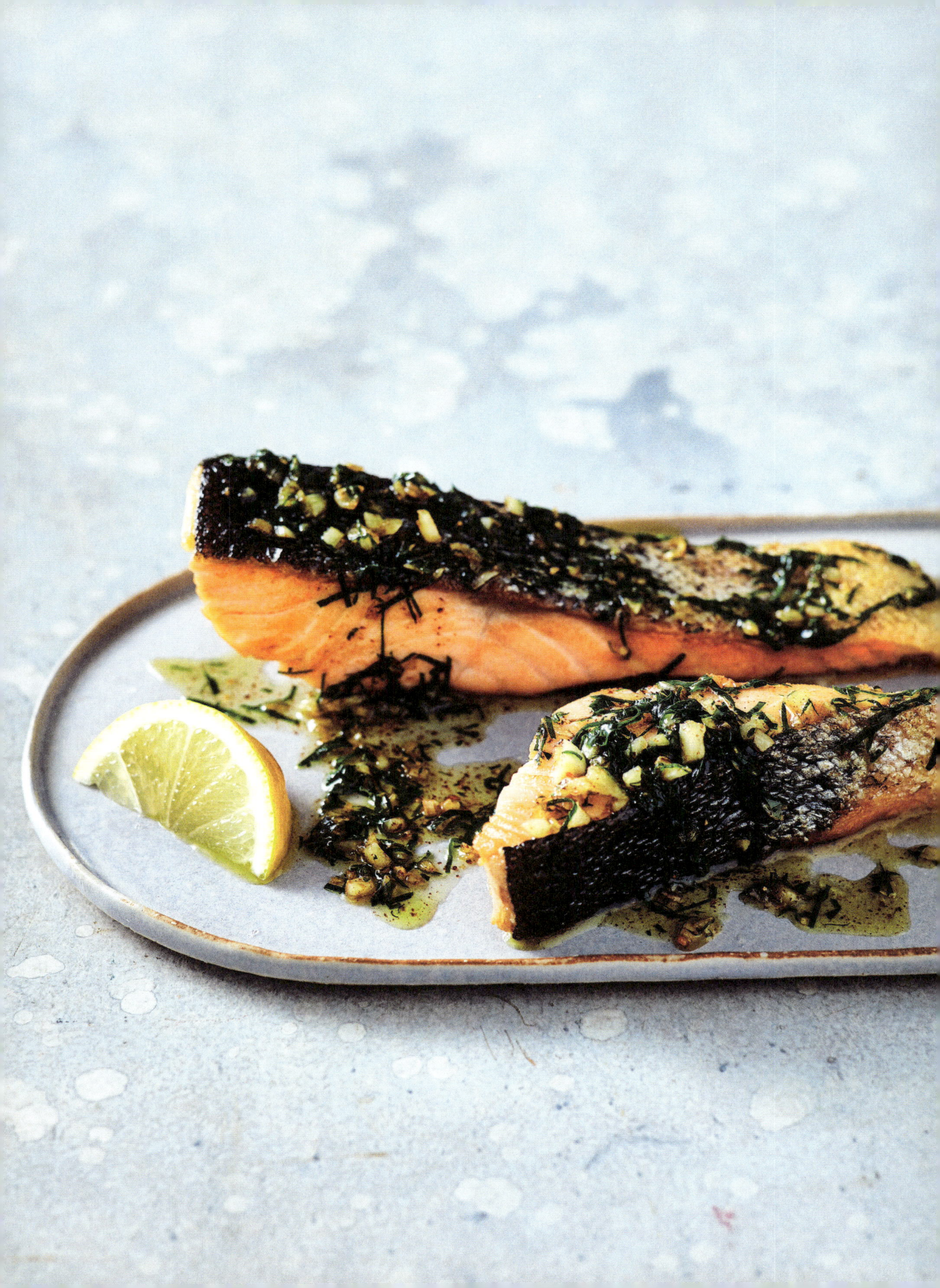

Winter lamb shank navarin

—

Serves 4
Prep 20 minutes
Cook 2 hours 45 minutes

This classic French lamb stew is often made in spring using vegetables such as green beans and peas, but for a more wintery version you can use lamb shanks and beautiful winter kale. The only non-negotiable part is the turnips, which are perfect for the dish — and are actually what gives a 'navarin' its name.

4 large carrots, peeled

1 tablespoon vegetable oil

4 French-trimmed lamb shanks

25 g (1 oz) butter

1 large brown onion, diced

4 garlic cloves, crushed

¼ cup (35 g/1¼ oz) plain (all-purpose) flour

1 cup (250 ml/8½ fl oz) white wine

4 cups (1 litre/34 fl oz) chicken stock

400 ml (13½ fl oz) tomato passata (puréed tomatoes)

1 teaspoon salt

2 rosemary sprigs, leaves finely chopped

6 thyme sprigs, leaves finely chopped

2 bay leaves

3 turnips, peeled and quartered

10 baby onions, peeled

½ bunch kale, stalks removed

1 teaspoon white-wine vinegar

If you feel like turning the carrots, see the Tips below. If not, just cut the carrots into 5 cm (2 in) lengths and skip to the next step.

Heat your oven to 180°C (350°F) fan-forced. Heat a large flameproof casserole dish over a medium heat and add the oil. Brown the lamb shanks on all sides and set aside.

Add the butter to the dish and fry the onion and garlic until fragrant. Add the flour and stir for about 3–4 minutes until the flour mixture starts to brown. Stir in the wine and bring to a simmer, then stir in the stock a little at a time to avoid lumps.

Return the lamb shanks to the pot and add the passata, salt and herbs. Top up with enough water to cover the lamb. Bring to a simmer, cover with the lid, then transfer to the oven to cook for 2 hours.

Remove from the oven, then mix in the carrots, turnips and onions. Bake with the lid on for a further 30 minutes until the vegetables are tender.

Stir in the kale and vinegar, adjust the seasoning and serve.

TIPS Turning carrots is a huge waste of time, and yet I always do it for this dish, and not for any other dish. I honestly don't know why, other than that it's traditional. Food isn't always about efficiency. There's love and art in it, too — even in something as simple as a carrot.

To turn a carrot, cut each carrot into 7 cm (2¾ in) lengths. Using a sharp turning or paring knife, cut seven curved cuts down the length of the carrot, shaving it into a football shape. Save the carrot offcuts for stock.

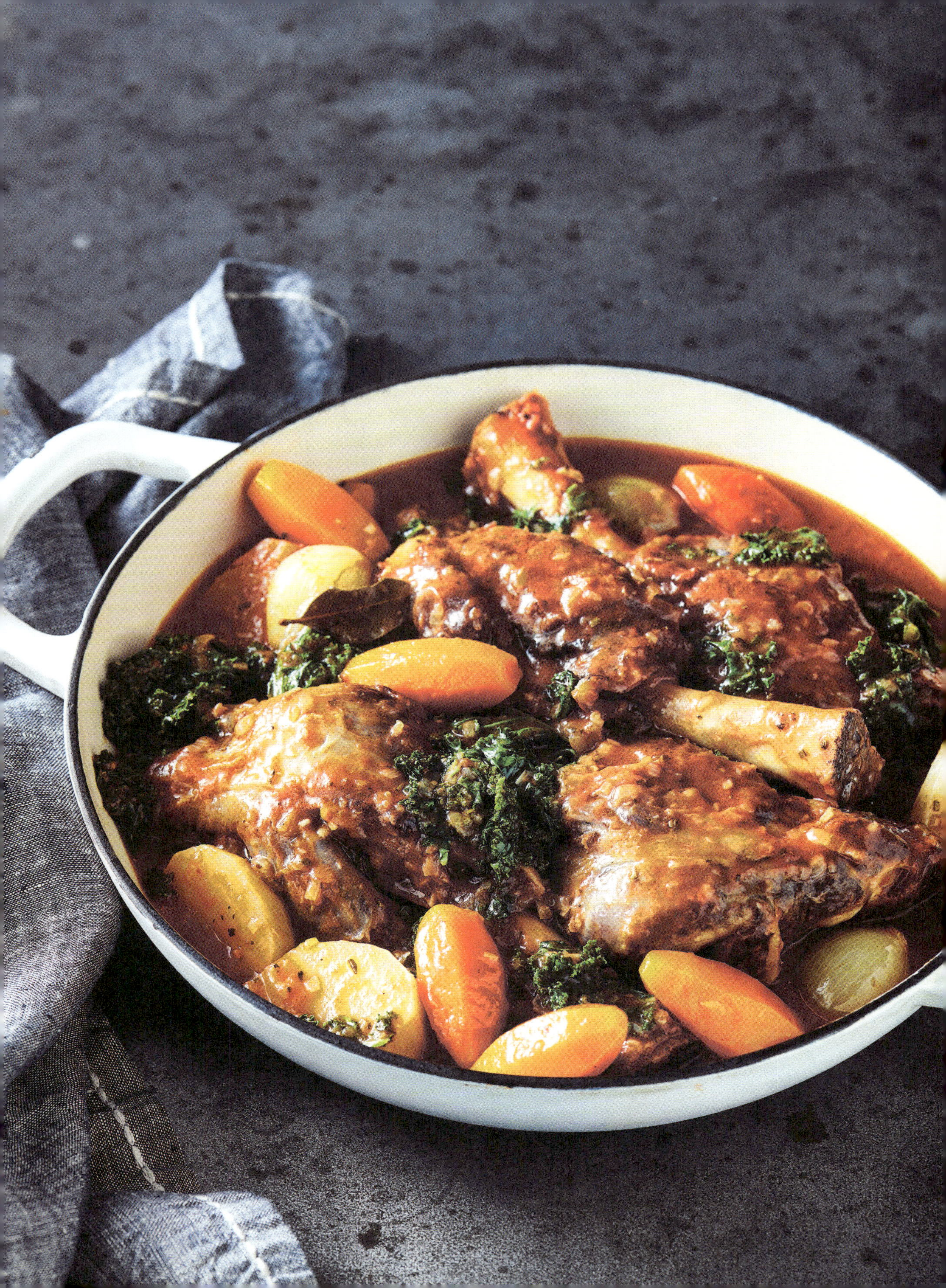

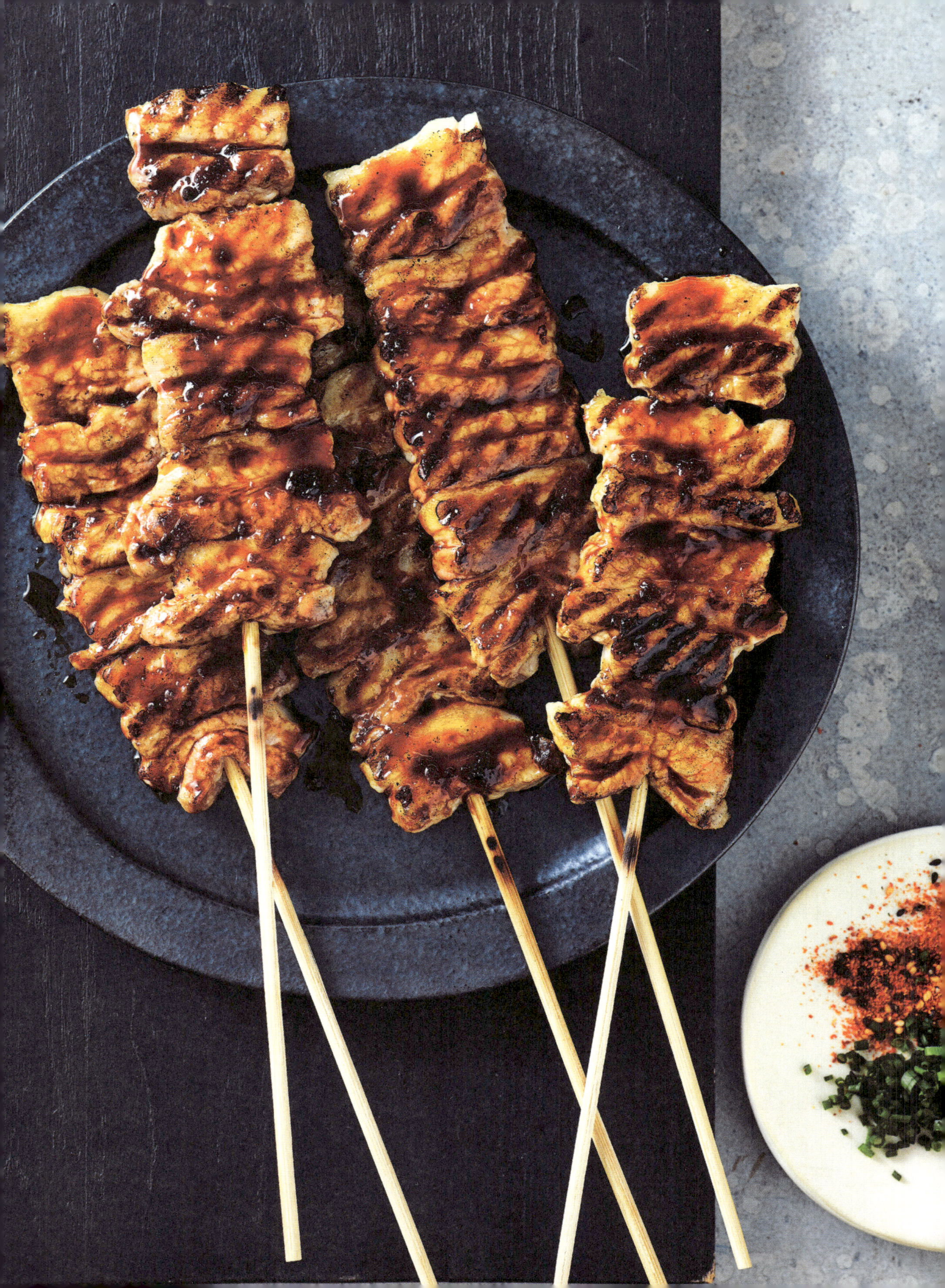

Ginger pork skewers

—

Serves 6 skewers
Prep 20 minutes
Soak 1 hour
Cook 10 minutes

These are a barbecue favourite of ours, both at home and when we go camping, inspired by the jumbo kushiyaki skewers you get at Japanese festivals.

600 g (1 lb 5 oz) pork belly, skin removed

1 tablespoon vegetable oil

¼ cup (60 ml/2 fl oz) soy sauce

2 tablespoons mirin

2 tablespoons sake

1 tablespoon sugar

1 teaspoon grated fresh ginger

1 tablespoon finely chopped chives

½ teaspoon shichimi togarashi (Japanese seven-spice)

Soak six large bamboo skewers (about 20 cm/8 in long) in water for at least an hour.

Cut the pork belly into 1 cm (½ in) strips, then cut each strip into 5 cm (2 in) pieces. Thread five or six pieces of pork onto each skewer and brush with the oil.

Grill the skewers on a chargrill pan (or on a barbecue) over a medium–high heat for about 3 minutes each side until cooked through.

Combine the soy sauce, mirin, sake, sugar and ginger in a small saucepan. Bring to a simmer and cook for a few minutes until reduced to a thick glaze about the consistency of maple syrup.

Brush or pour the glaze over the skewers and serve with the chives and shichimi togarashi.

TIP You can also make this sauce from teriyaki sauce reduced with some grated ginger. Or leave it out completely. I'll often just grill the pork skewers with a good seasoning of salt and serve them simply with a wedge of lemon.

Seafood & dill pie
—

Serves 4
Prep 20 minutes
Cook 20 minutes

There's no rule with pies that the lid has to seal in the filling. In fact, for seafood it's better to have more control over how the seafood cooks, rather than trying to bake it all together — so baking a pastry lid separately and placing it on top is a much easier option.

1 sheet of butter puff pastry

1 egg, beaten

½ cup (125 ml/4 fl oz) white wine

700 g (1 lb 9 oz) seafood marinara mix (see Tip)

8 extra-large raw prawns (shrimp), peeled and deveined, tails on

1 teaspoon fish sauce

200 ml (7 fl oz) thickened (whipping) cream

2 tablespoons finely shredded dill

lemon wedges, to serve

ONION BÉCHAMEL

2 garlic cloves, bruised

½ onion

1 bay leaf

1½ cups (375 ml/12½ fl oz) milk

3 tablespoons butter

3 tablespoons plain (all-purpose) flour

salt and ground white pepper, to season

Heat your oven to 200°C (400°F) fan-forced. To make the pie lids, cut the pastry sheet into quarters. Brush with the beaten egg and bake for 20 minutes until risen and golden. Set aside.

To make the béchamel, place the garlic, onion, bay leaf and milk in a saucepan and bring to a simmer, then turn off the heat. In a separate saucepan, fry the butter and flour together, stirring for about 3 minutes until the roux is cooked but not yet browned. Strain in the milk a little at a time, stirring to form a white sauce. Season with salt and white pepper and set aside.

In a deep frying pan or shallow casserole dish, bring the wine to a simmer and let it reduce by half. Add the marinara mix, prawns and fish sauce, then the cream and béchamel and stir gently to combine. Simmer for about 4 minutes so that the seafood cooks through, then stir the dill through.

Spoon the mixture into individual serving bowls, top with a pastry square and serve with a wedge of lemon.

TIP A good marinara mix is the sign of a good fishmonger. Marinara mix shouldn't be a dumping ground for old seafood. Rather, it should be the offcuts from filleting quality fish that you can buy for much less than whole fillets. Find a good fishmonger and stick with them.

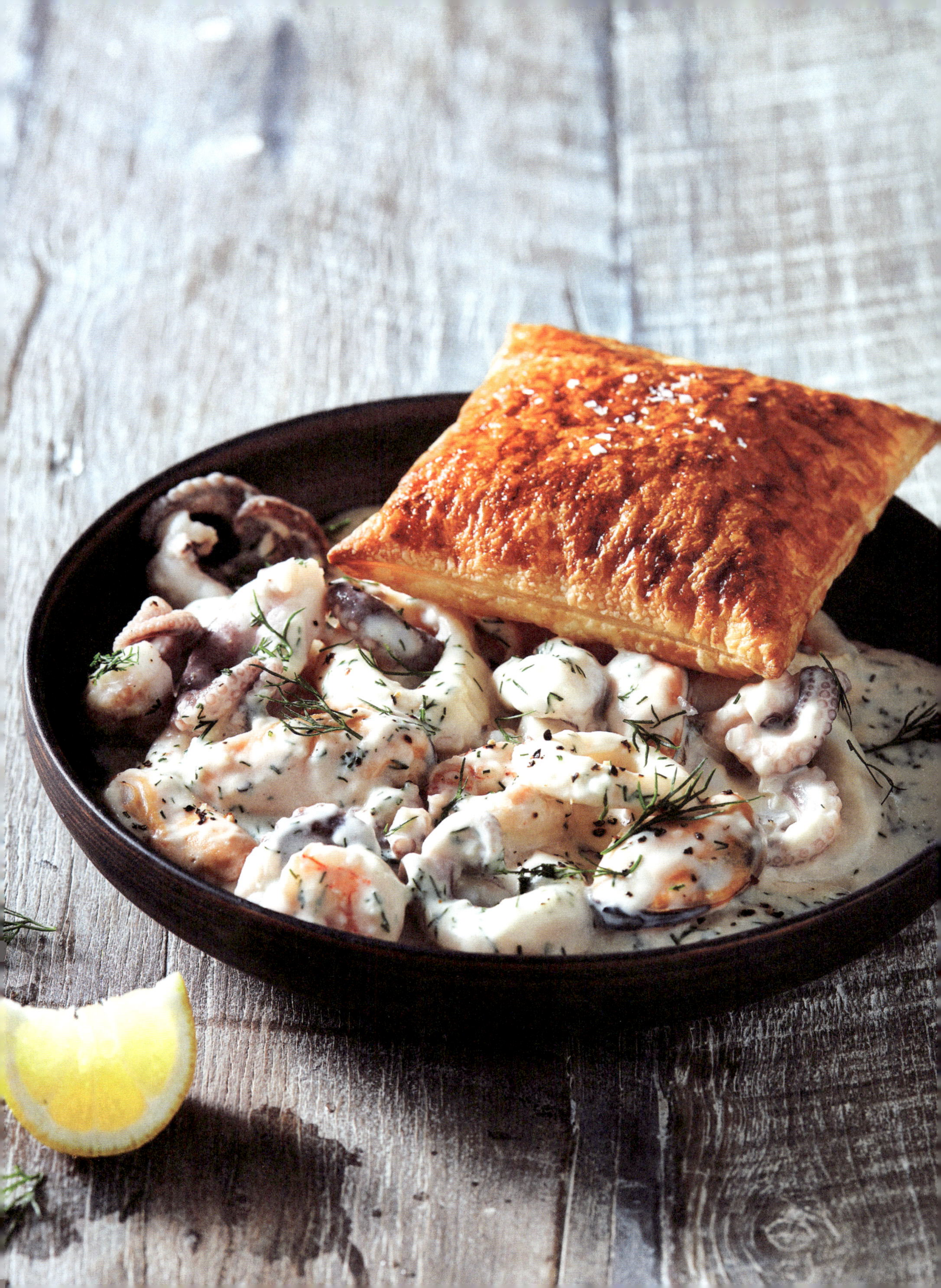

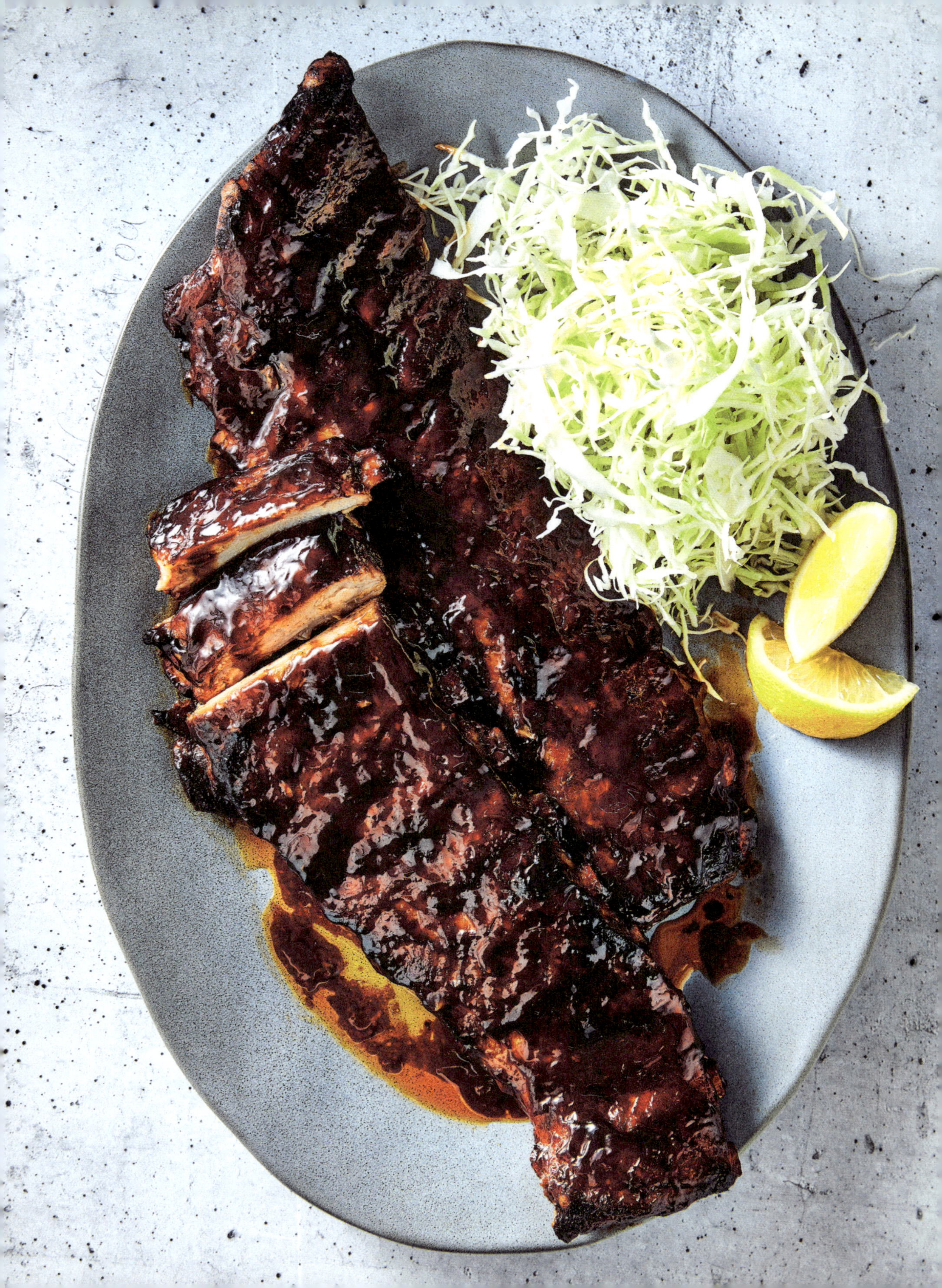

Tonkatsu ribs

—

Serves 4
Prep 5 minutes
Cook 3 hours 15 minutes

A big rack of ribs might look too difficult for a home cook to tackle, but it can be much, much easier than you think. At one end of the spectrum you can spend hours setting up an offset smoker, making sauces from scratch and blending your own rib rubs — but these ribs will literally take you only 5 minutes of hands-on time. Put the ribs in the oven in the afternoon and you've got an easy weekend dinner. I've used a Japanese tonkatsu sauce here, but you can use your favourite barbecue sauce instead.

2 kg (4 lb 6 oz) pork ribs
2 teaspoons smoked paprika
salt and black pepper, to season
2 tablespoons olive oil
¾ cup (190 ml/6½ fl oz) tonkatsu sauce, or other barbecue sauce

TO SERVE
½ head cabbage, finely shredded
lemon wedges

Heat your oven to 130°C (265°F) conventional. Place a sheet of baking paper on a large sheet of foil. Rub the ribs with the paprika, salt and pepper and drizzle with some of the olive oil. Wrap the foil and baking paper around the ribs into a parcel. Transfer to the oven and bake for 3 hours.

Remove the ribs from the oven and unwrap the parcel. Turn your oven's overhead grill (broiler) to high.

Mix the tonkatsu sauce with the remaining oil and brush over the ribs. Grill (broil) the ribs for a further 15 minutes until the sauce has caramelised and the ribs are charred in places.

Serve the ribs with the shredded cabbage and lemon wedges.

TIP Once you have the basic process down, try a Kansas City–style rub. Combine 4 tablespoons soft brown sugar, 2 tablespoons smoked paprika, 2 teaspoons black pepper, 2 teaspoons chilli powder, 2 teaspoons garlic powder, 2 teaspoons onion powder, 1 teaspoon mustard powder, ½ teaspoon ground cinnamon and ¼ cup salt flakes and rub it over the ribs before baking. Serve with your favourite barbecue sauce.

Jambalaya-style sausage rice

—

This affordable one-pot family meal could hardly be easier: fry a couple of sausages, then whack everything else into the pot and simmer away. Come back after 15 minutes and you've got dinner.

Serves 4
Prep 10 minutes
Cook 30 minutes
Stand 5 minutes

---

1 tablespoon vegetable oil

8 good-quality pork sausages

25 g (1 oz) butter

1 green capsicum (bell pepper), diced

1 brown onion, diced

2 celery stalks, diced

3 spring onions (scallions), finely sliced, whites and greens separated

4 garlic cloves, roughly chopped

3 bay leaves

2 teaspoons smoked paprika

½ teaspoon cayenne pepper (optional)

1 teaspoon dried oregano

1 teaspoon dried thyme

1 teaspoon salt

½ teaspoon ground black pepper

4 cups (1 litre/34 fl oz) chicken stock

400 g (14 oz) tinned diced tomatoes

2½ cups (500 g/1 lb 2 oz) uncooked jasmine rice

Heat a large, shallow casserole dish over a medium heat and add the oil. Brown the sausages and remove from the pan. The sausages don't need to be cooked through at this point.

Add the butter, capsicum, onion, celery and white part of the spring onions and cook for about 5 minutes until softened and fragrant. Add the garlic and cook for a further 5 minutes.

Add the bay leaves, spices, salt and pepper, mixing well. Pour in the stock and tomatoes and bring to a simmer. Stir in the rice to combine, then return to a simmer.

Push the sausages into the rice, then reduce the heat to very low, cover and simmer for 15 minutes.

Turn off the heat and stand for 5 minutes. Scatter with the spring onion greens to serve.

TIP An authentic jambalaya usually uses andouille sausages. Kielbasa and chorizo sausages are good substitutes, but I think this works fine with any garden variety sausage. Food doesn't have to be authentic as long as it tastes good.

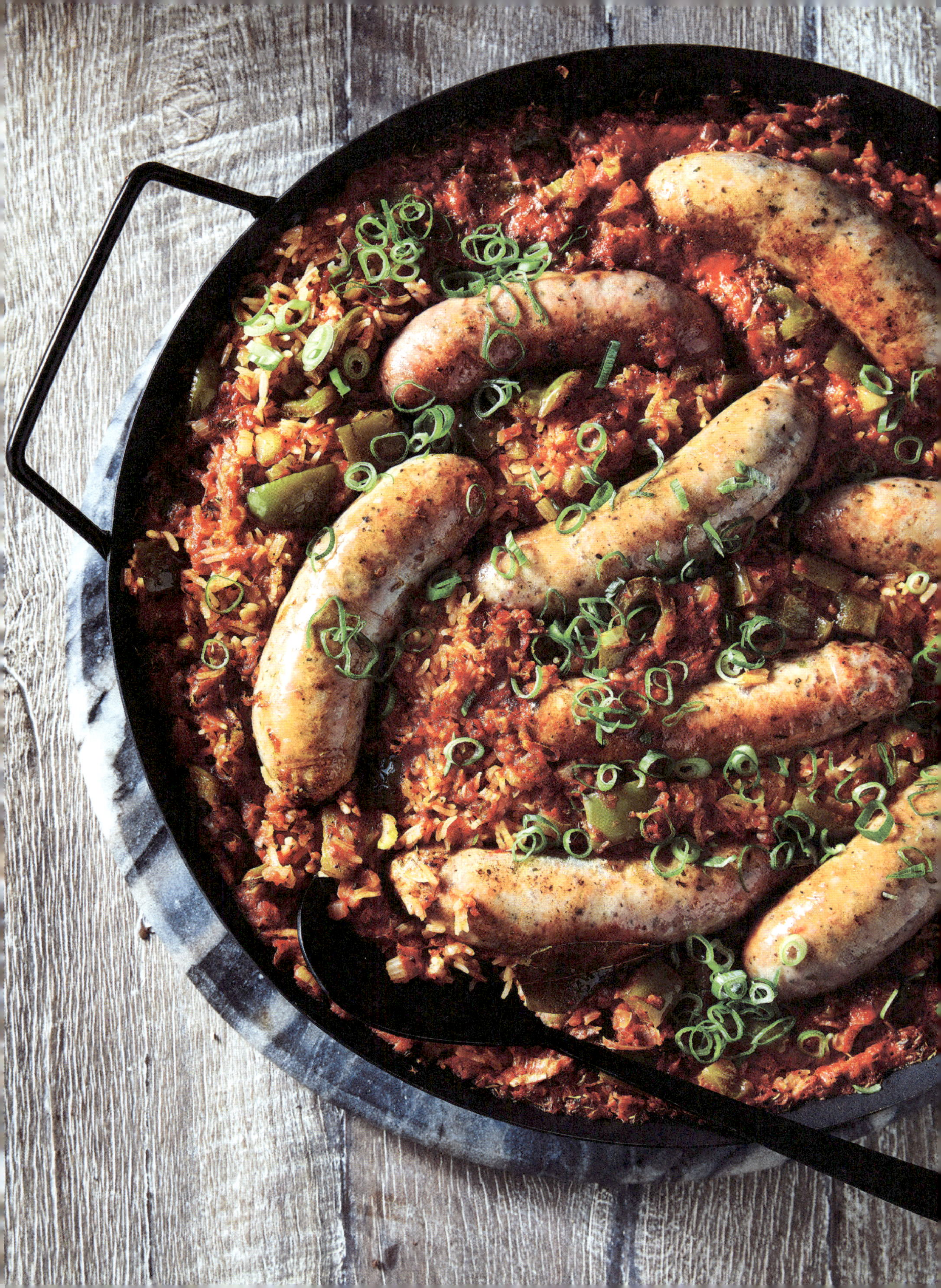

/mi:t/fri:/
adjective

1. (of food or a diet) not containing meat
2. vegan or vegetarian

MEAT FREE

Reducing the amount of meat we eat is often easier said than done.

We may have the best intentions of eating less meat and more vegetables, but we've become so used to building meals around a central block of meat that it can be hard to orient your cooking once you remove that.

Reducing meat intake makes a lot of sense from many different perspectives, and the shift doesn't need to be dramatic. Half the recipes in this book are vegetarian, and many more can easily be adapted.

My advice is to shift your thinking to individual vegetables as centrepieces of your table.

Roasted cauliflower can form the basis of a delicious red curry (page 100), fried broccoli (page 116) can be even tastier than fried chicken, and a generous piece of ratatouille slice (page 103) only needs a side salad to turn it into a full meal.

Red curry roast cauliflower

Serves 4
Prep 20 minutes
Cook 30 minutes

If you're trying to cut down on the amount of meat you're eating, a dish like this is an easy place to get started. The flavours are bold and strong, and there are lots of different textures going on. You won't miss the meat at all.

2 heads cauliflower

3 tablespoons vegetable oil

400 ml (13½ fl oz) tinned coconut cream

½ cup (130 g/4½ oz) red curry paste

5 makrut lime leaves

2 lemongrass stems, bruised

1 cinnamon stick

2 star anise

1 tablespoon cardamom pods

1 tablespoon palm sugar (jaggery), plus extra to season

1 cup (90 g/3 oz) halved button mushrooms

1 small bunch water spinach (kangkung), cut into 5 cm (2 in) lengths

150 g (5½ oz) cherry tomatoes

6 spears baby corn, halved

salt, to season

soy sauce, to season

1 loosely packed cup Thai basil leaves

½ cup picked coriander (cilantro) leaves

lime wedges, to serve

steamed rice, to serve

Heat your oven to 220°C (430°F) fan-forced. Cut the cauliflower into quarters and drizzle with 2 tablespoons oil. Place in a lined roasting pan and roast for 30 minutes until browned and cooked through.

Meanwhile, heat a large wok over a high heat and add the remaining oil and about half the coconut cream. Fry for about 5 minutes until the oil in the coconut cream starts to 'crack' and separate. Add the curry paste and fry for about 3 minutes, stirring constantly until very fragrant, then add the lime leaves, lemongrass, spices, palm sugar and about 700 ml (23½ fl oz) water. Bring to a simmer and cook for about 5 minutes.

Stir in the mushrooms and simmer for a few more minutes, then add the water spinach, tomatoes and corn and bring to a simmer. Stir in the remaining coconut cream and simmer again for just a minute or two. Taste, and adjust the seasoning with salt, soy sauce and palm sugar if needed.

Place the cauliflower in serving bowls. Spoon the curry over and scatter with the herbs. Serve with lime wedges and rice.

TIP Seasoning is all important for a dish like this; it's about the balance between salty, savoury, sweet and sour. Taste the curry and decide for yourself if it needs a little more salt, savouriness from soy sauce, or sugar, or a squeeze of lime.

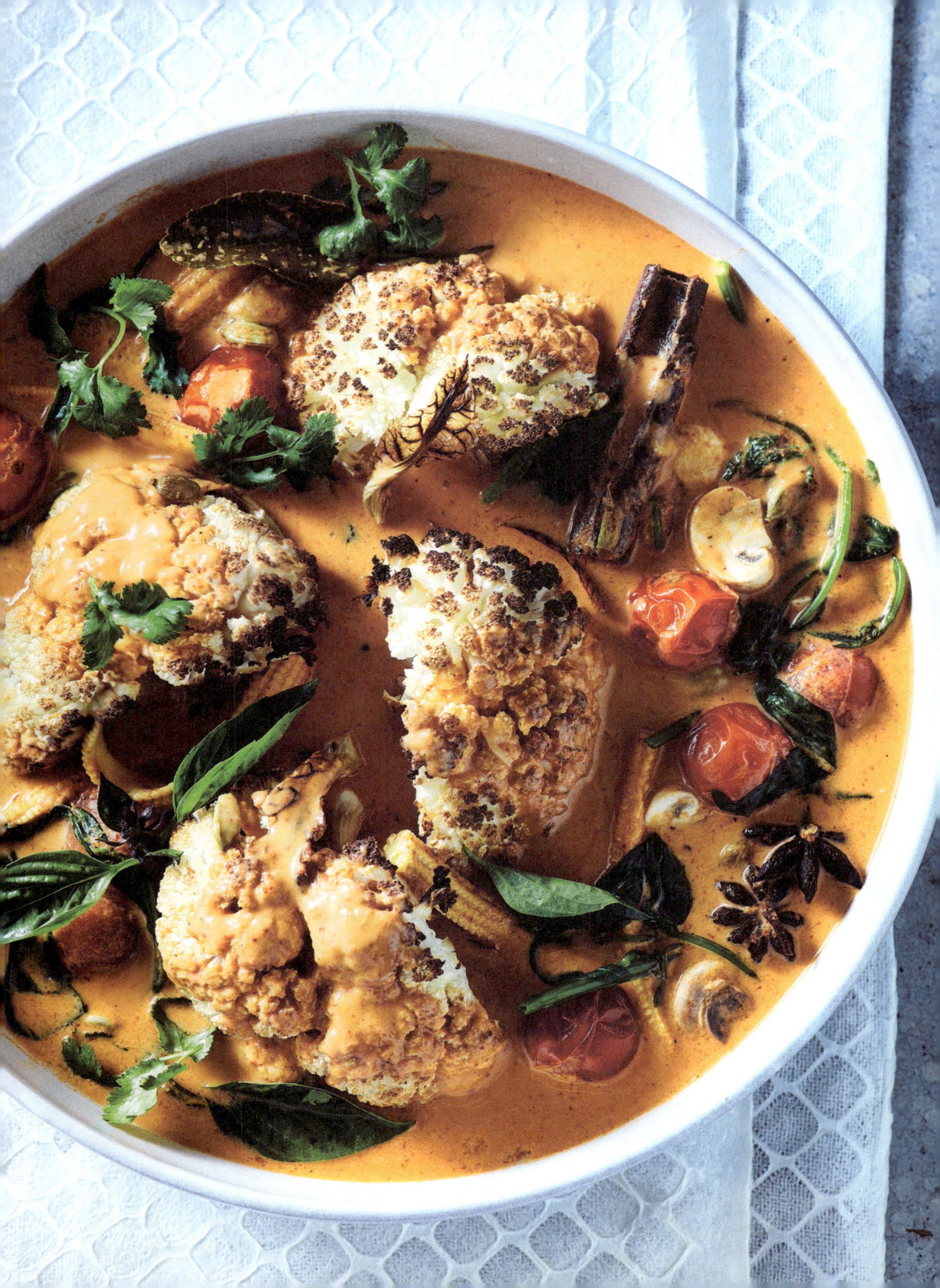

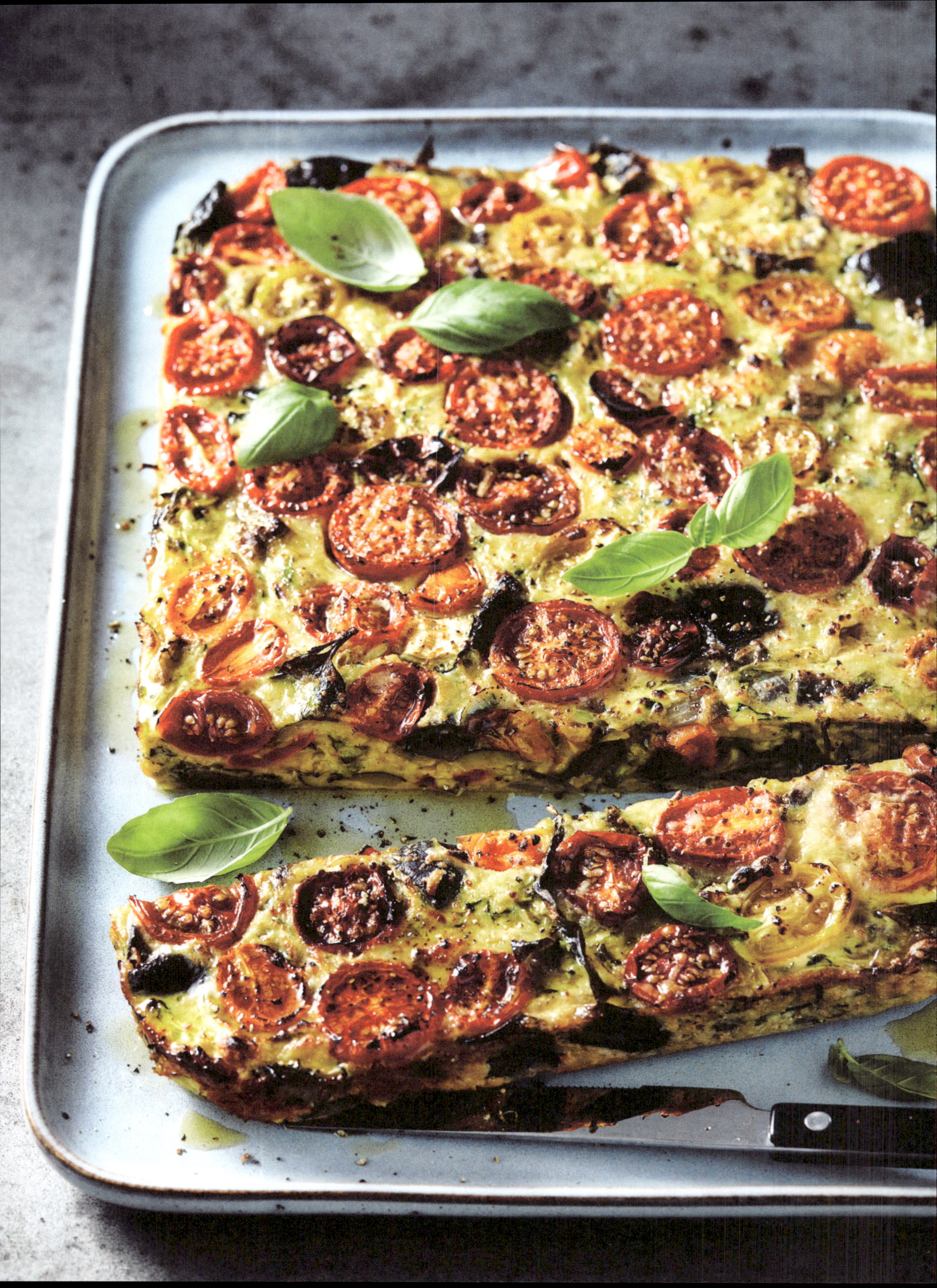

Ratatouille slice

—

Serves 4
Prep 20 minutes
Cook 1 hour 30 minutes
Cool 15 minutes

The classic Aussie zucchini slice gets a little makeover here with the addition of vegetables you might normally find in a Provençal ratatouille (page 45). Have it on its own as a savoury afternoon tea item, or put a green salad on the side for a simple and elegant lunch.

1 onion

1 eggplant (aubergine)

1 red capsicum (bell pepper)

4 zucchini (courgettes)

2 garlic cloves, roughly chopped

¾ cup (185 ml/6 fl oz) olive oil, plus extra to serve

salt and black pepper, to season

1 cup (150 g/5½ oz) self-raising flour

6 eggs, beaten

1 cup (125 g/4½ oz) grated cheddar

½ cup (50 g/1¾ oz) grated parmesan, plus extra for topping

6 thyme sprigs, leaves picked

handful of basil leaves

1 cup (150 g/5½ oz) mixed cherry tomatoes, halved

Heat your oven to 160°C (320°F) fan-forced. Cut the onion, eggplant, capsicum and one zucchini into 2 cm (¾ in) cubes. Toss in a large bowl with the garlic and ¼ cup (60 ml/2 fl oz) of the olive oil. Season with salt and pepper, spread on a lined baking tray and bake for 40 minutes. Remove from the oven and allow to cool slightly.

Increase the oven temperature to 180°C (350°F) fan-forced.

Grate the remaining zucchini into a large bowl (you can use the same one). Add the roast vegetables and the remaining ½ cup (125 ml/4 fl oz) olive oil, as well as the flour, eggs, cheeses, thyme and most of the basil. Mix well.

Transfer the ratatouille mixture to a lamington tray, or a deep-sided tray measuring about 16 × 30 cm (6¼ × 12 in). Press the cherry tomatoes into the top of the slice, then grate a little more parmesan over.

Bake for about 45 minutes until browned and cooked through.

Allow to cool for about 15 minutes, then cut into long slices. Serve with a drizzle of olive oil, scattered with the remaining basil.

TIP Just like the classic Provençal ratatouille, this slice works really well with tuna, and would be great packed in a lunchbox with a tin of tuna on the side.

Saffron risotto with roast tomatoes

—

Serves 8
Prep 15 minutes
Cook 1 hour

Risotto is all about stock. Good-quality stock makes good-quality risotto. It's as simple as that. Don't skip the smoked paprika butter, though. It's absolutely delicious.

6 cups (1.5 litres/51 fl oz) vegetable stock

2 large pinches of saffron threads

¼ cup (60 ml/2 fl oz) olive oil

1 onion, finely diced

3 garlic cloves, crushed

2 cups (440 g/15½ oz) risotto rice (vialone nano, arborio or carnaroli are popular)

½ cup (125 ml/4 fl oz) white wine

salt and black pepper, to season

50 g (1¾ oz) butter

1 cup (100 g/3½ oz) grated parmesan, plus extra to serve

1 tablespoon finely shredded parsley

ROAST TOMATOES
8 tomatoes, halved
¼ cup (60 ml/2 fl oz) olive oil
salt, to season

SMOKED PAPRIKA BUTTER
50 g (1¾ oz) butter
½ teaspoon smoked paprika

TIP Risotto doesn't need to be stirred non-stop. The creaminess is created through the mantecare (the stirring or mixing at the end), which emulsifies the rice starch with the cheese and butter fat.

Heat your oven to 200°C (400°F) fan-forced. Place the tomatoes on a baking tray lined with baking paper, drizzle with the olive oil and season with salt. Roast for 1 hour.

Bring the stock to a simmer and add the saffron. Turn off the heat, then cover and stand for 10 minutes for the saffron to infuse.

Heat a large saucepan over a medium heat and add the olive oil. Fry the onion for about 3 minutes until translucent, then add the garlic and fry for a further minute. Add the rice and toast in the oil for about a minute. Pour in the wine and stir until absorbed. Add about one-third of the hot stock and simmer for about 5 minutes, stirring occasionally until the stock is absorbed.

Repeat two more times for the remaining two-thirds of the stock, stirring occasionally throughout the cooking time, which should take about 20 minutes. Adjust the amount of stock added towards the end, so the risotto is still fluid and settling in the saucepan when stirred, not clumping. When the risotto is cooked, the grains should still be separate and al dente.

Taste the risotto and season with salt if needed (remembering that the cheese will be salty, too). Stir the butter and parmesan through to emulsify the risotto to a creamy texture; the hot risotto should still be quite soft and fluid, so that it spreads easily on a plate if you tap the bottom of the plate.

For the smoked paprika butter, place the butter in a small saucepan over a medium heat. When the butter is foaming, stir in the paprika and remove from the heat.

Divide the risotto among deep serving plates, top with the roast tomato and drizzle with the smoked paprika butter. Scatter with more parmesan, pepper and parsley to serve.

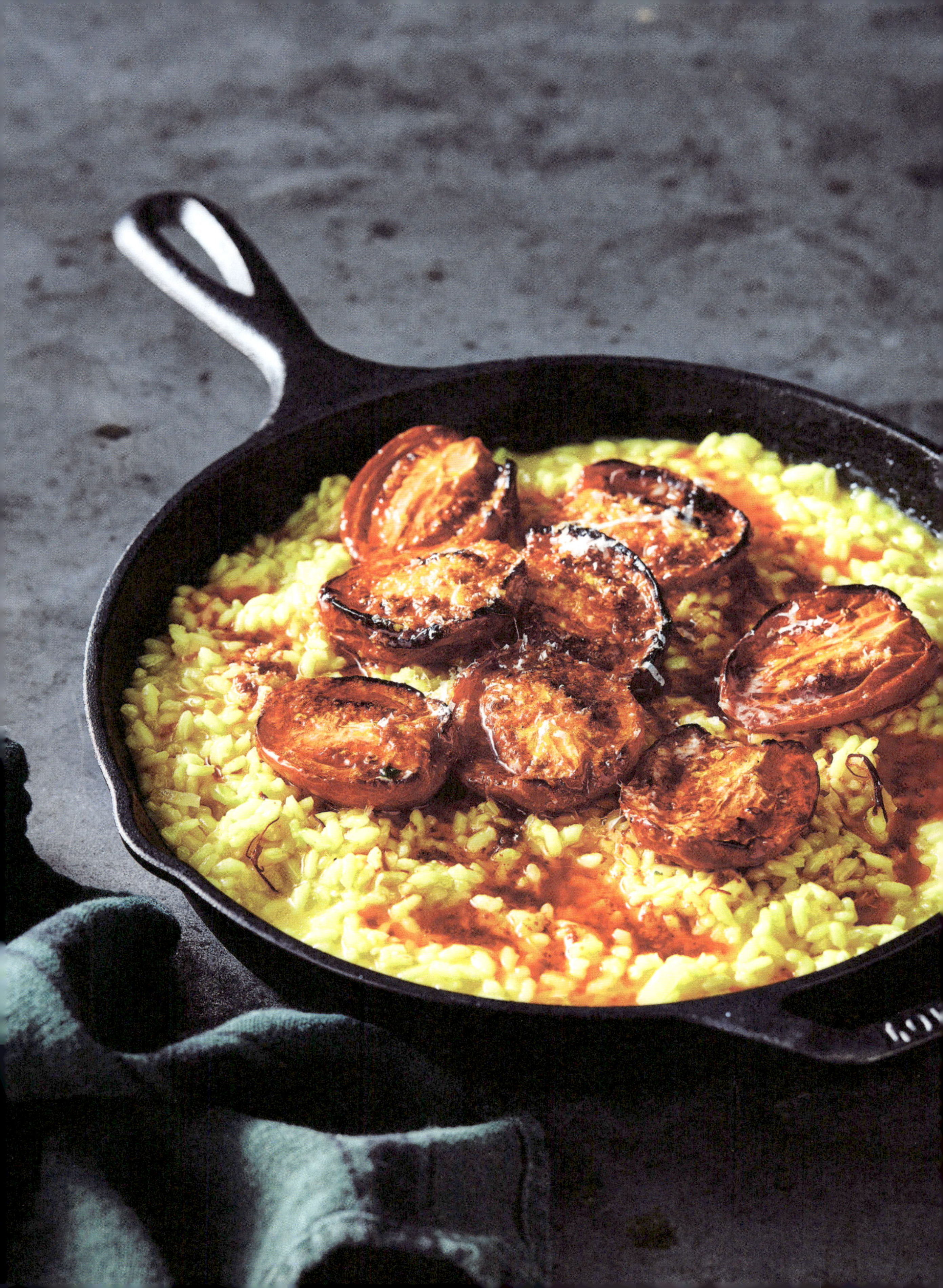

Salt, pepper & seaweed tofu

—

Serves 6, as part of a shared meal
Prep 10 minutes
Rest 10 minutes
Cook 10 minutes

Nori is a staple in our house. We use it for wrapping onigiri (rice balls), making hand-rolled sushi, and in donburi (page 40). But nori is even more versatile than that. Its toasty and ocean-y aroma works brilliantly with this simple salt and pepper tofu.

1 nori sheet

600 g (1 lb 5 oz) medium-soft tofu (see Tip)

1 cup (120 g/4½ oz) potato starch (or cornflour/cornstarch)

2–4 cups (500 ml–1 litre/ 17–34 fl oz) vegetable oil, for deep-frying

3 garlic cloves, roughly chopped

2 spring onions (scallions), sliced

salt and black pepper, to season

Toast the nori by waving it over an open flame for just a few seconds until crisp. Alternatively, you can grill (broil) it under an overhead grill (broiler) until crisp and fragrant. Transfer to a small blender or food processor and blend to a fine powder.

Place the tofu on a tray or chopping board between two pieces of paper towel and place a plate on top. Stand for about 10 minutes to remove the excess moisture. Cut the tofu into 5 cm (2 in) cubes and roll in the potato starch. Allow to stand for 5 minutes while you heat the oil to 175°C (345°F).

Fry the tofu in batches for about 3 minutes each batch, then drain on a wire rack. Don't wait for the tofu to turn golden brown: potato starch (and cornflour) don't contain much protein, so they don't brown when fried.

Heat a wok over a medium heat and add about 1 tablespoon of oil. Fry the garlic and spring onion for about 30 seconds until fragrant. Add the tofu, season very well with salt and pepper and gently toss to coat the tofu in the fried aromatics.

Remove to a plate, scatter liberally with the nori powder and serve.

TIP You want a tofu that isn't too soft, but also isn't too firm. Different brands will have different textures, so find one that is firm enough to handle gently without breaking apart, but not so firm that it has 'bite'.

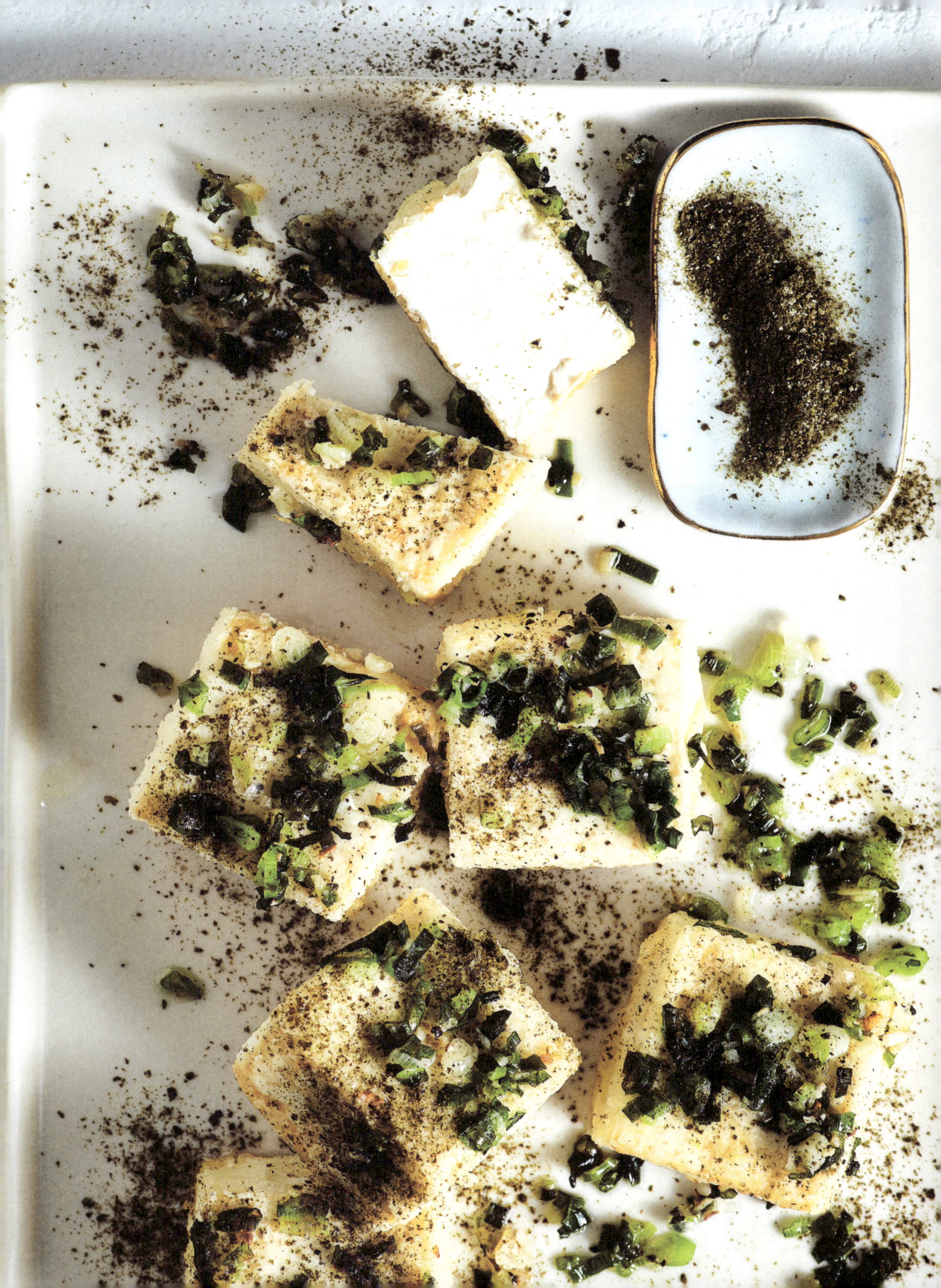

Roast cauliflower with zucchini cheese sauce

Serves 2–4
Prep 20 minutes
Cook 40 minutes

1 head cauliflower

2 tablespoons olive oil, plus 1 teaspoon

salt and black pepper, to season

4 zucchini (courgettes)

½ onion

½ cup (125 ml/4 fl oz) vegetable stock

1 cup (125 g/4½ oz) grated cheese, such as tasty or cheddar

½ cup (50 g/1¾ oz) grated parmesan

The idea for this low-carb cauliflower cheese came from a fan of *The Cook Up* — a 'mostly retired' food scientist named John who emailed me to share his side dish for my Scarborough Fair chicken from volume 1 of *Tonight's Dinner*. John's recipe uses zucchini purée to thicken a delicious low-carb cheese sauce.

Heat your oven to 220°C (430°F) fan-forced. Place the whole cauliflower in a baking dish. Drizzle with 2 tablespoons of olive oil and season well with salt. Roast the cauliflower for 40 minutes, or until well browned on the surface.

While the cauliflower is roasting, peel the zucchini and grate it using the large holes of a box grater. Do the same with the onion. Heat a small saucepan over a medium heat, add the remaining teaspoon of olive oil and sweat the zucchini and onion for about 10 minutes until most of the moisture is removed. Leave to cool slightly.

Transfer the zucchini mixture to a high-speed blender and blend with a little of the stock to form a thick sauce, adding enough of the remaining stock to bring the sauce to the consistency of pouring cream. Return to the saucepan and whisk in the cheeses until melted and combined. Keep warm.

Serve the roasted cauliflower with the sauce poured over.

TIP This sauce works by replacing the starch of flour with cellulose from zucchini — essentially fibre. John says the zucchini sauce base is non-gelling, which means it doesn't stick to pans and is easy to wash off. Also, you can't really overcook it, or undercook it: if it's too thick, simply add a little water to thin it. If it's too thin, cook it a bit longer to evaporate some of the water, which will thicken it. An added bonus is that the sauce is non-allergenic, gentle on the digestive tract and nutritious, too.

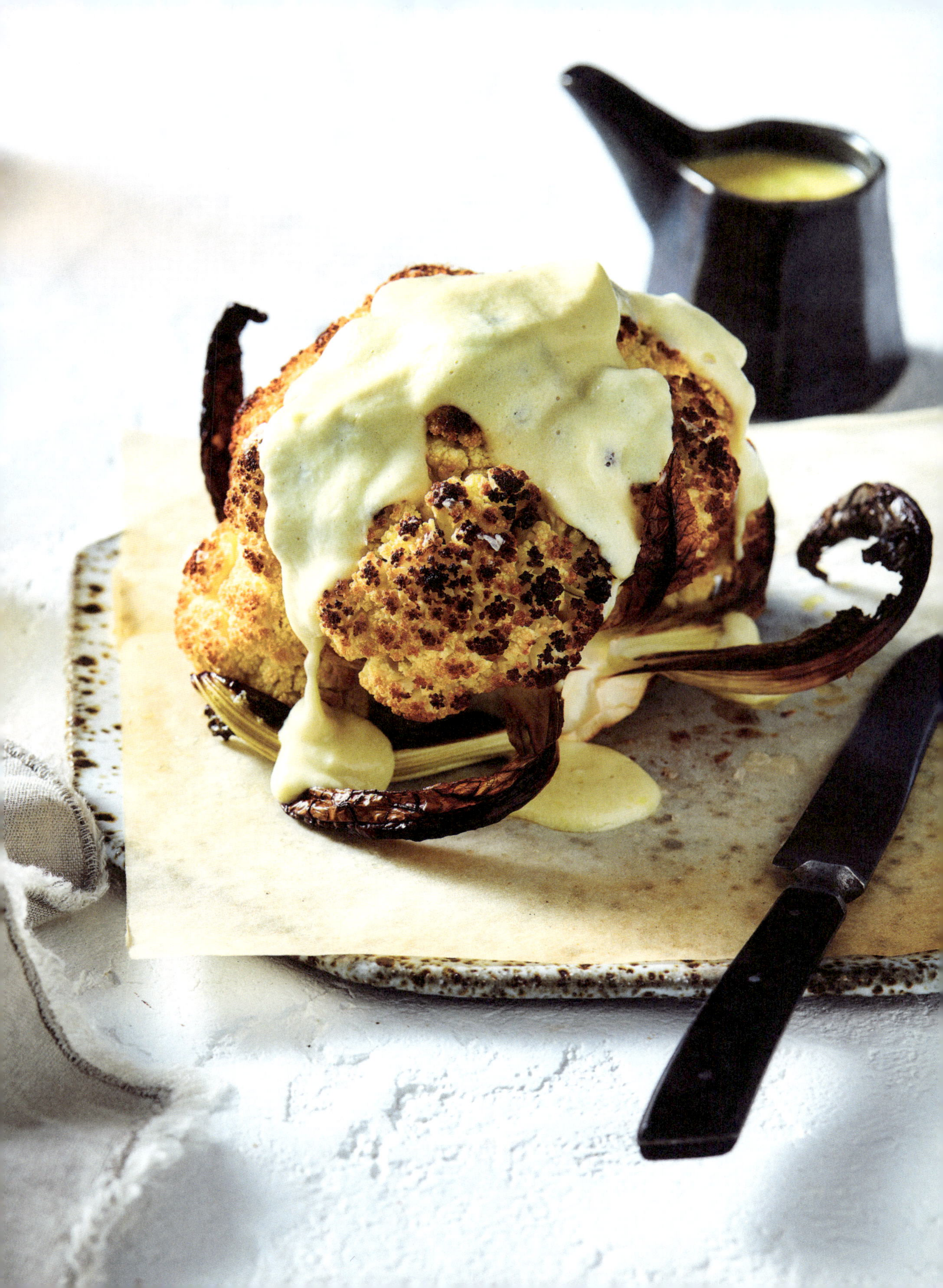

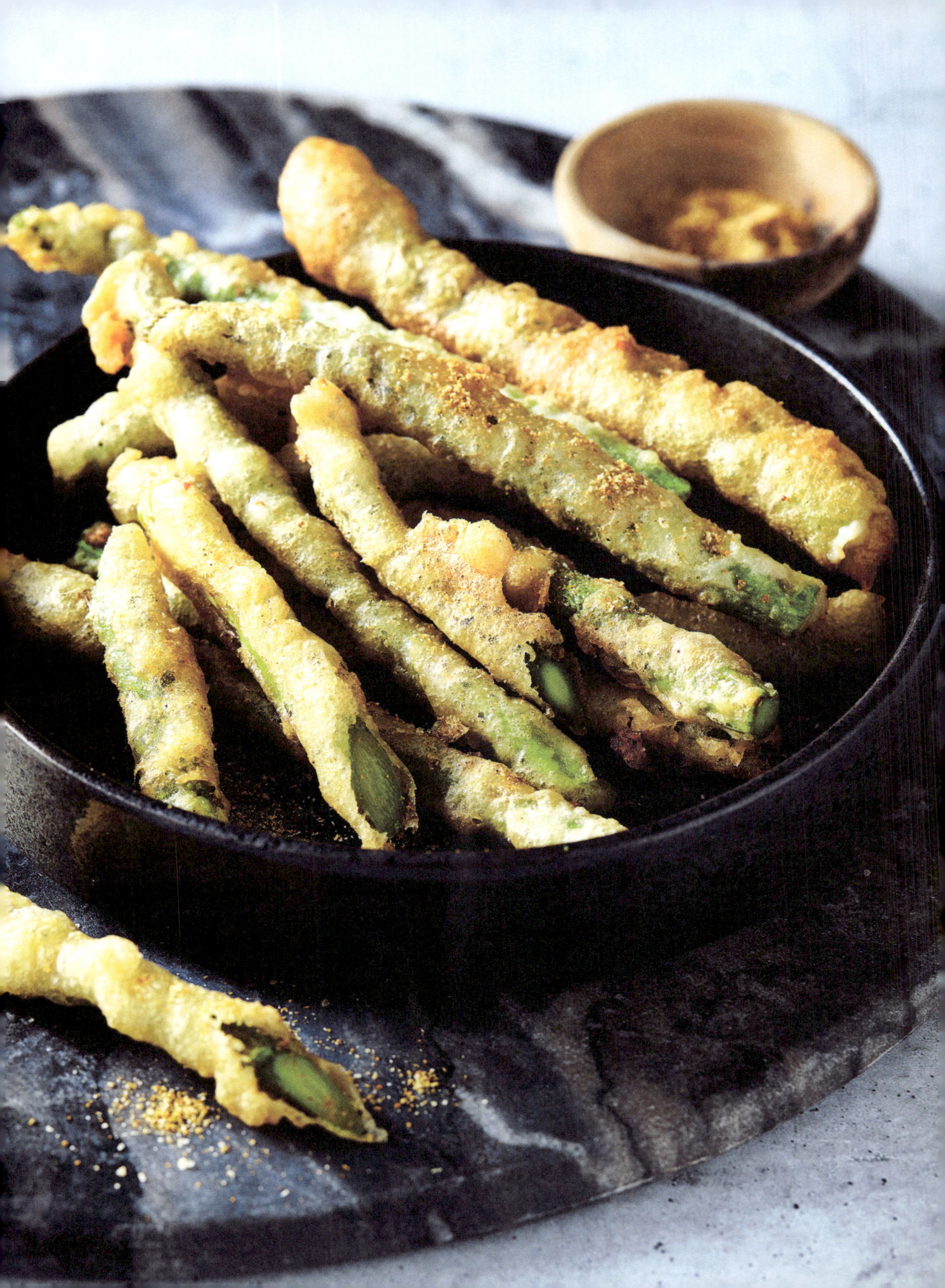

Beer-battered asparagus with curry salt

—

Serves 2–4
Prep 15 minutes
Cook 10 minutes
Soak 15 min

330 ml (11 fl oz) light-flavoured beer

1½ cups (225 g/8 oz) self-raising flour

1 bunch asparagus

4 cups (1 litre/34 fl oz) vegetable oil, approximately, for deep-frying

lemon wedges, to serve

mayonnaise, to serve (optional)

CURRY SALT (MAKES EXTRA)

2 teaspoons curry powder

black pepper, to taste

2 tablespoons salt

The best batter is made from two things: beer and flour. There's no point complicating a recipe when it's fine just as it is. With large asparagus, this is substantial enough to be a main meal with some rice and pickles, or you could serve it as a side dish if you prefer.

To make the curry salt, place the curry powder in a heatproof mortar with some pepper. Heat the salt in a small saucepan until hot, then pour the hot salt into the mortar and grind to a smooth powder. Set aside.

In a bowl, gently whisk the beer into the flour until just combined but still lumpy; you don't want to overwork the batter. Trim the asparagus and place in the batter.

Heat your oil to 180°C (350°F) in a medium saucepan. Fry the asparagus in batches for about 4 minutes until crisp and golden brown, then drain on a wire rack.

Serve the asparagus with the curry salt and lemon wedges, and a little mayonnaise if you like.

TIPS Pouring the hot salt onto the curry powder provides a bit of heat to release the aromas of the spices.

You'll have plenty of curry salt left over. Store it in a clean jar in the pantry and use for sprinkling over fried or roast chicken, French fries or even boiled or scrambled eggs.

Tempered roast vegetables

Serves 4
Prep 15 minutes
Cook 1 hour 10 minutes

Tempering (also known as tadka or chauk) is a process of heating aromatic ingredients to flavour oil, then using the oil to add a distinctive aroma to a dish. It's an often-missed but fundamentally important step in making curries, but it can also be used for flavouring other things too, like these roast vegetables.

150 ml (5 fl oz) ghee, melted

200 g (7 oz) brussels sprouts, cut in half

1 head cauliflower, separated into florets

1 head broccoli, separated into florets

½ small head cabbage, cut into 4 wedges

salt and black pepper, to season

1 small onion, sliced

2 garlic cloves, roughly chopped

1 large green chilli, sliced

1 teaspoon black mustard seeds

1 teaspoon cumin seeds

1 teaspoon coriander seeds

1 teaspoon fennel seeds

½ teaspoon ground turmeric

15–20 curry leaves

thick yoghurt, to serve

lemon wedges, to serve

Heat your oven to 220°C (430°F) fan-forced.

Heat a heavy roasting pan over a high heat and add 50 ml (1¾ fl oz) of the ghee. Fry the brussels sprouts cut side down for about 3 minutes until browned, then remove to a plate. Fry the cauliflower and broccoli for about 5 minutes until browned on one side, then remove.

Add the cabbage wedges to the pan and cook on one side for about 5 minutes until browned. Flip the cabbage over, transfer the pan to the oven and roast the cabbage alone for 25 minutes.

Return the brussels sprouts, cauliflower and broccoli to the pan. Season well with salt and pepper and roast for a further 20 minutes until softened and well browned. Transfer the roasted vegetables to a serving dish.

Heat the remaining ghee in a small saucepan over a medium heat. Fry the onion for about 3 minutes until golden, then add the garlic, chilli, spices and curry leaves and cook for a further minute until the spices are crackling and fragrant. Pour the seasoned ghee over the vegetables. Season again with salt and black pepper.

Season the yoghurt well with salt and pepper and serve with the vegetables, along with some lemon wedges.

TIP Brassicas such as brussels sprouts, cabbage, cauliflower and broccoli are fabulous when roasted and almost blackened. Frying one side of the vegetables in the roasting pan, as we do here, gives them a head start on the colouring process.

This is great with Indian breads and chutneys, or even just on its own.

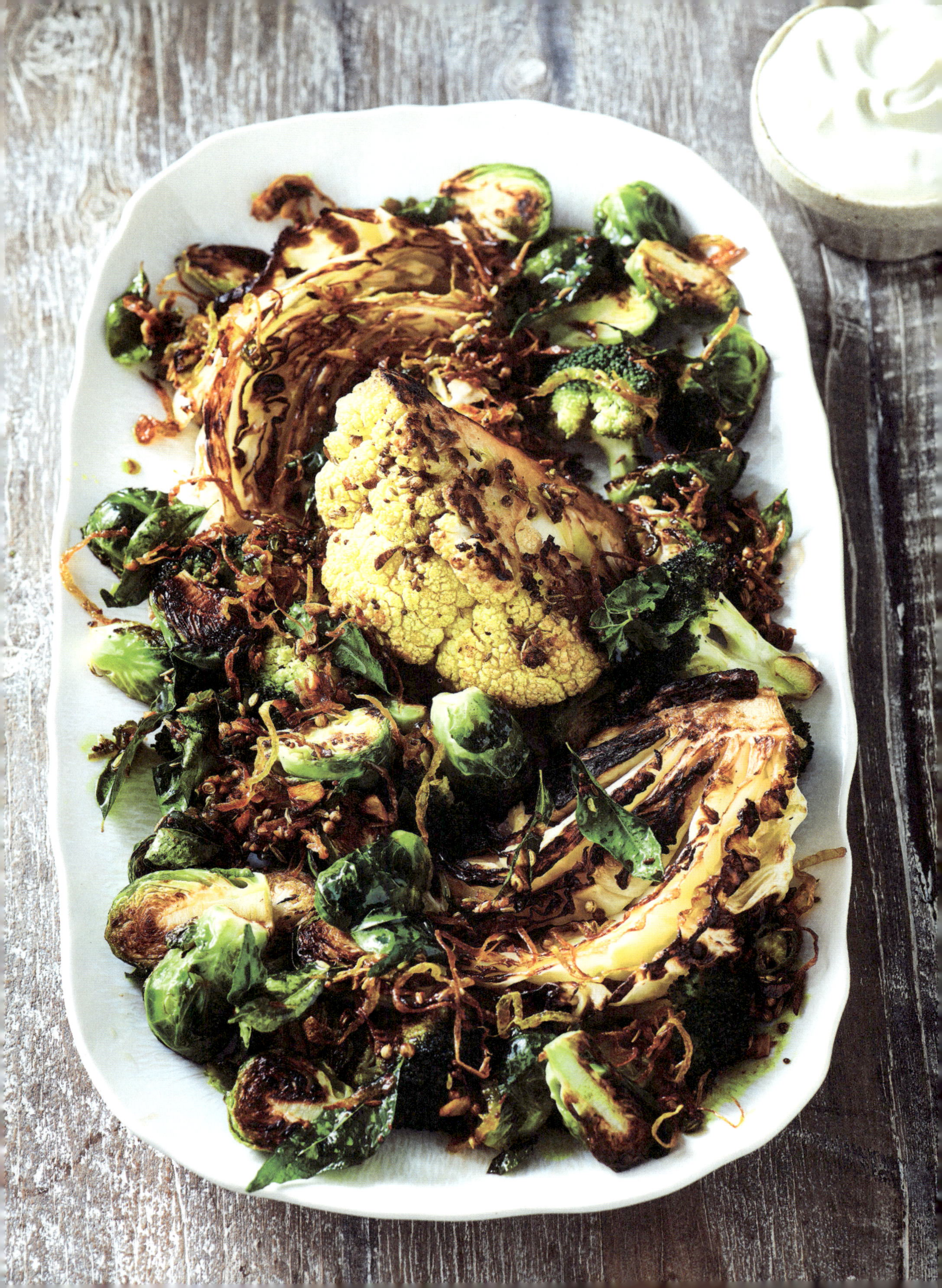

Red wine baked beans

Serves 4
Prep 15 minutes
Soak Overnight
Cook 3 hours 15 minutes

These vegetarian baked beans cook for hours in the oven to a deliciously rich stew consistency. To make them completely vegan you can simply replace the butter with olive oil, but I think butter and baked beans are a match made in heaven.

500 g (1 lb 2 oz) dried great northern or navy beans

1 teaspoon salt

50 g (1¾ oz) butter

1 onion, diced

1 carrot, diced

1 celery stalk, diced

400 g (14 oz) tinned diced tomatoes

2 tablespoons tomato paste

1 tablespoon worcestershire sauce

2 cups (500 ml/17 fl oz) red wine

2 cups (500 ml/17 fl oz) vegetable stock

6 thyme sprigs

3 bay leaves

2 rosemary sprigs

salt and black pepper, to season

TO SERVE

25 g (1 oz) butter

¼ cup finely shredded parsley

buttered sourdough

Put the beans in a large saucepan, cover with plenty of water and stir in the 1 teaspoon of salt. Leave to soak overnight.

Drain the beans. Return to the pan, cover with fresh water and bring to a simmer, then cook for 15 minutes. Drain and set aside.

Meanwhile, heat your oven to 160°C (320°F) fan-forced. Heat a large, shallow flameproof casserole dish over a medium heat. Fry the butter, onion, carrot and celery for about 5 minutes until the onion is translucent and fragrant.

Add the remaining ingredients, except the beans, mixing well. Simmer for 5 minutes, then add the beans and pour in enough hot water to cover the beans. Cover with a tight-fitting lid, transfer to the oven and bake for 3 hours. Check the beans every hour and add more hot water to cover if needed.

When the beans are tender, stir the butter through and scatter with the parsley. Season with salt and pepper and serve with buttered sourdough.

TIP Baked beans on toast are the classic, but try them with a baked potato, or on top of corn chips with cheese to make nachos. Or, top with mashed potato (or potato gems) and bake for a further 30 minutes for a baked bean pie.

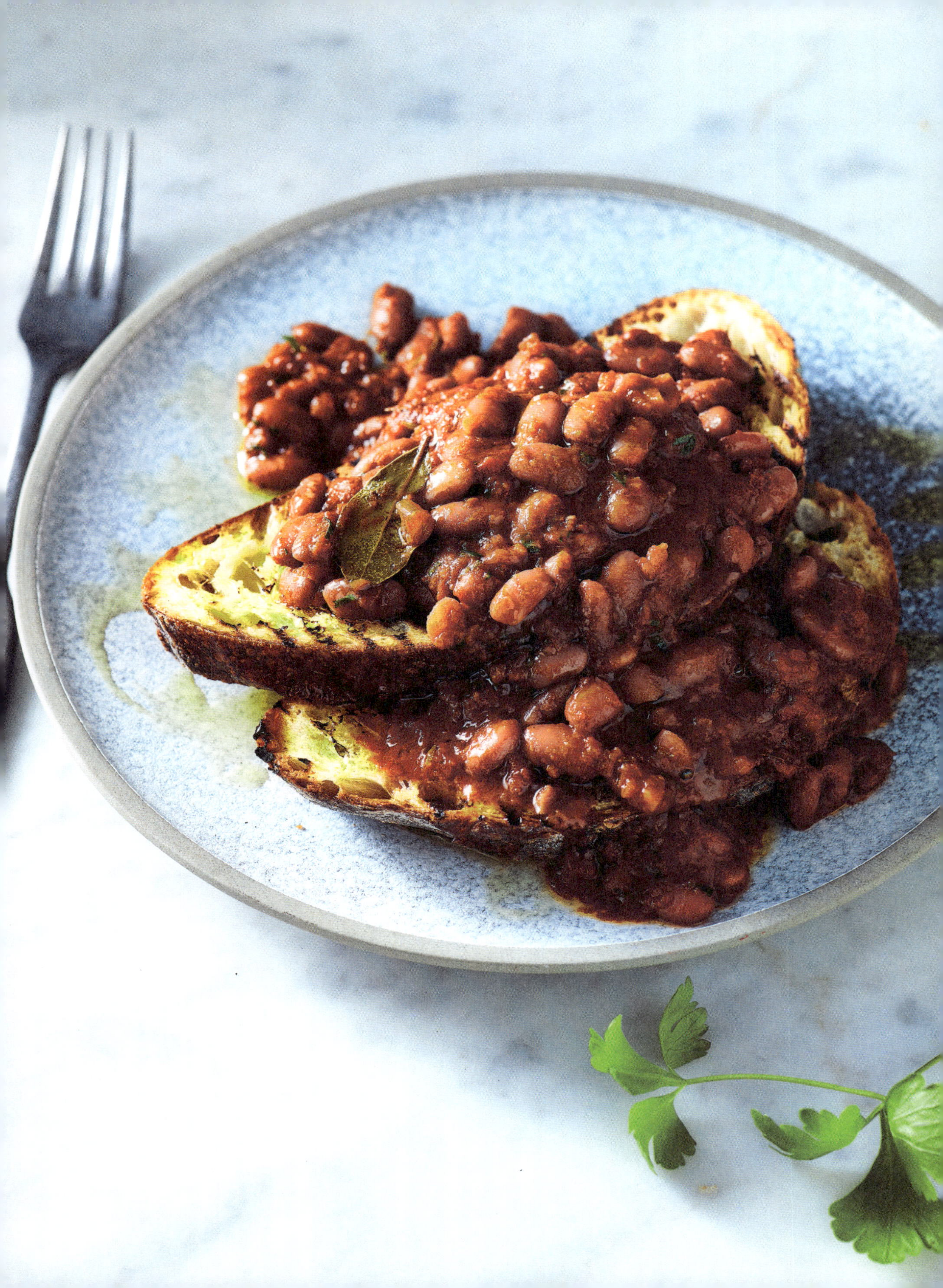

Spicy fried broccoli

Serves 4
Prep 10 minutes
Cook 15 minutes

These broccoli bites make for a great vegetable alternative to fried chicken, but would also be wonderful with some mayonnaise and salad in a delicious bun, for a veggie burger of a different kind.

1 cup (150 g/5½ oz) plain (all-purpose) flour

salt and black pepper, to season

2 heads broccoli, separated into florets

2 eggs, beaten

1 cup (100 g/3½ oz) dry fine breadcrumbs

4 cups (1 litre/34 fl oz) vegetable oil, approximately, for deep-frying

2 teaspoons salt

lemon wedges, to serve

SPICE MIX

1 teaspoon smoked paprika

1 teaspoon onion powder

1 teaspoon garlic powder

1 teaspoon Korean chilli powder (see Tip)

½ teaspoon ground cumin

½ teaspoon ground coriander

½ teaspoon ground allspice

In a large bowl, combine the ingredients for the spice mix. Remove half to a small bowl and set aside for serving. Add the flour to the remaining spice mix and season well with salt and pepper. Toss the broccoli through, then add the eggs and ¾ cup (180 ml/6 fl oz) water and mix well until the broccoli is coated in a batter. Toss the broccoli through the breadcrumbs to coat.

Heat the oil to 170°C (340°F) in a medium saucepan. Fry the broccoli pieces in batches for about 5 minutes until the breadcrumbs are golden brown and crisp. Remove to a wire rack.

While the broccoli is frying, heat 2 teaspoons of salt in a dry frying pan until hot, then mix the hot salt through the reserved spice mix.

Season the fried broccoli with some of the spiced salt and serve with lemon wedges.

TIPS I prefer Korean chilli powder for most purposes because it has slightly larger granules than other chilli powders and a more vibrant colour. It also comes in mild and hot versions so you can choose your heat level.

This spiced salt can be used to season potatoes, fries or roast chicken – it's great with just about anything.

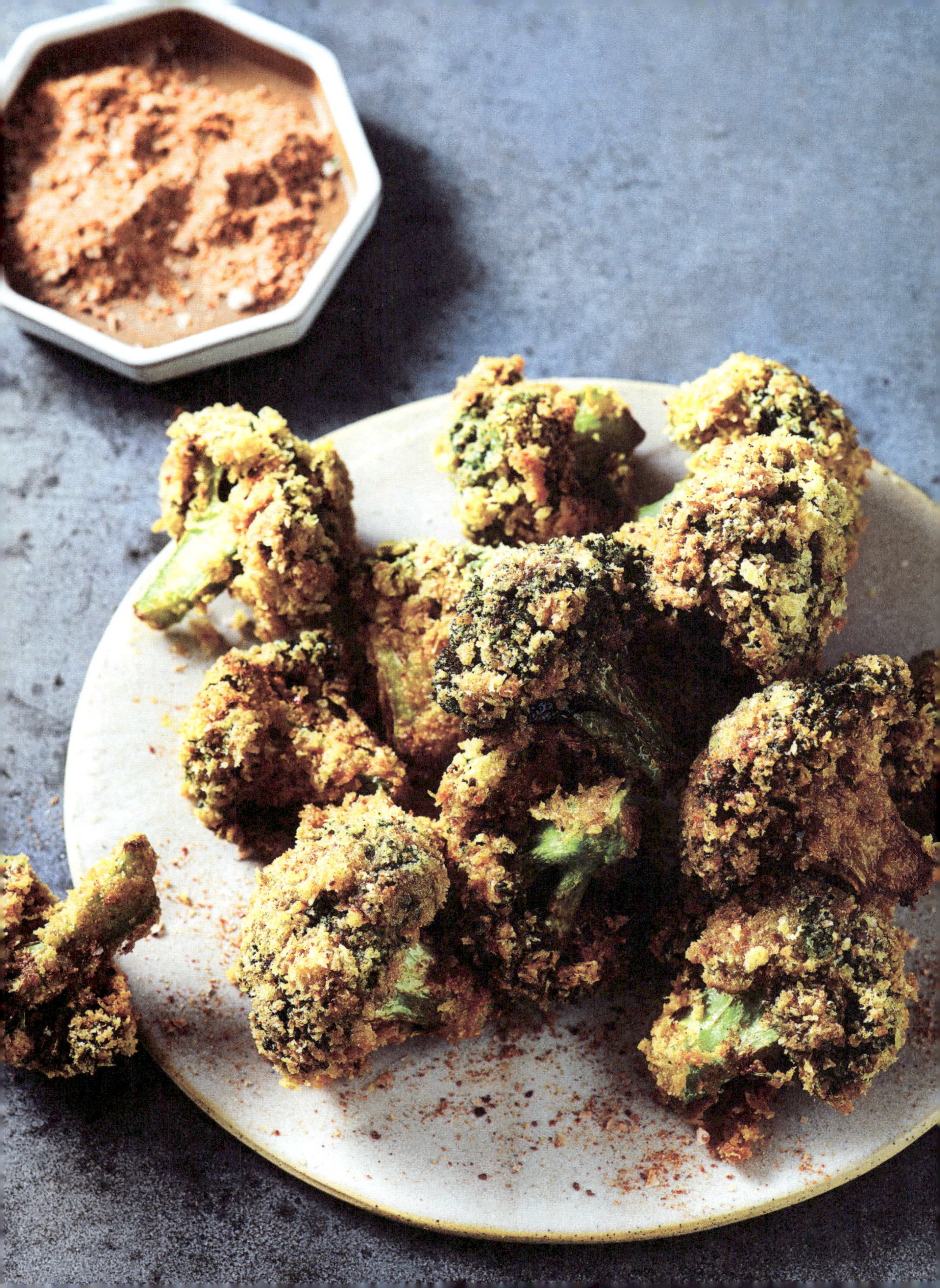

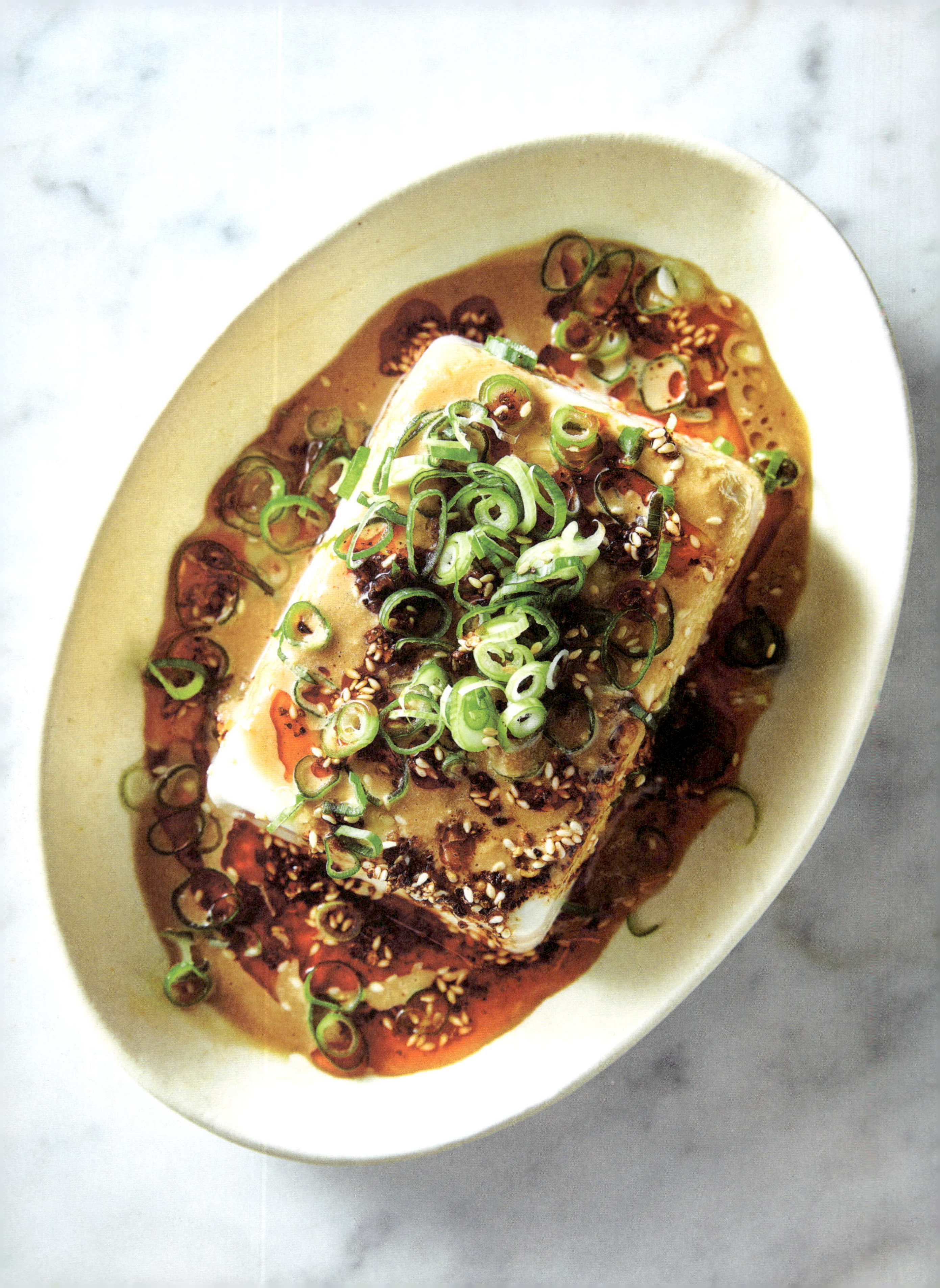

Tofu with sesame, garlic & chilli oil

—

Serves 4, as part of a shared meal
Prep 10 minutes
Stand 10 minutes
Cook 10 minutes

300 g (10½ oz) silken tofu

2 teaspoons vegetable oil

2 garlic cloves, roughly chopped

2 teaspoons soy sauce

2 spring onions (scallions), finely sliced

toasted sesame seeds, for sprinkling

SESAME SAUCE (MAKES EXTRA)

¼ cup (40 g/1½ oz) sesame seeds

2 tablespoons sake

2 tablespoons soy sauce

1 tablespoon rice vinegar

1 tablespoon sesame oil

1 tablespoon sugar

QUICK CHILLI OIL (MAKES EXTRA)

1 tablespoon Sichuan peppercorns (optional)

1 teaspoon Korean chilli powder or chilli flakes

½ teaspoon sesame seeds

¼ cup (60 ml/2 fl oz) vegetable oil

Silken tofu is something we have at home about once a week. Often I'll top it with a bit of fried garlic, onion and soy sauce; sometimes just with a bit of salt, raw grated ginger and spring onion. This version with sesame sauce and chilli oil is absolutely delicious. If you have the sesame sauce and chilli oil already on hand, this dish is ready in a flash.

For the sesame sauce, toast the sesame seeds in a dry frying pan over a medium–low heat until fragrant. Transfer to a high-speed blender, add the remaining ingredients and blend to a smooth paste. Mix about a tablespoon of the sesame sauce with enough cold water to form a loose sauce. Transfer the remaining sauce to an airtight container; it will keep in the fridge for several weeks.

For the chilli oil, if using the Sichuan peppercorns, toast them in a dry frying pan until fragrant, then grind to a coarse powder using a mortar and pestle. Add the chilli powder and whole sesame seeds. Heat the oil in a small saucepan until smoking, then pour over the mixture. Cool to room temperature, then transfer to an airtight container to keep in the pantry, where it will keep for several weeks.

Turn the tofu out of its container and sandwich between two sheets of paper towel. Stand for 10 minutes to absorb the excess moisture. Use the container to transfer the tofu to a serving plate (so it doesn't break up).

Heat a small frying pan over a medium heat and add the oil. Fry the garlic for a minute or two until lightly browned. Add the soy sauce and remove from the heat.

Pour the soy sauce and garlic mixture over the tofu. Spoon the loose sesame sauce over and as much of the chilli oil as you like. Serve scattered with the spring onion and toasted sesame seeds.

TIP I've given you this recipe for the sauces as much as the final dish. Use the sesame sauce as a salad dressing mixed with a little vinegar. Dilute it down with some water and use it as a dipping sauce. And the chilli oil? That goes with everything.

Shiitake, garlic & spring onion noodles

—

Serves 4
Prep 10 minutes
Stand 15 minutes
Cook 10 minutes

4 dried shiitake mushrooms

2 tablespoons oyster sauce

2 tablespoons dark soy sauce

1 tablespoon light soy sauce

2 teaspoons sugar

½ cup (125 ml/4 fl oz) vegetable oil

8 large spring onions (scallions), julienned

6 garlic cloves, finely chopped

500 g (1 lb 2 oz) thin egg noodles

black vinegar, to serve (optional)

It might surprise you that something this delicious could be this easy, but dishes like these never fail to remind me of one of the great truths in cooking — that there is no correlation between how hard something is to cook and how good it tastes.

Place the dried mushrooms in a bowl and cover with 1 cup (250 ml/8½ fl oz) boiling water. Stand for 15 minutes to rehydrate.

Remove the shiitake, reserving the steeping water. Using scissors, snip off and discard the stalks, and very thinly slice the caps (see Tip). Place the steeping water and sliced caps in a small saucepan and bring to a simmer for 2 minutes. Remove from the heat and stir in the sauces and sugar.

Heat the oil in a separate saucepan over a medium heat and add the spring onion. After a few minutes, when the spring onion is starting to brown, add the garlic, then fry for another minute or two until the garlic is lightly browned and the onion crisp. Scoop them out with a slotted spoon and drain on paper towel, reserving the oil for the noodles.

Cook the noodles for just 30 seconds to 1 minute in plenty of boiling water. Drain, then place in a large bowl with the garlicky oil and mushroom sauce. Stir to coat the noodles.

Transfer the noodles to serving bowls. Top with the crisp spring onion and garlic and serve with a little black vinegar if desired.

TIP Be sure to slice the mushrooms very thinly. If they're too thick they'll absorb too much of the salty sauces.

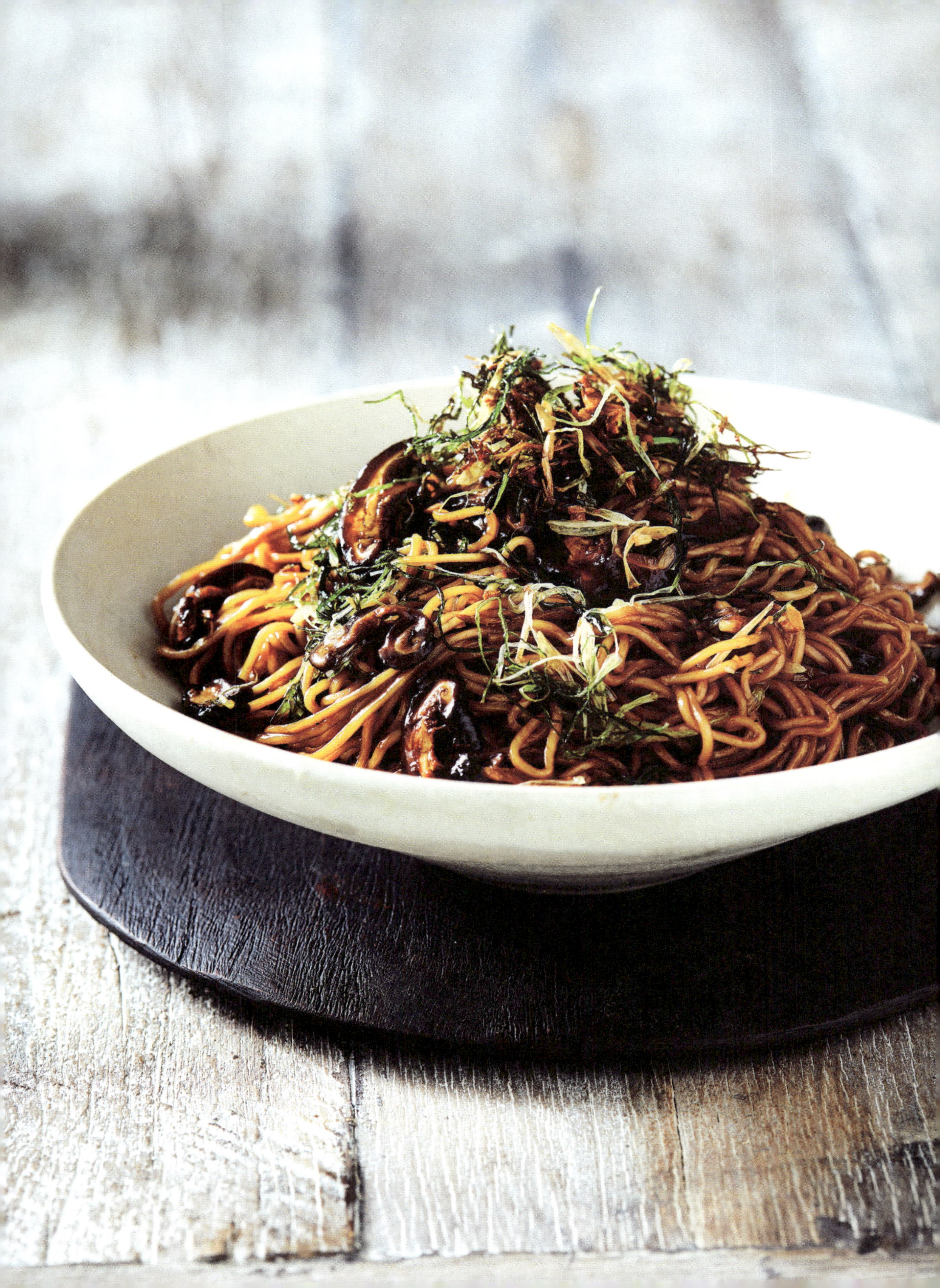

/piːtsə/pastə/
noun

1. dough-based dishes characteristic of Italian cuisine

PIZZA & PASTA

There's barely a country in the world that hasn't fallen in love with Italian food to some extent. Pizza and pasta are dinnertime staples not just in Rome, but from London to Paris and Tokyo to Timbuktu.

Pasta especially is quick and affordable and comes in a nearly endless number of varieties, so you never have to get bored with it. For me, the key to good pasta is two-fold. First, you have to get the texture right: undercooked and it's unpleasant; overcooked, there's no al dente resistance and it just ends up as a tasteless noodle. Secondly, make the pasta the focus of the dish. The sauce is there to enhance the pasta, not compete with it. The 'mantecare' process — tossing the pasta with the sauce — is important for bringing the two elements together.

Pizza, on the other hand, tends to be something we order in rather than make at home. The irony here is that I actually don't think pizza travels all that well. The difference between pizza fresh from the oven and one that's been sitting in a cardboard box for 40 minutes is like chalk and cheese.

It's true that it's not easy to recreate the authentic conditions of a Neapolitan wood-fired oven in a home kitchen, but who ever said you had to? Try my technique for simple pizza dough (page 127) and cooking great homestyle pizzas and you'll never look back.

Pizza basics
—

Up until now, the idea of making pizza at home has been a question of, why bother? We can order pizza when we want and it's going to be fine. But since I worked out this pizza dough and the process for cooking the pizzas in an ordinary home oven, pizza-making has become one of our most enjoyable family activities.

For me, the thing that clicked was realising that you don't have to replicate the pizzas you get at pizzerias. There are hundreds of different styles of pizza around the world. This one is ours — and it can be yours, too.

We still order in pizza sometimes when we want something specific or quick, but now pizza night at home is an occasion for us, and the pizza tastes like home.

All-in pizza dough

Makes 4 pizzas (26 cm/10¼ in)
Prep 10 minutes
Rest up to 3 days

This pizza dough isn't a traditional Napoli-style pizza, nor is it like those you'd get from a home-delivery chain. There's no rolling, no flour on the bench, no mess. It's literally just all-in.

1 kg (2 lb 3 oz) strong flour (see Tips) or '00' flour
20 g (¾ oz) salt
1 sachet (7 g/¼ oz) dried yeast
3 tablespoons olive oil, plus extra for oiling

Combine all the ingredients with 650 ml (22 fl oz) water in a stand mixer fitted with the dough attachment. Knead for about 6 minutes until a smooth dough forms.

Divide into four equal pieces and transfer to individual oiled containers of about 2 cup (500 ml/17 fl oz) capacity with airtight lids. The dough will rise, so if the container is too small, the expanding dough will not fit, and if the container is too large it will hold too much air and the dough may dry out.

Place in the fridge to prove for up to 3 days (see Tips); the dough will develop more flavour the longer you leave it.

Bake as directed in any of the pizza recipes in this book.

TIPS Cold-proving the dough in the fridge allows the yeast to develop and multiply slowly, producing better flavour in the dough. If you're in a hurry, you could simply leave the dough to prove for 1 hour at room temperature before using.

'Strong' flour refers to flour that is high in gluten — the protein in wheat flour that allows it to stretch and gives your pizza a crisper base. You can use ordinary flour if that's all you have, but your pizza will taste a little more cake-y.

One of the great things about pizza at home is being able to add fresh ingredients for different textures. Try topping a pizza with dressed rocket or thin shavings of prosciutto. I like to be focused with my toppings, adding just one or two per pizza (like the mushroom pizza on page 133), but if you want to load up a full super-supreme that's entirely okay too. After all, it's your pizza. And ham and pineapple on pizza is totally fine.

For great garlic bread, you can bake the dough just with olive oil and garlic or herbs.

Basic pizza sauce

—

This simple tomato-based pizza sauce can sit at the base of just about any topping.

Makes 2 cups (500 ml/17 fl oz)
Cook 5 minutes

2 cups (500 ml/17 fl oz) tomato passata (puréed tomatoes)

1 garlic clove, grated

1 teaspoon salt

pinch of sugar

¼ teaspoon dried oregano (optional)

Combine all the ingredients in a small saucepan. Cover and simmer for 5 minutes, just until the raw taste of the tomato is gone. Allow to cool before using. This sauce will keep refrigerated in an airtight container for about a week.

Classic margherita pizza

—

The classic margherita is near upon the perfect pizza. Fresh mozzarella can release moisture as it melts, but if you tear the pieces quite small this shouldn't be a problem.

Makes 2 pizzas
Prep 5 minutes
Cook 5 minutes each

½ **quantity All-in pizza dough (page 127)**

¼ **quantity Basic pizza sauce (page 128)**

200 g (7 oz) fresh mozzarella, approximately

a few basil leaves

olive oil, for drizzling

Remove the pizza dough from the fridge about 30 minutes before you want to cook.

Take a 26 cm (10¼ in) frying pan with a handle that can go in your oven. Tear a piece of baking paper slightly larger than the pan and lay it on a cutting board. Place a ball of dough in the centre and, with your fingertips, press and stretch the dough out to about the same size as the frying pan. Press the dough from the centre out, leaving a slightly raised lip around the edge.

Spoon ¼ cup (60 ml/2 fl oz) of the pizza sauce over the dough, spreading it out with the back of a large spoon. Tear half the mozzarella into pieces and arrange over the top.

Heat your oven's overhead grill (broiler) as high as it can go.

Place your frying pan on the stove over a high heat until very hot. Drop the paper holding the pizza onto the hot frying pan, then immediately transfer the pan to the oven. Cook for about 5 minutes until the dough is cooked through, risen and the crust is browned.

Serve hot, garnished with torn basil leaves and drizzled with a little olive oil. Repeat for the remaining pizza.

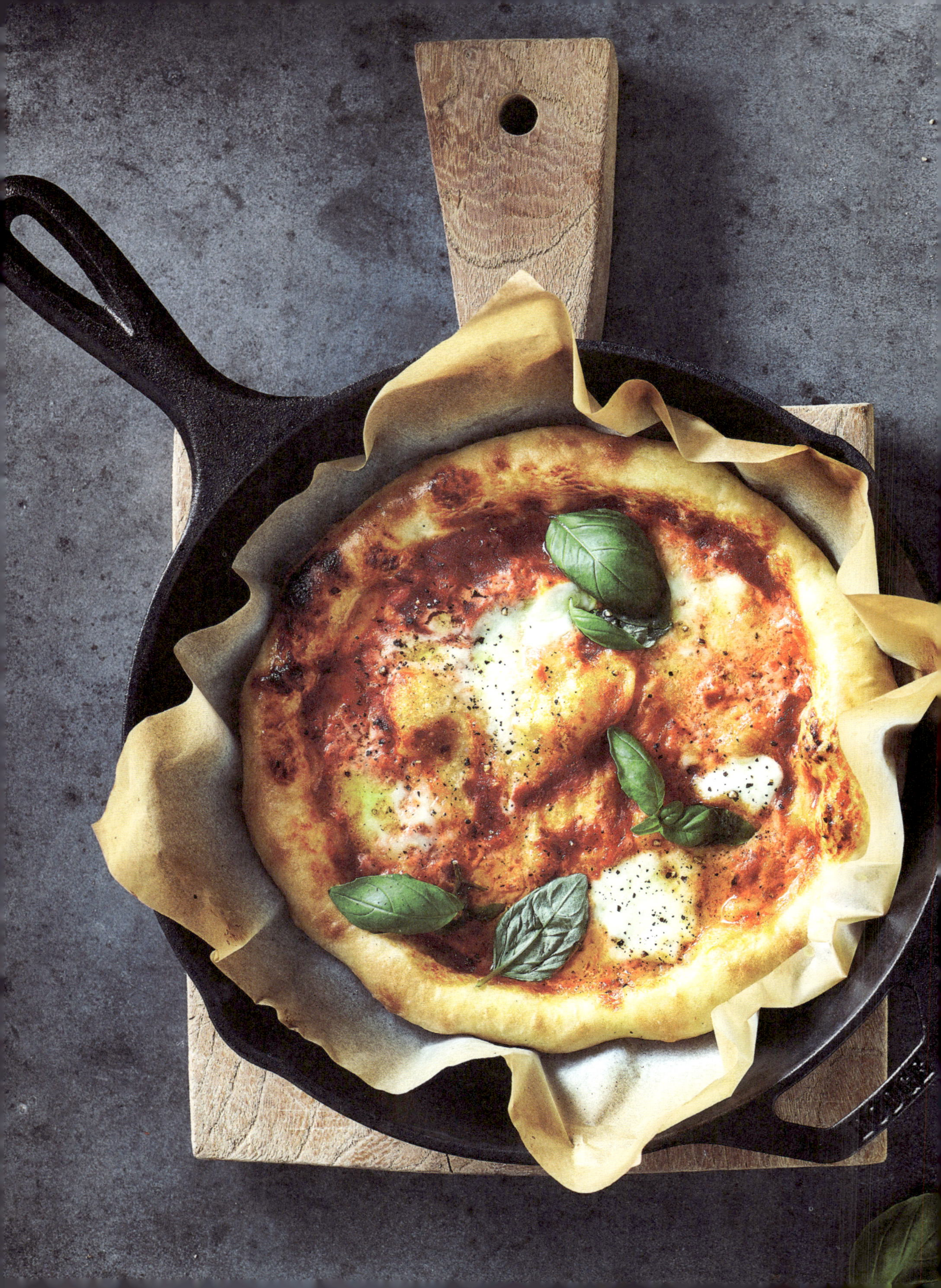

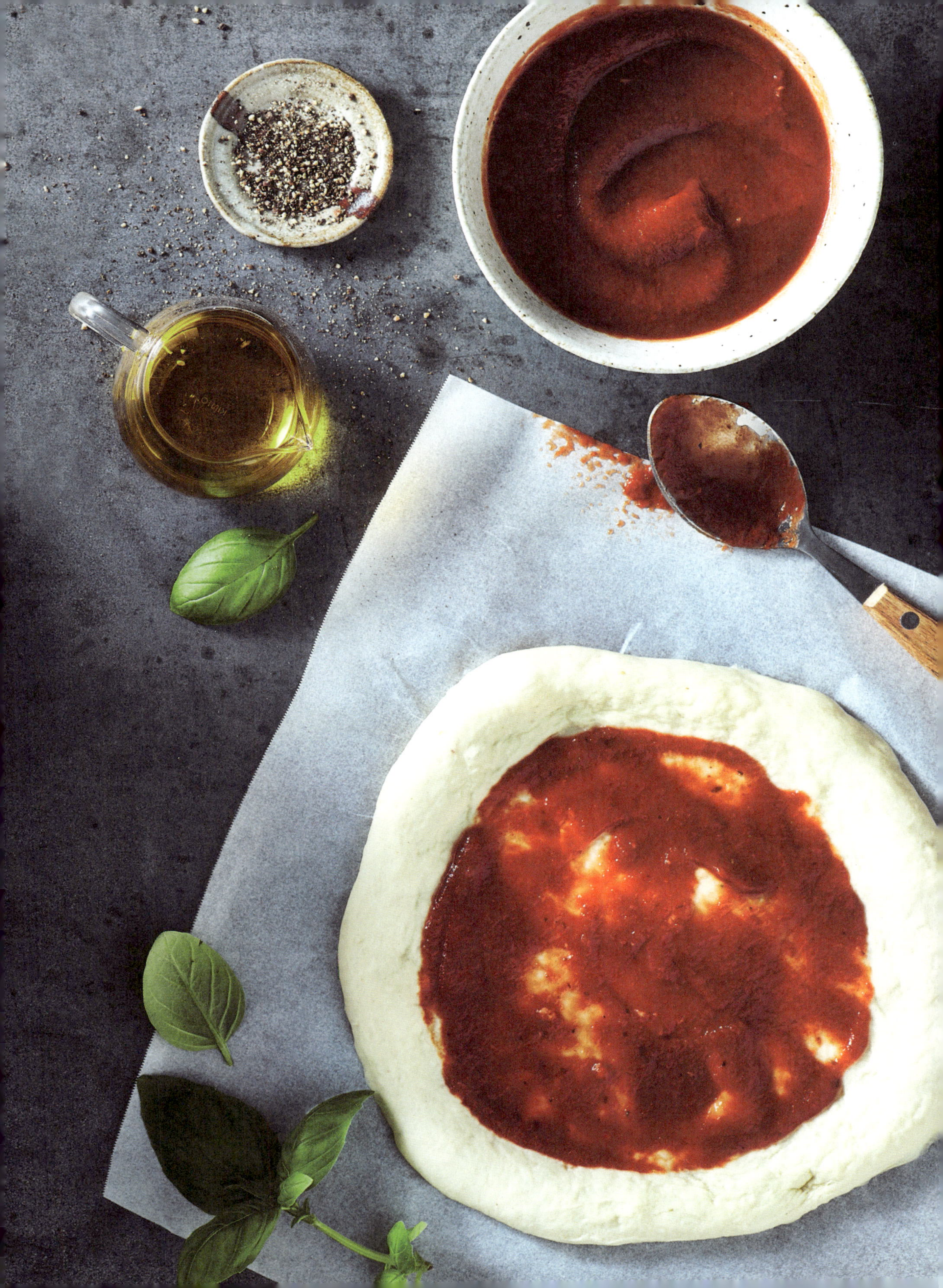

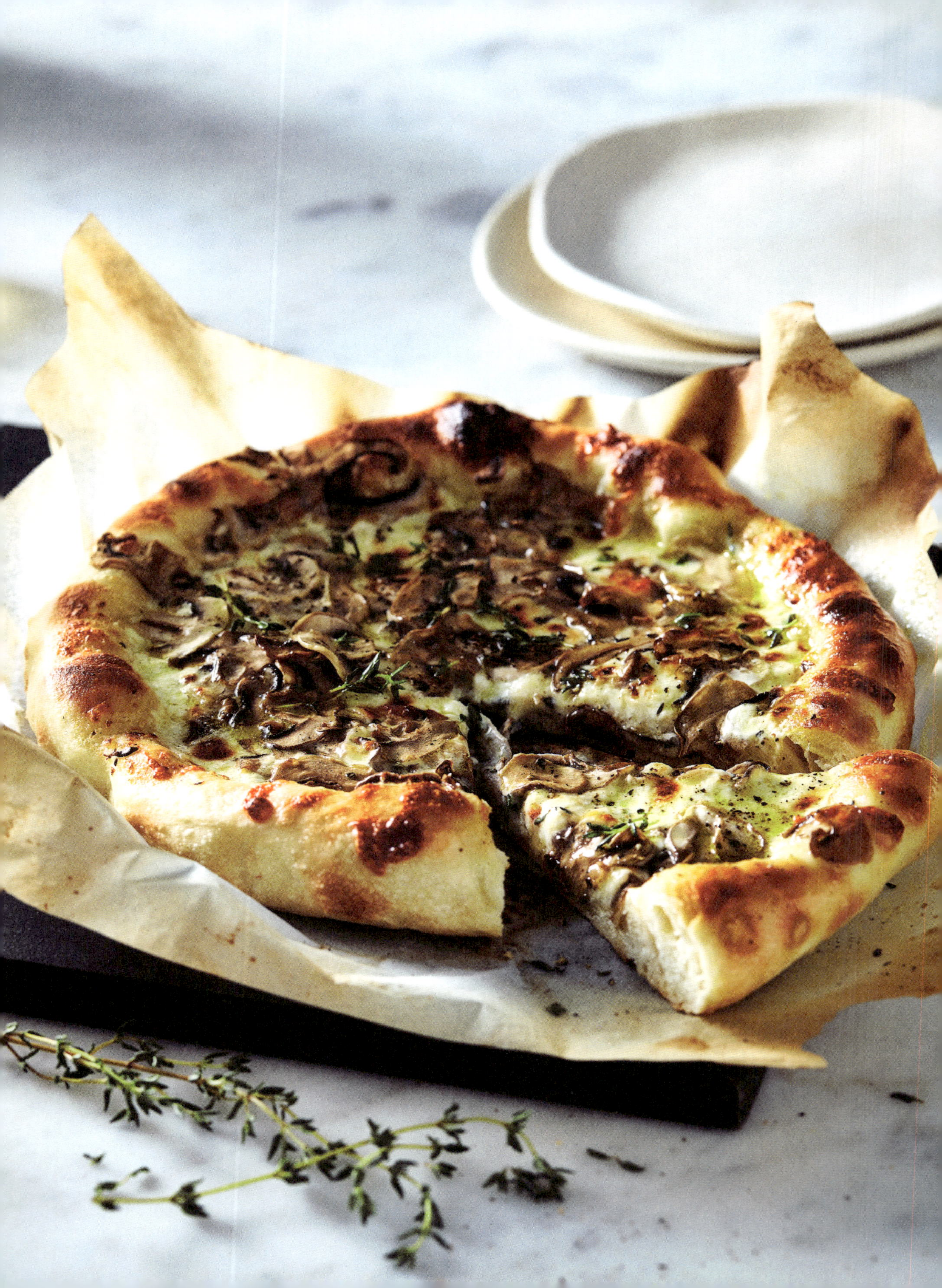

White mushroom pizza

Makes 4 pizzas
Prep 10 minutes
Cook 5 minutes each

A good white-sauce pizza is a brilliant change from the standard tomato bases. But really, why choose one or the other? These pizzas are all so quick you could make every pizza in this chapter for one big pizza party.

1 quantity All-in pizza dough (page 127), or pre-made pizza bases

500 g (1 lb 2 oz) button mushrooms, thinly sliced

3 garlic cloves, finely crushed

2 tablespoons olive oil

6 thyme sprigs, leaves stripped, plus extra to serve

salt and black pepper, to season

2–3 cups (300–450 g/ 10½ oz–1 lb) shredded mozzarella

WHITE SAUCE

½ cup (125 g/4½ oz) sour cream

½ cup (125 ml/4 fl oz) thickened (whipping) cream

3 tablespoons grated parmesan

2 garlic cloves, crushed

¼ teaspoon black pepper

Remove the pizza dough from the fridge about 30 minutes before you want to cook.

In a bowl, combine the white sauce ingredients, mixing well.

In another bowl, combine the mushrooms, garlic, olive oil and thyme and season well with salt and pepper.

Take a 26 cm (10¼ in) frying pan with a handle that can go in your oven. Tear a piece of baking paper slightly larger than the pan and lay it on a cutting board. Place a ball of dough in the centre and, with your fingertips, press and stretch the dough out to about the same size as the frying pan. Press the dough from the centre out, leaving a slightly raised lip around the edge.

Spread one-quarter of the white sauce over the dough, then scatter with one-quarter of the cheese, then the mushrooms.

Heat your oven's overhead grill (broiler) as high as it can go.

Place your frying pan on the stove over a high heat until very hot. Drop the paper holding the pizza onto the frying pan, then immediately transfer the pan to the oven. Cook for about 5 minutes until the dough is cooked through, risen and the crust is browned.

Scatter with a little fresh thyme and more black pepper. Repeat for the remaining pizzas.

TIP In case you're re-reading this to work out where to actually cook the mushrooms, they sit on top of the cheese raw, so that they can cook together with the pizza.

Bolognese pizza

—

Makes 4 pizzas
Prep 10 minutes
Cook 5 minutes each

Home cooking is all about making things work for you — and often that can just mean cooking smarter. Making more bolognese sauce (see page 136) than you need for one meal saves both time and energy — and then you can use the leftovers to make quick and easy stuff like this.

1 quantity All-in pizza dough (page 127)

2 cups (500 ml/17 fl oz) leftover bolognese sauce (page 136)

4 cups (600 g/1 lb 5 oz) shredded mozzarella

1 cup (100 g/3½ oz) grated parmesan

olive oil, for drizzling

2 tablespoons parsley or basil, to serve

Remove the pizza dough from the fridge about 30 minutes before you want to cook.

Take a 26 cm (10¼ in) frying pan with a handle that can fit in your oven. Tear a piece of baking paper slightly larger than the pan and lay it on a cutting board. Place a ball of dough in the centre and, with your fingertips, press and stretch the dough out to about the same size as the frying pan. Press the dough from the centre out, leaving a slightly raised lip around the edge.

Spread one-quarter of the bolognese sauce over the dough, and scatter with one-quarter of the mozzarella. Sprinkle a little parmesan over and drizzle a little oil onto the crust.

Heat your oven's overhead grill (broiler) as high as it can go.

Place your frying pan on the stove over a high heat until very hot. Drop the paper holding the pizza onto the hot frying pan, then immediately transfer the pan to the oven. Cook for about 5 minutes until the dough is cooked through, risen and the crust is browned.

Serve hot, scattered with more parmesan and a little parsley or basil. Repeat for the remaining pizzas.

TIP If you don't want to make your own pizza dough (though it's so easy I strongly suggest you do), you can use pre-made pizza bases, or even good, thick pitas. Alternatively, ask your local pizzeria if they'll sell you some dough!

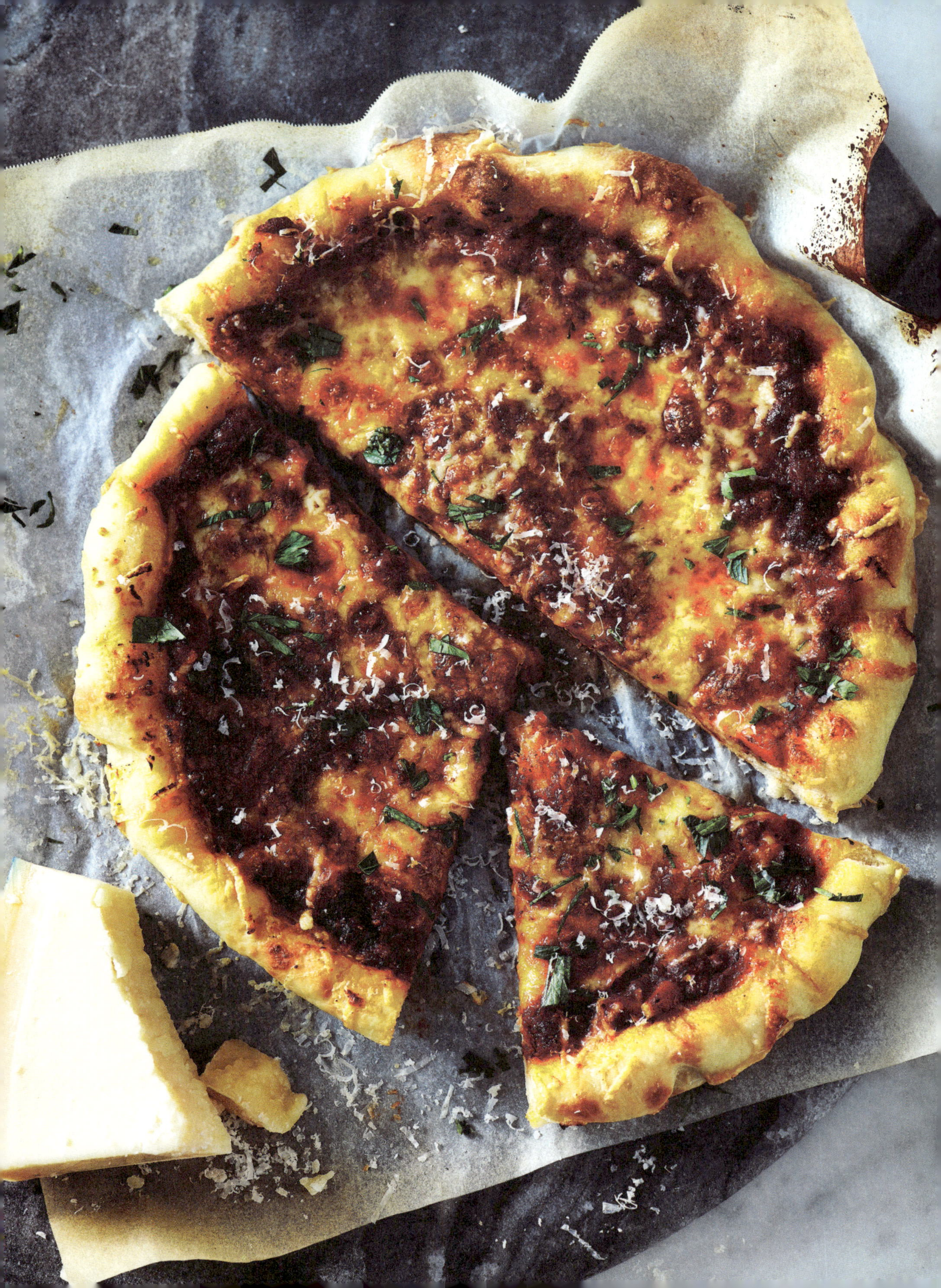

Spaghetti bolognese

—

Serves 6, with leftover sauce
Prep 15 minutes
Cook 3 hours

In a hundred different households in Australia you'll find a hundred different versions of spaghetti bolognese, but to my mind three things are most important. First, the magic happens in the third hour of cooking the sauce. Second, combine the pasta and sauce together to serve it, rather than just serving the sauce on top. And third, always make extra sauce.

2 large brown onions
2 celery stalks
2 carrots
4 garlic cloves
2 tablespoons olive oil
500 g (1 lb 2 oz) extra mixed vegetable offcuts (optional), such as broccoli stems, mushrooms, zucchini (courgette), eggplant (aubergine)
500 g (1 lb 2 oz) minced (ground) beef
500 g (1 lb 2 oz) minced (ground) pork
1 teaspoon dried oregano
2 bay leaves
2 × 700 ml (23½ fl oz) bottles of tomato passata (puréed tomatoes)
2 tablespoons tomato sauce (ketchup)
1 teaspoon salt, plus extra to season
750 g (1 lb 11 oz) dried spaghetti
25 g (1 oz) butter (optional)
finely shredded parsley, to serve
grated parmesan, to serve

Cut the onions, celery and carrots into 1 cm (½ in) cubes, and roughly chop the garlic. Heat a large flameproof casserole dish over a medium heat and add the olive oil. Fry the vegetables, vegetable offcuts, if using, and garlic for about 10 minutes until fragrant and softened. Add the beef and pork and fry until lightly browned.

Stir in the passata, tomato sauce, salt and about 2 cups (500 ml/ 17 fl oz) water. Simmer over a low heat for 2½ hours, stirring occasionally and topping up with a little water if the mixture is getting too dry. Taste and adjust the seasoning.

Just before serving, cook the pasta in plenty of boiling salted water according to the packet directions, but start checking it about 2 minutes before the time recommended on the packet. Drain the pasta, reserving about ¼ cup (60 ml/2 fl oz) of the pasta water.

When the pasta is nearly finished cooking, heat a very large frying pan over a medium heat and add about a third to half of the bolognese sauce (you can always add more later). Add the pasta to the sauce, along with the reserved pasta water, and stir or toss to combine with the sauce. This also allows the flavour of the sauce to be absorbed by the pasta.

Add the butter, if using, and mix to combine. Serve topped with a little shredded parsley and a lot of grated parmesan.

TIP If you're here to argue about a traditional ragù alla bolognese from Bologna, save your breath, this ain't it. The reason I've given you such a large quantity of sauce is for practicality. Use a third to half of it for this dish, then mix in a few Japanese curry roux cubes to make the Japanese-style dry curry on page 68 — and then you can still reserve a couple of cups for the Bolognese pizza on page 134.

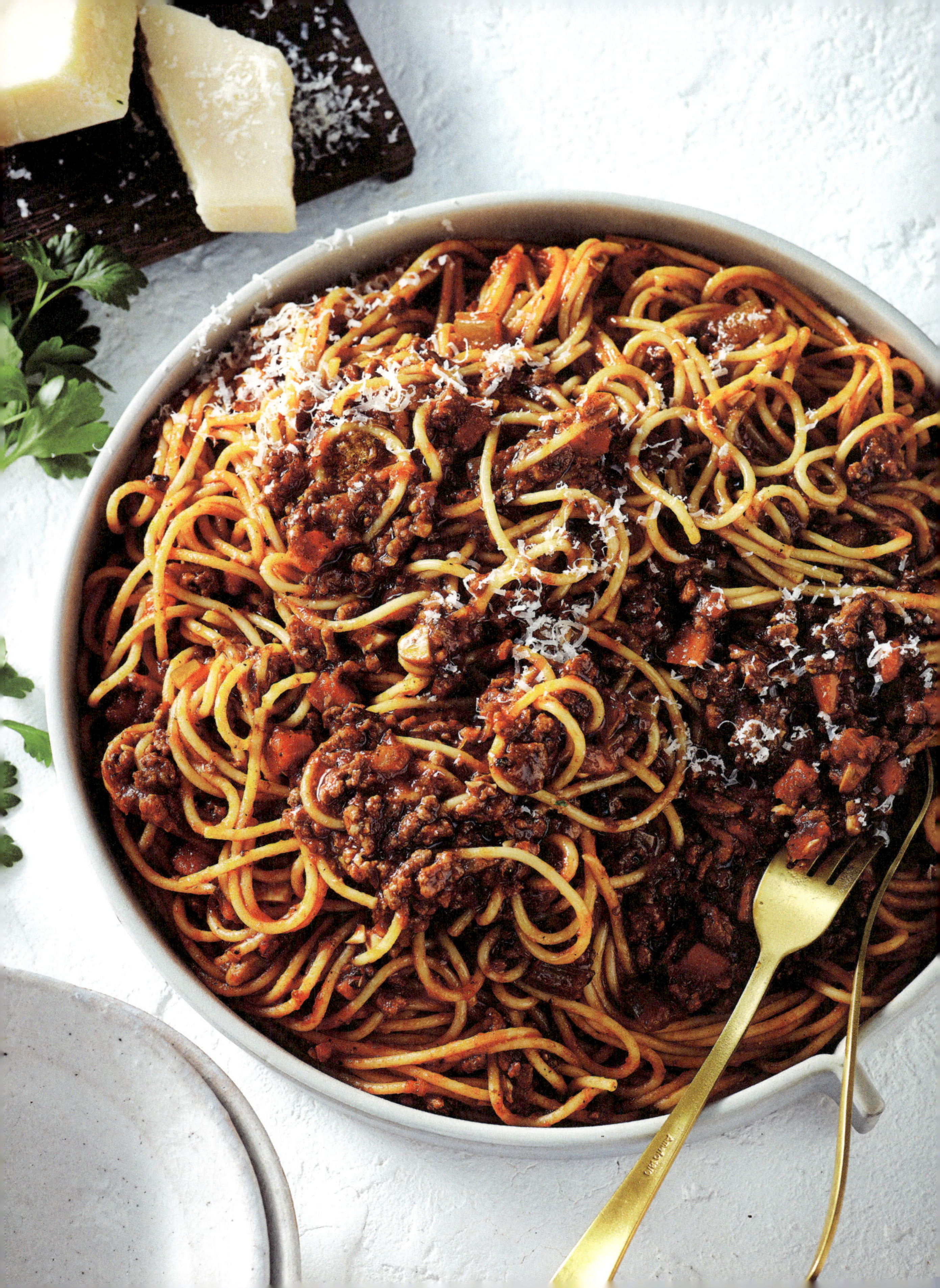

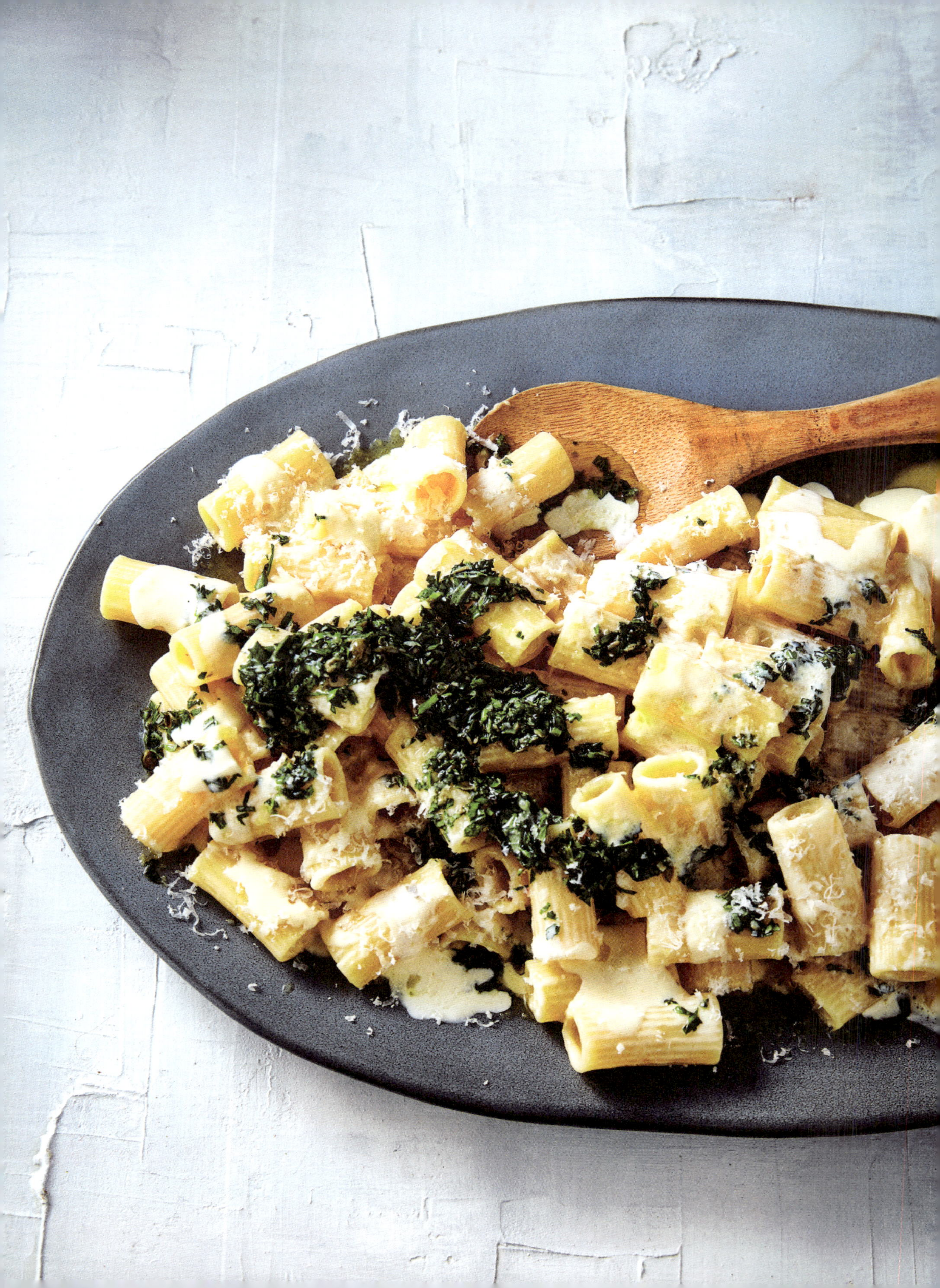

Rigatoni alfredo

—

Serves 6
Prep 10 minutes
Cook 15 minutes

Fettuccini alfredo was the creamy pasta everyone loved in the 1980s and into the '90s. I'm shaking it up a bit with rigatoni, which I think is fabulous with thick, creamy sauces. I've added a lemony salsa verde to cut through the richness.

500 g (1 lb 2 oz) dried rigatoni

salt and black pepper, to season

75 g (2¾ oz) butter

1 French shallot, very finely chopped

300 ml (10 fl oz) thickened (whipping) cream

1 cup (100 g/3½ oz) grated parmesan, plus extra to serve

ROUGH SALSA VERDE

¼ cup parsley leaves, roughly chopped

¼ cup basil leaves, roughly chopped

2 teaspoons capers, roughly chopped

1 garlic clove, crushed

¼ cup (60 ml/2 fl oz) olive oil

juice of ½ lemon

Mix the salsa verde ingredients in a bowl and set aside.

Cook the pasta in plenty of boiling salted water according to the packet directions, but start checking it about 2 minutes before the time recommended on the packet. Drain the pasta, reserving about ¼ cup (60 ml/2 fl oz) of the pasta water.

While the pasta is boiling, heat a very large frying pan over a medium heat and add the butter. Fry the shallot for 4 minutes until softened, then add the cream and bring to a simmer for 2 minutes. Stir the parmesan through.

Add the drained pasta directly to the pan, along with the reserved pasta water. Toss to emulsify and coat the pasta in the creamy sauce.

Serve the pasta with the salsa verde spooned over, plenty of black pepper and a bit of extra cheese.

TIP The original Roman fettuccini alfredo (invented by Alfredo di Lelio in 1908) was simply pasta emulsified in the pasta water with butter and parmesan — like cacio e pepe, without the pepper. And as with the cream in a carbonara, purists would frown on creamy versions of alfredo such as this one. It goes without saying that I'm no purist.

Fried egg & chilli linguine

—

Serves 4
Prep 10 minutes
Cook 15 minutes

This dish has no right to be as delicious as it is. The thing is, it plays to the natural affinity foods sometimes share in the most unlikely places. Both eggs and olive oil-based pasta dishes should be cooked with a liberal amount of oil, so why not combine the two together.

500 g (1 lb 2 oz) dried linguine

⅔ cup (170 ml/5½ fl oz) olive oil

6 eggs

6 garlic cloves, roughly chopped

3 large red chillies, roughly chopped

salt and black pepper, to season

½ cup (50 g/1¾ oz) grated parmesan, to serve

Cook the pasta in plenty of boiling salted water according to the packet directions, but start checking it about 2 minutes before the time recommended on the packet. Drain the pasta, reserving about ¼ cup (60 ml/2 fl oz) of the pasta water.

While the pasta is cooking, heat a very large frying pan over a medium heat. Add the olive oil and fry the eggs until crisp and lightly browned around the edges, but with soft yolks. Remove from the pan and set aside. Add the garlic and chilli and fry for just a minute or two until fragrant.

Transfer the pasta and the reserved pasta water to the pan and toss to coat.

Return the eggs to the pan and stir gently. Season with salt and black pepper and scatter with parmesan to serve.

TIP When eating this dish, crack the yolks open first, so that the runny egg yolk forms a bit more of a sauce with the pasta.

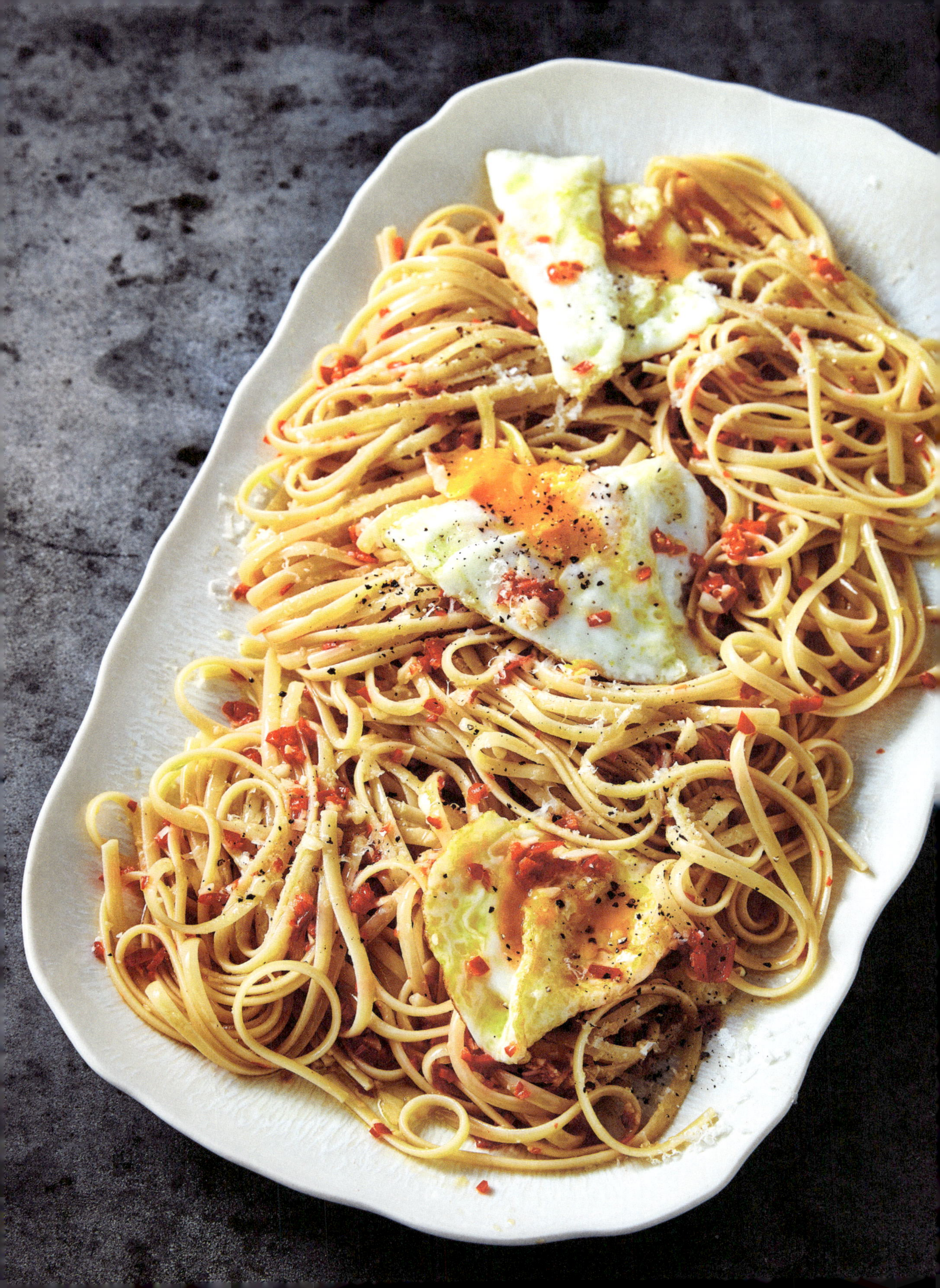

Lion's head meatball spaghetti

—

Serves 4
Prep 20 minutes
Cook 2 hours 20 minutes

Spaghetti and meatballs meets the classic Shanghainese dish known as lion's heads. Tofu works as a fabulous protein-rich base to lighten the meatballs — much better than stodgy breadcrumbs.

2 tablespoons olive oil

1 onion, finely chopped

3 garlic cloves, roughly chopped

½ cup (125 ml/4 fl oz) red wine

2 tablespoons tomato paste (concentrated purée)

700 ml (23½ fl oz) tomato passata (puréed tomatoes)

2 bay leaves

½ teaspoon dried oregano

salt and black pepper, to season

500 g (1 lb 2 oz) dried spaghetti

1 cup (100 g/3½ oz) grated parmesan

LION'S HEAD MEATBALLS

1 tablespoon olive oil

1 onion, finely chopped

2 garlic cloves, finely chopped

2 zucchini (courgettes), grated

500 g (1 lb 2 oz) mix of minced (ground) beef and pork

300 g (10½ oz) medium-firm tofu, crumbled

1 egg

1 teaspoon salt

black pepper, to season

TIP If you find the idea of giant meatballs daunting, make smaller ones and bake them under the oven grill for about 15 minutes.

Heat your oven to 200°C (400°F) fan-forced, and switch on the overhead grill (broiler).

For the meatballs, heat a small saucepan over a medium heat and add the olive oil, onion, garlic and zucchini. Fry for 5 minutes, stirring occasionally, until the onion is translucent and the zucchini softened. Cool slightly, then tip into a bowl with the remaining ingredients and mix well. Form into four large meatballs. Place on a lined baking tray and bake for 30 minutes until browned.

Turn the oven down to 180°C (350°F), and turn off the grill setting.

Take an ovenproof saucepan or flameproof casserole dish that is just large enough to fit the meatballs in a single layer. Heat over a medium heat and add the oil. Fry the onion for a minute, then add the garlic and fry for a further minute until fragrant. Add the wine and boil for about 2 minutes, then stir in the tomato paste, passata, bay leaves, oregano and about 1 cup (250 ml/8½ fl oz) water (or stock) and bring to a simmer. Season well with salt and pepper.

Add the meatballs, spooning a bit of the sauce over them. Cover and bake for about 1½ hours, spooning the sauce over the meatballs once in a while. Taste and adjust the seasoning.

Just before serving, cook the pasta in plenty of boiling salted water according to the packet directions, but start checking it about 2 minutes before the time recommended on the packet.

Remove the meatballs from the sauce and set aside. Place the pan of sauce over a low heat. When the pasta is al dente, drain it, reserving about ¼ cup (60 ml/2 fl oz) of the pasta water. Stir both the pasta and reserved pasta water through the sauce over a low heat for about a minute to combine the sauce and pasta.

Divide the pasta among four shallow bowls and place a single meatball in the centre of each. Scatter with parmesan and serve.

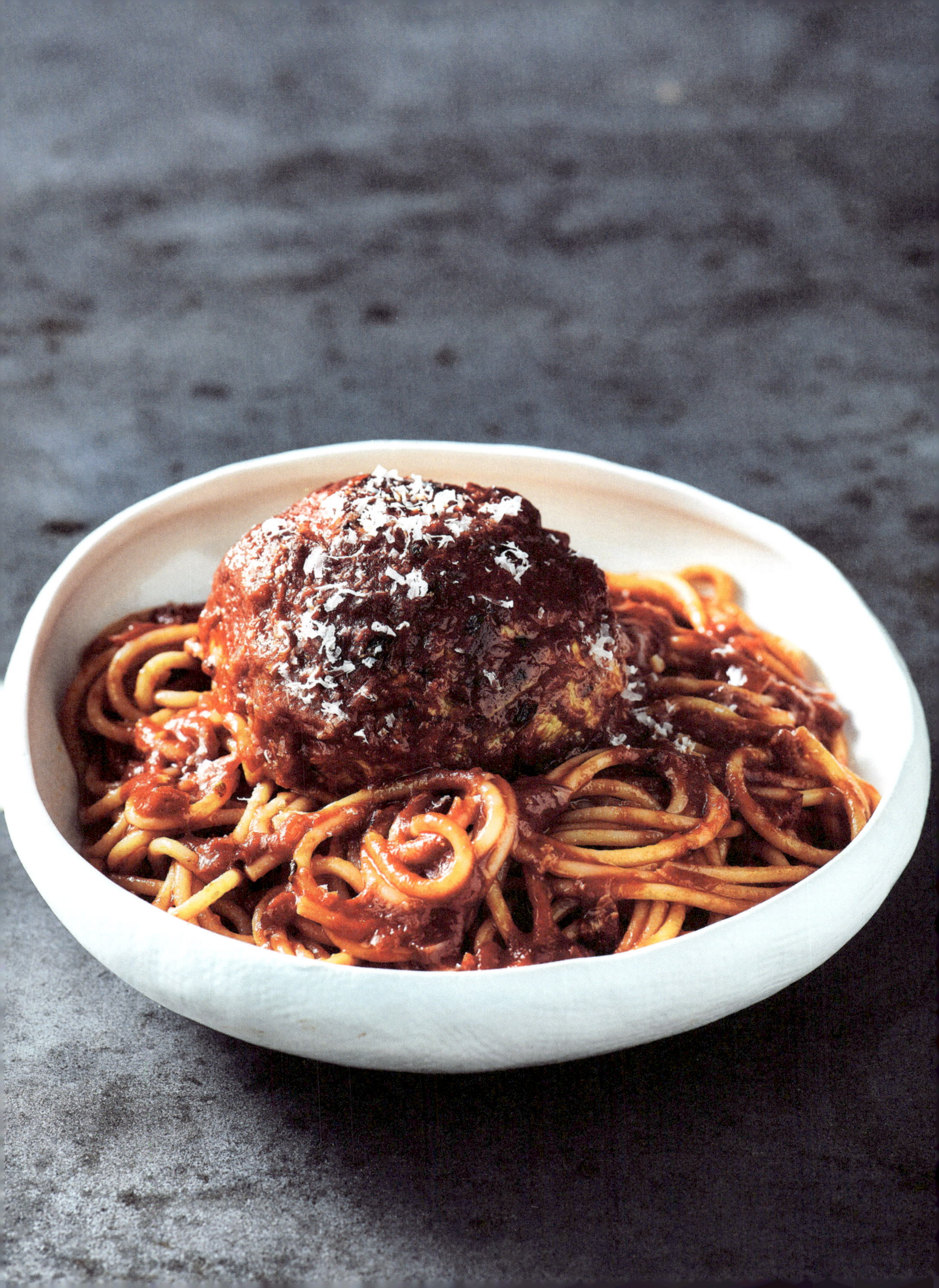

Roasted cherry tomato & olive fusilli

—

Serves 4
Prep 5 minutes
Cook 35 minutes

I can't impress on you enough how easy this is — a few ingredients thrown into a roasting pan and whacked in the oven. Then you just have to cook your pasta. The only thing you have to pick up a knife for is chopping the garlic, chilli and parsley.

450 g (1 lb) mixed cherry tomatoes

1 cup mixed marinated olives

½ cup (125 ml/4 fl oz) olive oil (see Tip)

½ teaspoon dried oregano

3 garlic cloves, roughly chopped

1 red bird's eye chilli, sliced (optional)

salt and black pepper, to season

500 g (1 lb 2 oz) dried fusilli (spirals), or other short pasta

1 tablespoon finely chopped parsley

handful of torn basil leaves

Heat your oven to 180°C (350°F) fan-forced. Combine the cherry tomatoes, olives, olive oil, oregano, garlic and chilli in a roasting pan, season with salt and pepper and stir to combine. Roast for 30 minutes until the tomatoes are bursting and the olives are warm and wrinkled.

Cook the pasta in plenty of boiling salted water according to the packet directions, but start checking it about 2 minutes before the time recommended on the packet. Drain the pasta, reserving about ¼ cup (60 ml/2 fl oz) of the pasta water.

Add the pasta and reserved pasta water to the roasting pan, along with the parsley and basil. Toss to coat the pasta in the sauce, then serve.

TIP If you have olives marinated in good extra-virgin olive oil, you can substitute the marinating oil for the olive oil in this recipe, but in many cases, commercial marinated olives will be marinated in vegetable oil or cheaper oil rather than good olive oil.

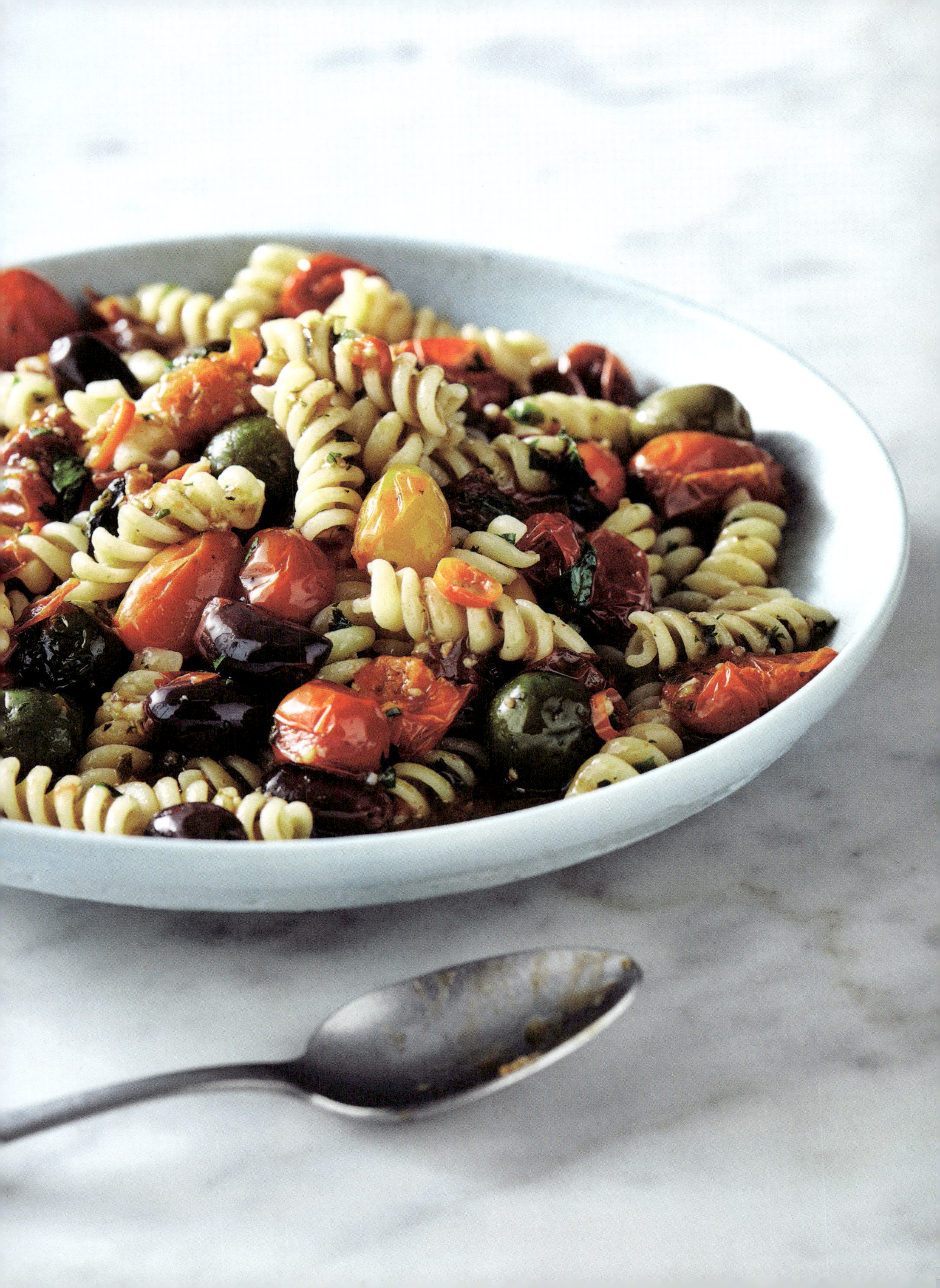

Rosé prawn linguine

Serves 4
Prep 15 minutes
Cook 20 minutes

Rosé pasta sauces that combine tomato and cream are tremendously unfashionable — but then a great many delicious things are very unfashionable indeed.

35 g (1¼ oz) butter

1 small brown onion, finely chopped

4 garlic cloves, crushed

2 cups (500 ml/17 fl oz) tomato passata (puréed tomatoes)

500 g (1 lb 2 oz) dried linguine (see Tip)

12–16 large raw prawns (shrimp), peeled, deveined and butterflied

1 tablespoon brandy (optional)

150 ml (5 fl oz) thickened (whipping) cream

salt and black pepper, to season

¼ cup torn basil leaves

Heat a medium saucepan over a medium heat and add 25 g (1 oz) of the butter, the onion and garlic. When the garlic just starts to brown, stir in the passata. Cover and simmer for about 15 minutes. Remove from the heat and set aside.

Cook the pasta in plenty of boiling salted water according to the packet directions, but start checking it about 2 minutes before the time recommended on the packet. Drain the pasta, reserving about ¼ cup (60 ml/2 fl oz) of the pasta water.

Heat a very large frying pan over a medium heat and add the remaining butter. Fry the prawns for about 2 minutes until they look half-cooked. Add the brandy, if using. Stir in the cream and your passata sauce mixture and bring to a simmer. Season well with salt and pepper.

Add the pasta and reserved pasta water. Toss to mix, then stir the basil through and serve.

TIP Linguine is a great pasta shape with seafood, but for something different, try mafaldine — a long, flat and crinkly pasta that looks like a fancy ribbon.

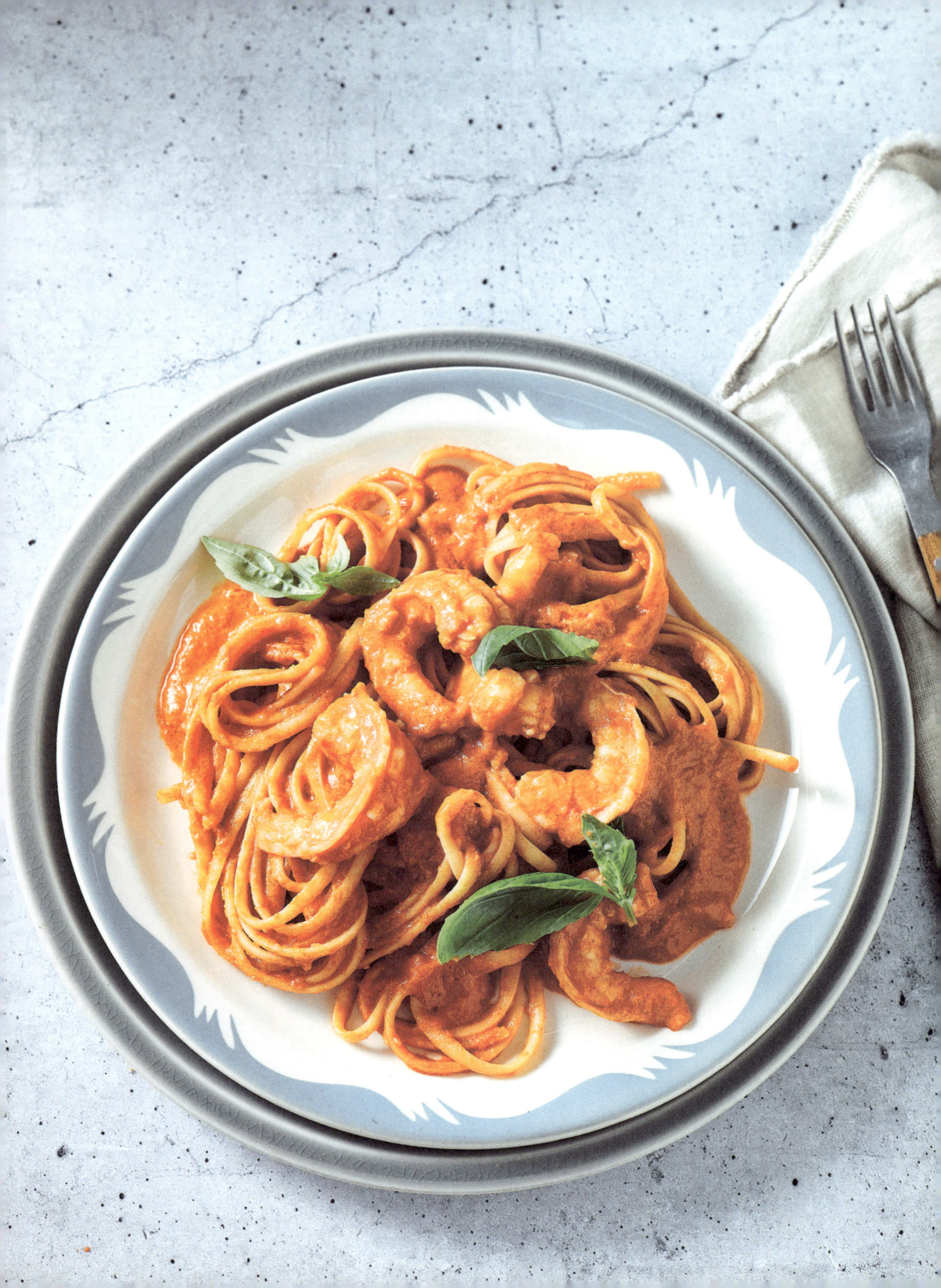

Midnight spaghetti

Serves 4
Prep 5 minutes
Cook 10 minutes

The idea behind midnight spaghetti is that it's a meal you can make with just what's in your pantry (or fridge), in the time it takes to cook the pasta. Here, the addition of a simple pangrattato made from quick-fried panko breadcrumbs provides a delicious texture.

500 g (1 lb 2 oz) dried spaghetti

salt and black pepper, to season

100 ml (3½ fl oz) good-quality extra-virgin olive oil, plus extra for the panko

6 anchovy fillets in oil, roughly chopped

6 garlic cloves, sliced

1 tablespoon baby capers

1 teaspoon chilli flakes

1 teaspoon tomato paste (concentrated purée)

1 cup (60 g/2 oz) panko, or other coarse breadcrumbs

Cook the pasta in plenty of boiling salted water according to the packet directions, but start checking it about 2 minutes before the time recommended on the packet. Drain the pasta, reserving about ¼ cup (60 ml/2 fl oz) of the pasta water.

While the pasta is cooking, heat a very large frying pan over a medium heat and add the olive oil, anchovies, garlic, capers, chilli and tomato paste. Stir until the garlic starts to brown.

Add the pasta to the pan, along with the reserved pasta water, and toss to mix everything well together. Grind over plenty of black pepper.

In a separate pan, heat a few more tablespoons of olive oil and fry the panko until browned and crisp. Season well with salt.

Scatter the panko over the pasta and serve.

TIP Other than the spaghetti, garlic and oil, every other ingredient here is optional. This is essentially an aglio e olio ('garlic and oil') style of pasta, but the most important point is tossing the pasta and oil together with a little of the pasta cooking water, so that the oil and starchy water will combine into a sauce that coats the pasta.

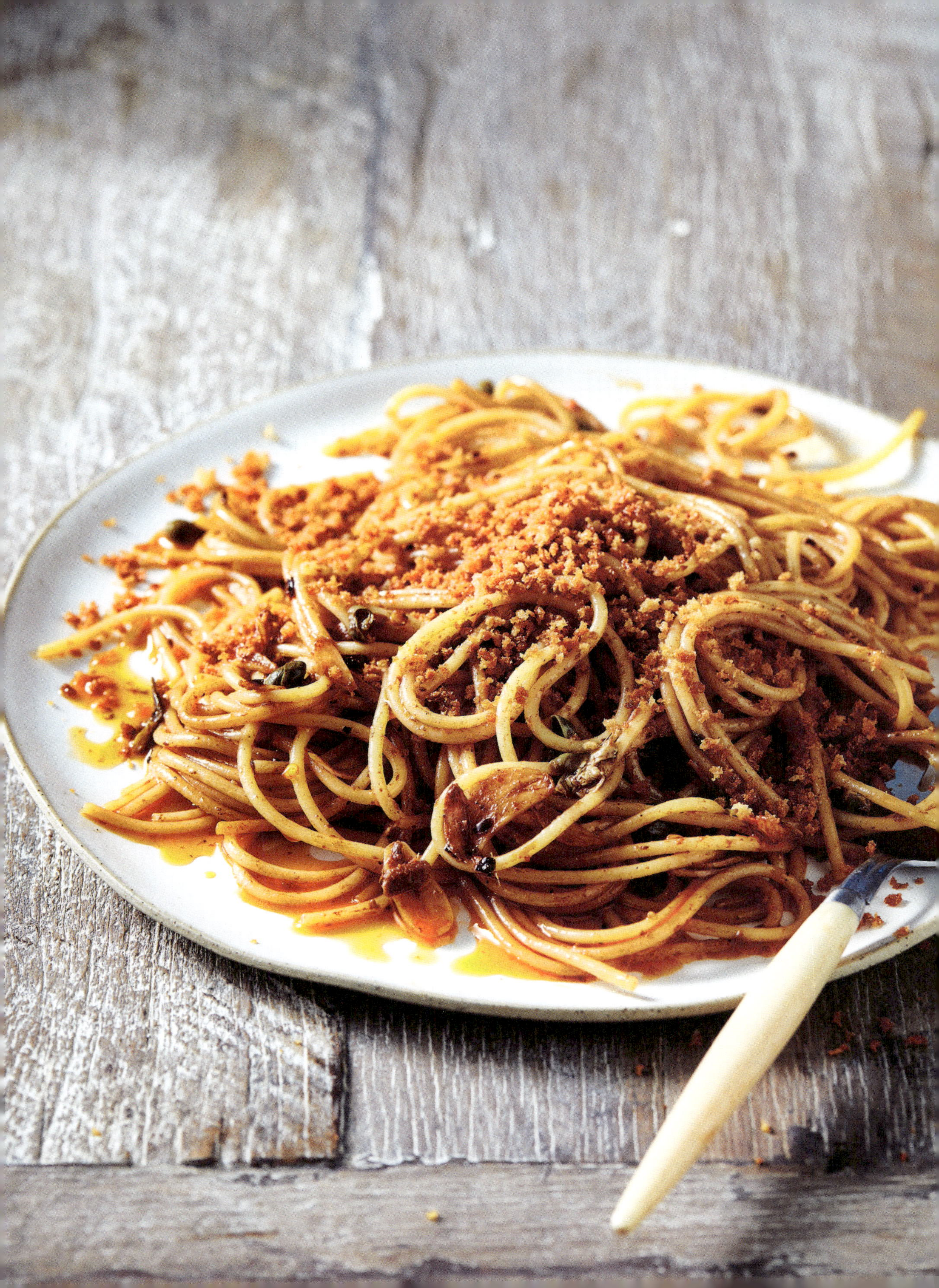

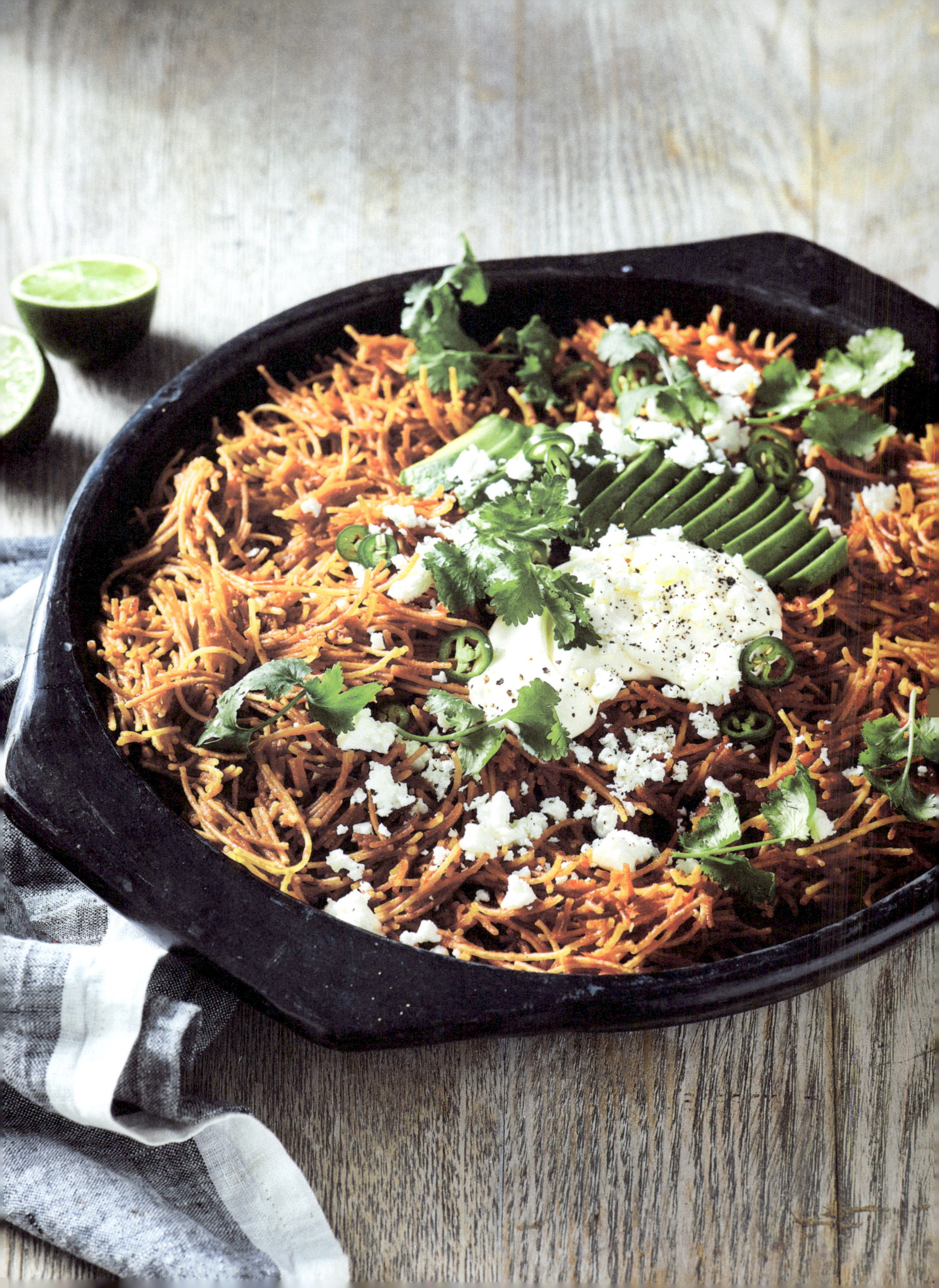

Mexican noodles

Sopa seca de fideos

—

Makes 4
Prep 10 minutes
Cook 20 minutes

This 'dry soup' of angel hair pasta that starts by frying the dried pasta in oil might seem strange at first, but it's a good reminder of how pasta has travelled around the world. Nearly every country has its own versions that have become family favourites.

500 g (1 lb 2 oz) dried angel hair pasta

6 ripe tomatoes, roughly chopped (see Tip)

1 small brown onion, roughly chopped

2 garlic cloves, roughly chopped

2 tablespoons chipotle chillies in adobo sauce

½ teaspoon salt

½ cup (125 ml/4 fl oz) vegetable oil

TO SERVE

1 avocado, cut into wedges

2 tablespoons sour cream

100 g (3½ oz) feta, crumbled

1 large green chilli, thinly sliced

¼ cup picked coriander (cilantro) leaves

Break the pasta into smaller pieces by smacking the packet of pasta with a rolling pin (before opening the packet, please).

Place the tomatoes, onion, garlic, chillies (and sauce) and salt in a blender and blitz to a smooth sauce.

Heat a large frying pan over a medium heat and add the oil. Fry the dried pasta pieces for about 3 minutes until golden and crisp. Add your tomato sauce and bring to a simmer. Stir in about 1 cup (250 ml/8½ fl oz) water and simmer for 10–15 minutes until the liquid is absorbed by the noodles and the sauce has thickened. Taste and season as needed with salt.

Transfer the noodles to a serving plate. Serve topped with the avocado, sour cream, feta, chilli and coriander.

TIP If you're fussy, you can peel the tomatoes before blending. Using a sharp knife, cut a cross into the base of each tomato, then plunge them into boiling water (or place in a heatproof bowl and pour a kettle of boiling water over them) for 30 seconds to 1 minute. The skin should peel back from the tomatoes, allowing you to remove it easily.

/wɒk/
noun

1. a rounded, multi-purpose cooking vessel often used in Asian cooking

WOK

Wok cooking is one of the most valuable disciplines for putting food on the dinner table each night with minimal effort or fuss. At its most basic, it's a very simple formula.

All you need is a few key ingredients (one meat and one vegetable; one seafood and one vegetable; maybe even just one vegetable), an aromatic or two (take your pick from any or all of onion, garlic and ginger — the holy trinity of Chinese cooking), and a light hand with one or two seasonings — oyster sauce, soy sauce, cooking wine, or just a pinch of salt. That's it.

What you'll end up with after a few minutes might be chicken and mushrooms (page 156), pork belly and capsicum (page 159), prawns and chilli (page 164) or chicken and leeks (page 171); you can turn any ingredients you have into a dish.

Take a look at some of the menus on page 216 to see how a few quick dishes can make for a very simple but memorable meal. Serve them with steamed rice, or don't — it's really up to you.

Read the tips throughout this chapter for some pointers on the techniques of wok cooking.

Chicken & mushrooms

Serves 4
Prep 10 minutes
Cook 10 minutes

The key to good stir-frying is keeping it simple. Fewer ingredients mean simpler flavours, and better technique. This is a dish of chicken and mushrooms, with just a hint of aromatic ginger and garlic. Everything else in here — the oil, oyster sauce, wine — is added in service of achieving that simplicity of flavour.

500 g (1 lb 2 oz) boneless, skinless chicken thighs, cut into 3 cm (1¼ in) pieces

300 g (10½ oz) mixed fresh enoki, shiitake and king oyster (eringi) mushrooms

2–3 tablespoons vegetable oil

1 brown onion, sliced

2 cm (¾ in) piece fresh ginger, unpeeled, sliced and bruised

2 tablespoons oyster sauce

1 tablespoon Shaoxing wine

pinch of sugar

1 teaspoon cornflour (cornstarch), mixed with ¼ cup (60 ml/2 fl oz) cold water

CHICKEN MARINADE

1 teaspoon soy sauce

1 teaspoon sesame oil

1 teaspoon cornflour (cornstarch)

¼ teaspoon bicarbonate of soda (baking soda)

Combine the marinade ingredients and mix through the chicken. Set aside for few minutes while you prepare the mushrooms.

Trim the dirty ends from the enoki and separate them into small bunches. Slice the shiitake in half on an angle, and slice the king oyster mushrooms into thick chunks.

Heat a wok over a high heat and add the oil. Fry the chicken in two batches for about 3 minutes until browned, then remove to a bowl and set aside.

Brush out the wok if necessary. Add a little more oil if needed and fry the mushrooms, onion and ginger for about 3 minutes until the mushrooms are softened.

Return the chicken to the wok, along with any collected juices. Add the oyster sauce and pour the Shaoxing wine against the metal of the wok (see Tips). Toss to combine. Take note of how much liquid is in the wok: you don't want it to be completely dry, but in the unlikely event that the wok is looking dry, add a little water or stock.

Add the sugar, then the cornflour mixture, a little a time, tossing it through to thicken the juices to a silky sauce that coats the chicken.

TIPS The quick 'marinade' for the chicken is really more of a coating, and each element is quite important. The bicarbonate of soda helps keep the chicken tender and juicy as it fries. The cornflour helps stick the sauce to the chicken. The soy sauce adds a bit of saltiness and umami, and the toasty sesame oil helps achieve the all-important wok-fried flavour.

Pouring the Shaoxing wine directly onto the metal of the wok allows the direct heat of the metal to remove some of the alcohol burn, and helps distribute the wine more evenly in the dish.

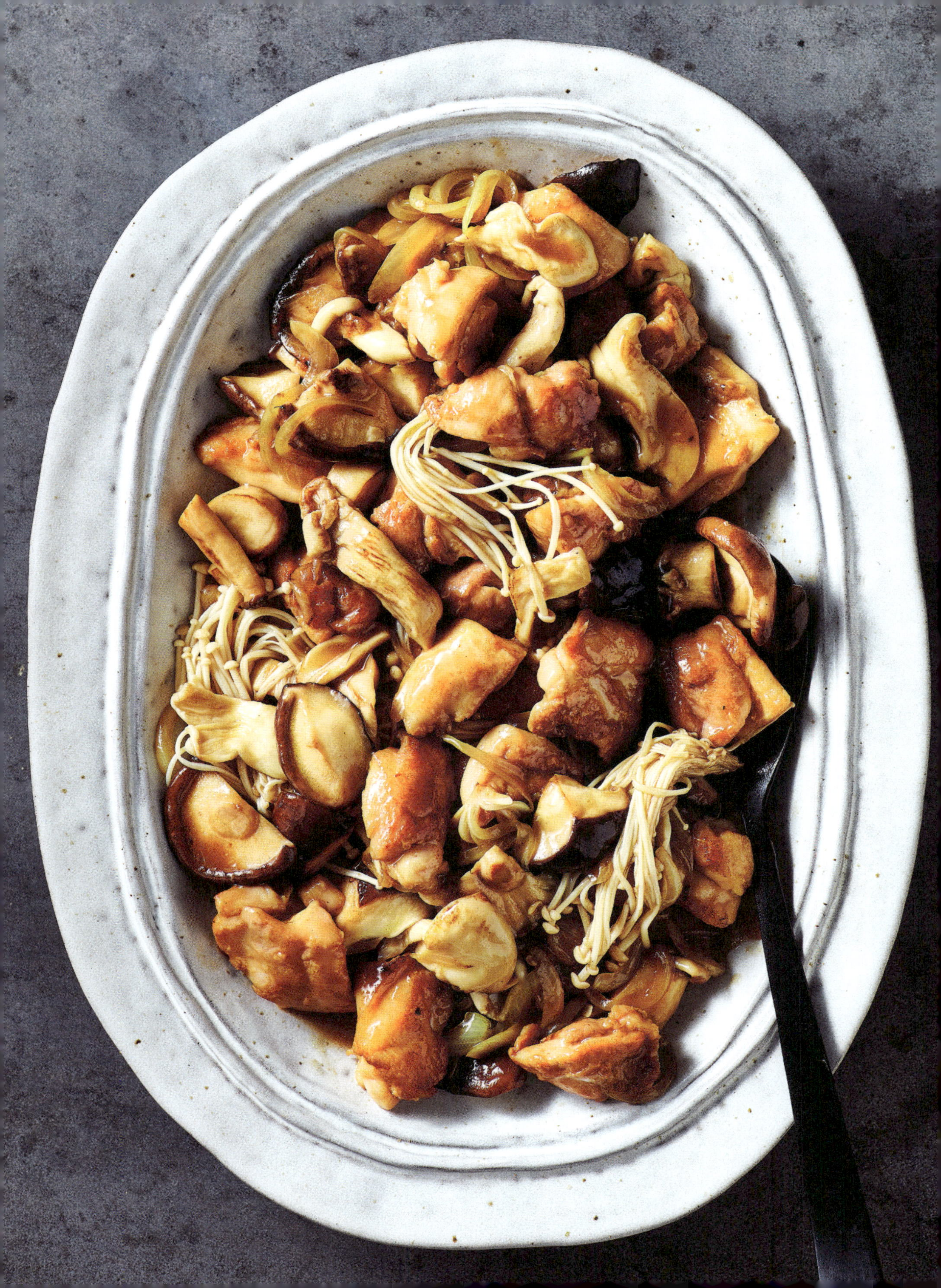

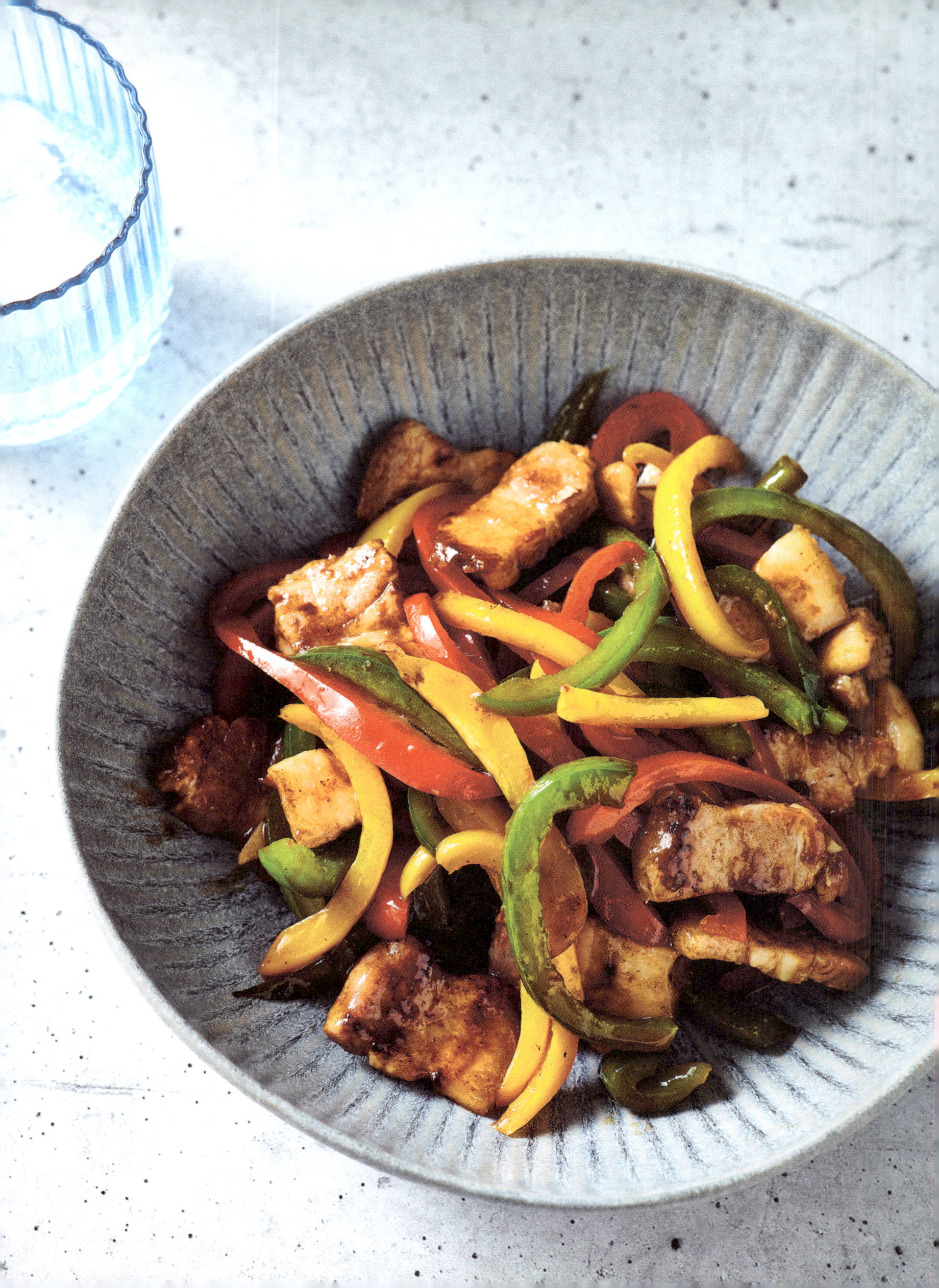

Fireworks

—

Serves 4, as part of a shared meal
Prep 10 minutes
Cook 10 minutes

This is a very minor variation on the ubiquitous Sichuan dish *qing jiao rou si* (sliced pork fried with green capsicum), using vibrantly coloured red, yellow and green capsicums. Other than the colour of the capsicum and a touch of oyster sauce, this is a pretty faithful reproduction of one of the most common wok dishes in Chinese cuisine.

300 g (10½ oz) pork belly, skin and bones removed

2 tablespoons vegetable oil

2 thick slices fresh ginger, bruised

2 garlic cloves, roughly chopped

½ each red, yellow and green capsicum (bell pepper), thinly sliced

1 tablespoon oyster sauce

1 tablespoon soy sauce

1 tablespoon Shaoxing wine

1 teaspoon sesame oil

½ teaspoon sugar

1 teaspoon cornflour (cornstarch), mixed with ¼ cup (60 ml/2 fl oz) water

PORK MARINADE

1 teaspoon soy sauce

1 teaspoon Shaoxing wine

½ teaspoon cornflour (cornstarch)

pinch of ground white pepper

Slice the pork into long thin strips about 1 cm (½ in) wide, then cut into 3 cm (1¼ in) lengths. Combine the pork with the marinade ingredients.

Heat a wok over a high heat until very hot, then add the vegetable oil. Add the pork to the wok, spreading it out into a single layer. Let it sit in the wok without stirring for about 2 minutes until one side of the pork is browned, then toss the wok and cook for another minute or two until the pork is just barely cooked through. Remove the pork to a bowl and set aside.

Return the wok to the heat and add a little extra oil if necessary. Add the ginger and garlic and toss for about a minute until fragrant. Add the capsicum and toss for a minute.

Return the pork to the wok with any juices, along with the oyster sauce, soy sauce, Shaoxing wine, sesame oil and sugar; you can also add a little water if the mixture is looking dry. Toss to combine.

Add a little of the cornflour slurry, tossing until the sauce thickens enough to coat the meat and vegetables. Serve immediately.

TIPS For a more traditional *qing jiao rou si*, slice the pork a little more thinly, replace the oyster sauce with another teaspoon of soy sauce, and only use green capsicum.

Sometimes translated as 'the breath of the wok', wok hei is the goal of wok cooking: basically, your wok-fried dishes should taste fried and not stewed. Allowing the pork to brown is very important, so don't stir when it's added to the wok; think of it like searing. It's totally fine if it only browns on one side.

Black pepper beef noodles

Serves 4
Prep 15 minutes
Stand 15 minutes
Cook 15 minutes

I like the slippery 'restaurant' texture that marinating the meat with bicarbonate of soda gives. If you run into trouble with fresh noodles breaking when you try to separate them, a quick zap in the microwave can solve all your problems. If you're concerned about the spiciness of the black pepper, you can simply reduce the amount, or even leave it out altogether.

500 g (1 lb 2 oz) beef topside or rump, very thinly sliced

1 teaspoon bicarbonate of soda (baking soda)

1 kg (2 lb 3 oz) hokkien noodles

⅓ cup (80 ml/2½ fl oz) vegetable oil

5 garlic cloves, roughly chopped

1 teaspoon grated fresh ginger

1 green capsicum (bell pepper), seeded and thinly sliced

1 bunch choy sum, cut into 5 cm (2 in) lengths

6 thick spring onions (scallions), sliced on a steep diagonal

MEAT MARINADE

1 tablespoon Shaoxing wine

1 teaspoon sesame oil

1 teaspoon dark soy sauce

2 teaspoons cornflour (cornstarch)

½ teaspoon black pepper

BLACK PEPPER SAUCE

3 tablespoons oyster sauce

2 tablespoons dark soy sauce

1 tablespoon coarsely ground black pepper

1 teaspoon caster (superfine) sugar

In a bowl, combine the beef, bicarbonate of soda and about 1 cup (250 ml/8½ fl oz) water. Mix and stand for 15 minutes. Rinse the beef well, massaging it in the water for a minute or so, then rinse and drain. Combine the beef with the marinade ingredients.

Poke a few holes in the bag of noodles with a sharp knife and microwave for about 4 minutes until softened. Allow to cool slightly, then massage the bag to loosen the noodles without breaking them. Set aside.

In a separate bowl, combine the black pepper sauce ingredients.

Heat a wok or large saucepan over a high heat and add the oil. Fry the beef in two or three batches for about 3 minutes until browned, then remove to a bowl. (If the wok becomes very dirty, wash it out, return to the heat and add more oil before continuing.)

Add a little more oil if needed, then fry the garlic and ginger for about a minute until fragrant. Add the capsicum, choy sum and spring onion. Toss for a minute or two to soften the vegetables.

Add the noodles and black pepper sauce and return the beef to the wok. Toss to combine, frying for about 2–3 minutes until the noodles are softened, adding a little water or stock as needed — about half a cup in total — to moisten the wok while frying.

Transfer to a plate and serve.

TIP The key with noodles like this is allowing them to be coated in flavourful oil, and also to absorb the flavour of the ingredients and sauce. Make sure you're using enough oil to coat the noodles.

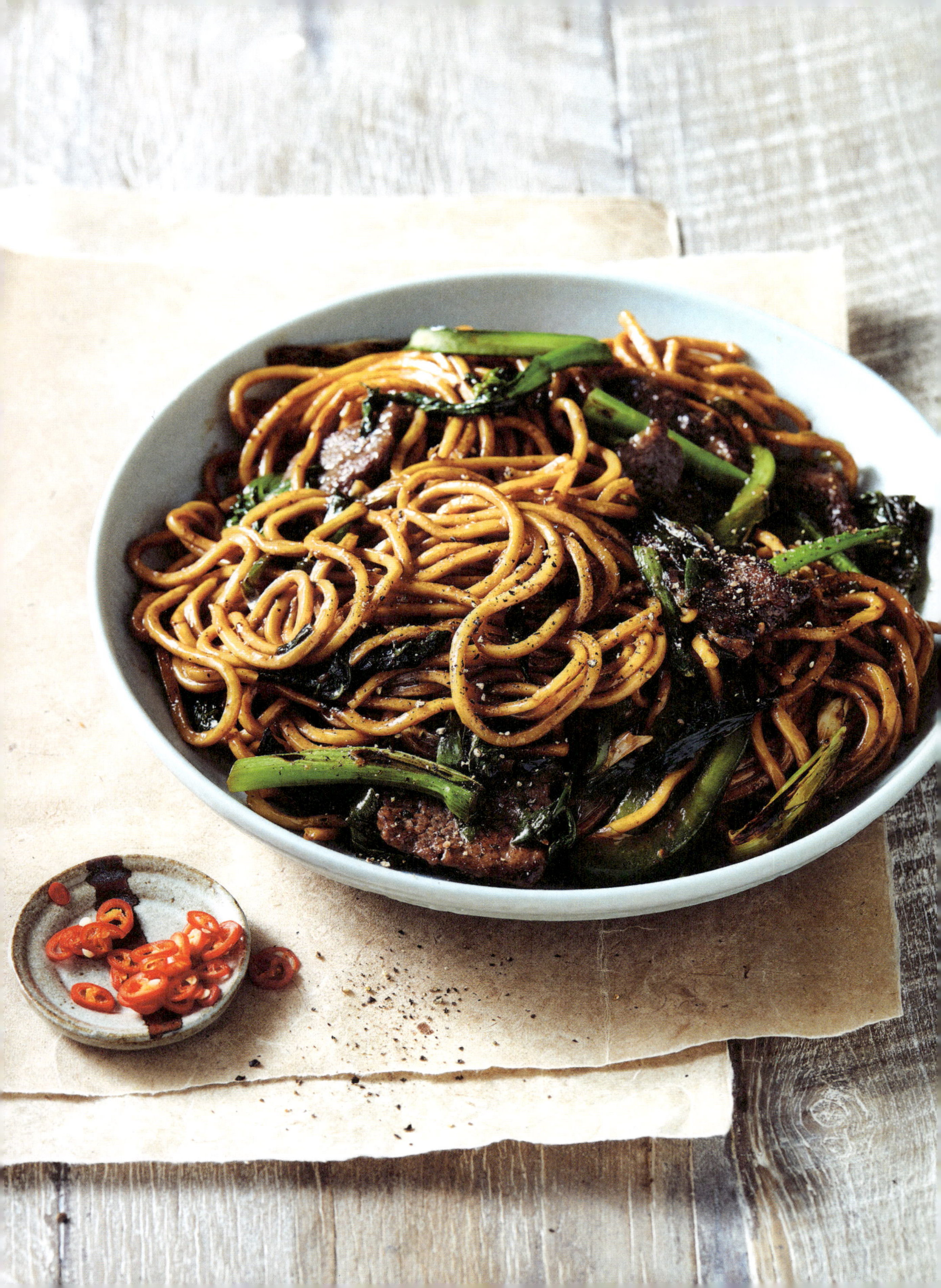

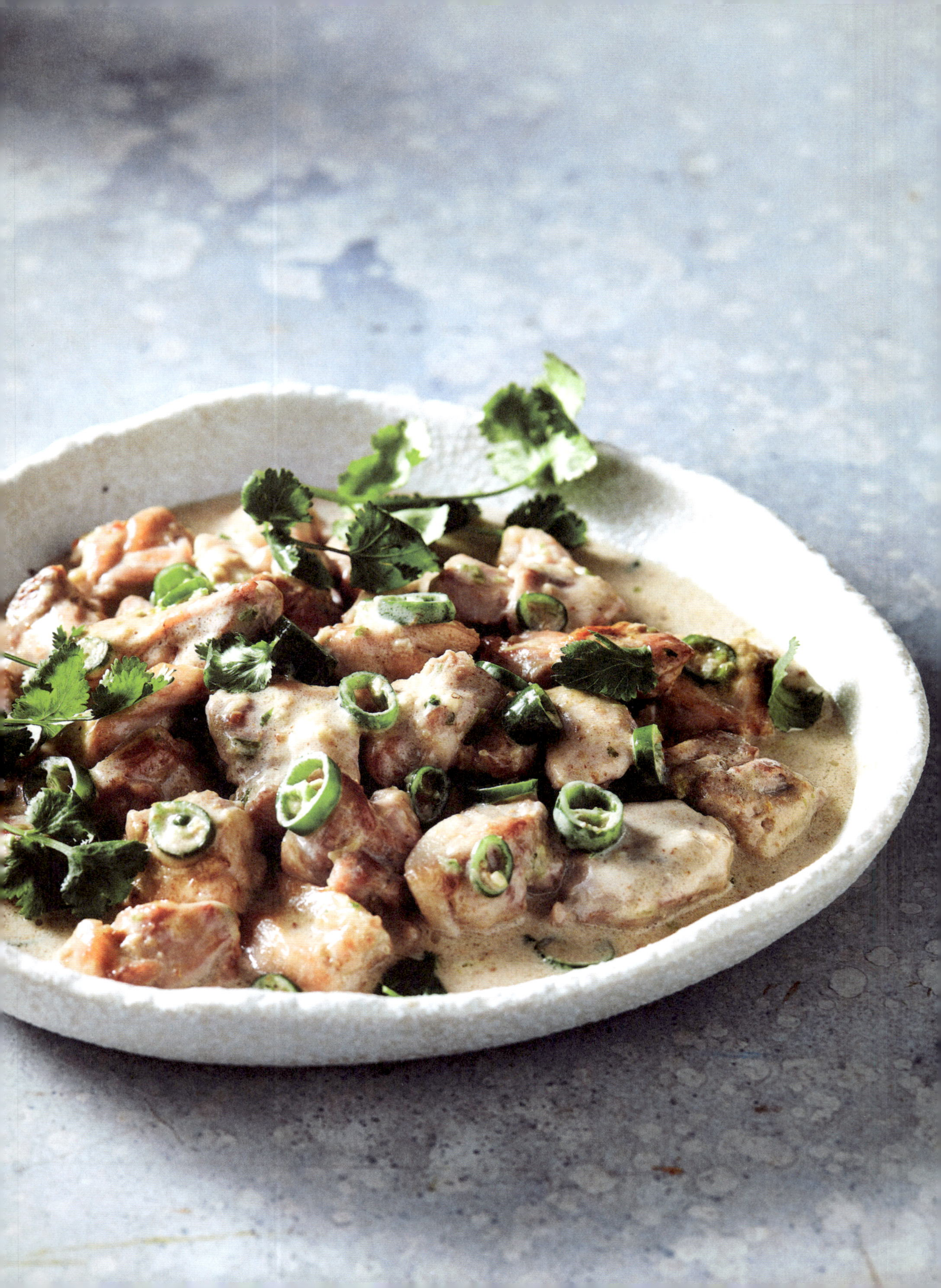

Double coriander chicken

Serves 4
Prep 10 minutes
Cook 10 minutes

Coriander is a stunning ingredient — unless you happen to be afflicted with the gene that makes it taste like soap. It not only has flavour from seed to plant and root to leaf, but each of those expressions has a different flavour. It's like four ingredients in one plant.

2 tablespoons vegetable oil

3 garlic cloves, roughly chopped

2 coriander (cilantro) plants, stalks and roots washed well and roughly chopped, leaves reserved

1 tablespoon ground coriander

4 boneless, skinless chicken thighs, cut into 3 cm (1¼ in) pieces

2 large green chillies, thickly sliced

2 tablespoons fish sauce

1 cup (250 ml/8½ fl oz) coconut cream

½ teaspoon sugar

lime wedges, to serve

Heat a wok over a high heat and add the oil. Stir-fry the garlic and coriander stalks and roots for about 1 minute until fragrant. Add the ground coriander and chicken and stir-fry for about 3 minutes until the chicken is lightly browned.

Stir in the chilli, fish sauce, coconut cream and sugar. Simmer for 5 minutes, or until the chicken is cooked through and the chilli softened. Taste and adjust the seasoning (see Tip).

Scatter with the reserved coriander leaves. Serve with lime wedges.

TIP Seasoning is the adjustment of taste — saltiness, sweetness, sourness, bitterness and savouriness (umami) — and it's a process that only requires you to know what you like. Taste the dish: if it's too sweet, add a little fish sauce, and if it's too savoury, add a bit of sugar. And remember, there'll be a squeeze of lime at the end to give a wonderful hit of acidity.

Prawns with chilli & basil

—

Serves 2–4, as part of a shared meal
Prep 10 minutes
Cook 10 minutes

The popular Thai dish *pad krapao* translates as 'fried (with) holy basil'. While the flavour of holy basil is distinct from Thai and Italian basil, there's no reason you can't use either of those here instead. I never let some misguided concept of 'authenticity' get in the way of a good and easy meal.

1 large red chilli, roughly chopped

1 large green chilli, roughly chopped

2 small dried red chillies, torn

6 garlic cloves, roughly chopped

4 tablespoons vegetable oil

8 extra-large raw prawns (shrimp), peeled and deveined, tails on

1 tablespoon fish sauce

2 teaspoons soy sauce

1 teaspoon oyster sauce

2 teaspoons kecap manis (sweet soy sauce)

1 teaspoon sugar

1 cup picked holy, Thai or Italian basil

2 eggs

steamed jasmine rice, to serve

Using a mortar and pestle, pound the fresh and dried chillies with the garlic to a very coarse paste.

Heat a wok over a high heat, add 1 tablespoon of the oil and fry the paste until very fragrant. Add the prawns and toss to coat. Add the sauces, sugar and about half a cup (125 ml/4 fl oz) water. After about 2–3 minutes, when the prawns are very nearly cooked, toss the basil leaves through and transfer to a serving plate.

Rinse out the wok. Heat the remaining oil in the wok and crack in an egg. Spoon a little oil on top of the egg so that it is crispy and cooked on top. Remove from the wok and repeat for the remaining egg.

Serve the prawns with rice, topped with the fried eggs.

TIPS Instead of prawns, apply this same recipe to roughly chopped chicken, squid, thinly sliced beef or pork, diced firm tofu ... you get the idea.

I like to take prawns and other seafood off the heat just before they're cooked (and eggs, too). They'll continue to cook from the heat of the dish, so they'll be perfect by the time you get them to the table.

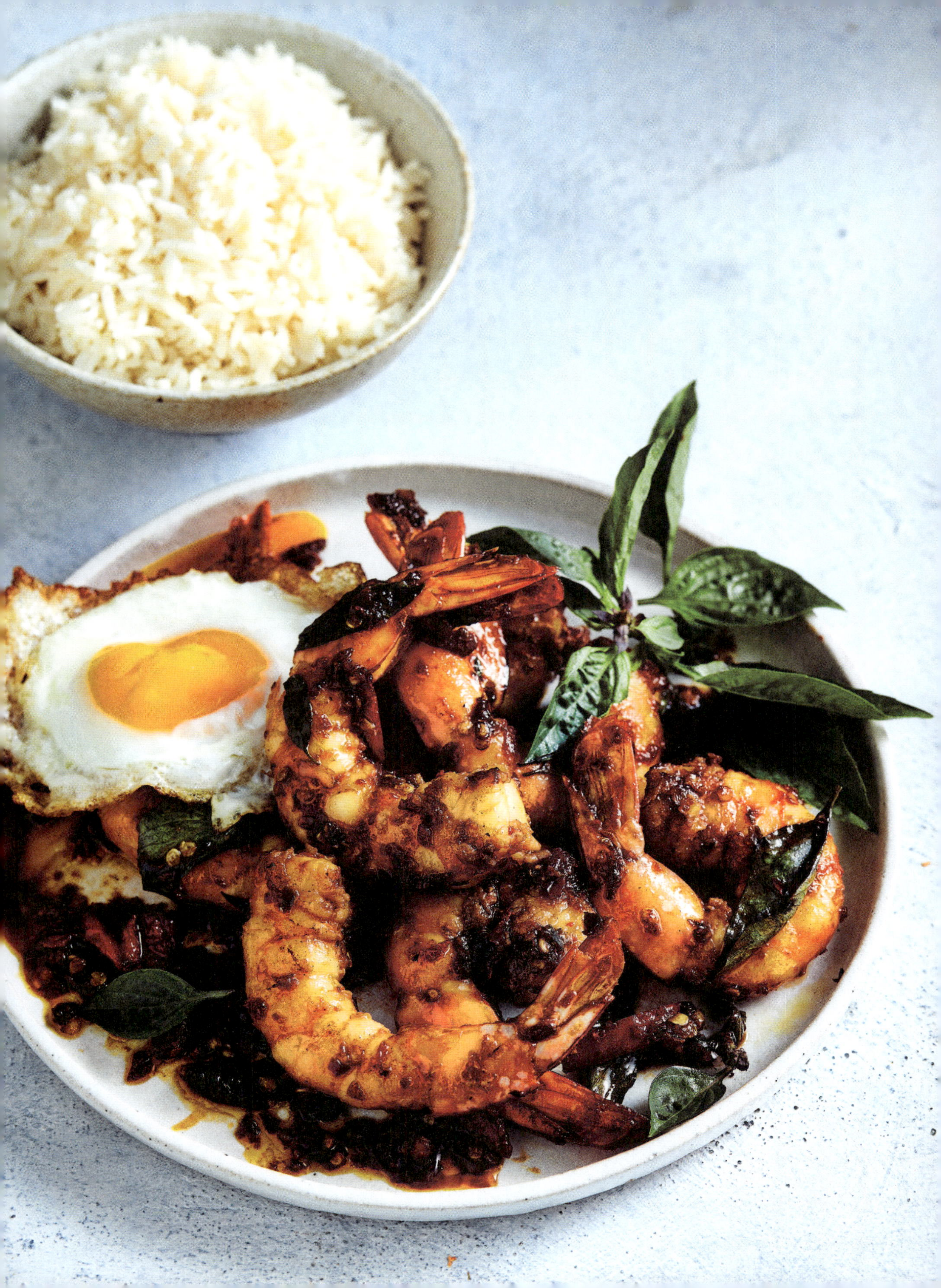

Spring onion omelette

—

Serves 4 as part of a shared meal
Prep 5 minutes
Cook 5 minutes

An omelette like this is a quiet achiever. It doesn't scream for attention, but I can't tell you the number of times I've served this as part of a Chinese meal with more elaborate and expensive dishes next to it, and seen people coming back to this plate again and again and finishing it long before the other dishes are done.

5 eggs

½ teaspoon salt

¼ teaspoon ground white pepper

1 teaspoon white vinegar

½ teaspoon cornflour (cornstarch), mixed with 2 tablespoons water

6 thin spring onions (scallions), sliced into rounds

3 tablespoons vegetable oil

Crack the eggs into a bowl. Add the salt, pepper, vinegar and cornflour slurry and beat well to combine. Stir the spring onion through.

Heat a wok over a medium heat. Add two-thirds of the oil, then two-thirds of the egg mixture. Mix occasionally for about a minute until the egg starts to set, and the raw egg stops flowing into the spaces made by mixing.

Pour the remaining egg mixture around the edges of the omelette. Cook for a further minute until lightly browned, then flip and drizzle the remaining oil around the wok so that it runs under the edges of the egg. Cook for about a minute more until the egg is just set, swirling the omelette around the wok so it colours evenly.

Transfer to a plate and serve.

TIP Adding the egg to the wok in two stages ensures the edges of the omelette don't overcook, given the curved shape of the wok. If using a flat-bottomed wok or frying pan, you can add all the egg mixture at once.

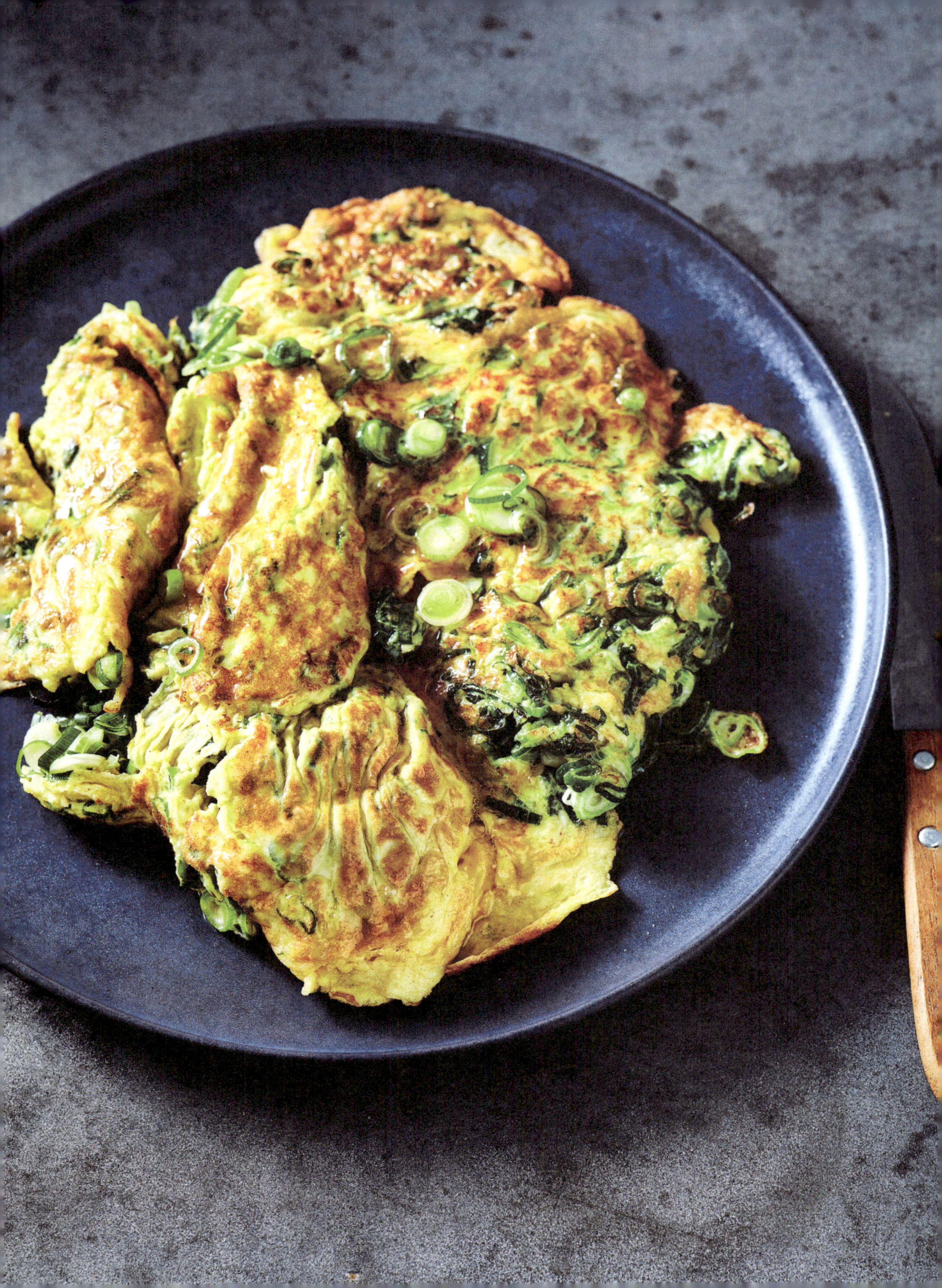

Chicken 65

—

Serves 4
Prep 20 minutes
Marinate 4 hours or overnight
Cook 15 minutes

We might think of the wok as the cornerstone of Chinese cuisines — and it is — but its influence certainly isn't limited to China. The wok has travelled around the world with Chinese cuisine. Chicken 65 originated at the Buhari Hotel in Chennai on the south-east coast of India (in 1965, many believe, hence the name), but has become a staple of Desi-Chinese restaurants all around the country.

15–20 curry leaves

600 g (1 lb 5 oz) boneless chicken thighs, skin on, cut into 5 cm (2 in) pieces

3 garlic cloves, grated

2 cm (¾ in) piece fresh ginger, peeled and grated

juice of 1 lemon

1 tablespoon ground coriander

1 tablespoon Korean or Kashmiri chilli powder (see Tips)

2 teaspoons ground turmeric

1 tablespoon garam masala

½ teaspoon ground black pepper

½ teaspoon salt

½ cup (60 g/2 oz) cornflour (cornstarch)

¼ cup (35 g/1¼ oz) plain (all-purpose) flour

4 cups (1 litre/34 fl oz) vegetable oil, for deep-frying (see Tips)

2 green bird's eye chillies

TO SERVE

½ red onion, thinly sliced

lemon wedges

Roughly chop about five curry leaves, then set the rest aside.

Combine the chicken in a large bowl with the chopped curry leaves, garlic, ginger, lemon juice, spices, salt, cornflour and plain flour, mixing well. Add about ¼–½ cup (60–125 ml/2–4 fl oz) cold water to produce a coating that is paste-y, not wet like a batter. Cover and marinate in the fridge for at least 4 hours, or preferably overnight.

Heat the oil in your wok to 170°C (340°F). Fry the chicken pieces in batches for 5 minutes until golden brown and just cooked through, removing each batch to drain on a wire rack. Pour most of the oil out of the wok, leaving about a tablespoon.

Fry the whole chillies until blistered, then add the reserved curry leaves and fry until crisp.

Return the chicken to the wok and toss together. Serve with the raw onion and lemon wedges.

TIPS I prefer Korean or Kashmiri chilli powder because of their vibrant red colour. While Kashmiri chilli powder is often quite hot, Korean chilli powder comes in mild versions and can be a good option for people who don't like too much spiciness.

You don't need to make this dish in a wok. You can fry the chicken in batches in a small saucepan using less oil, but it might take a little longer.

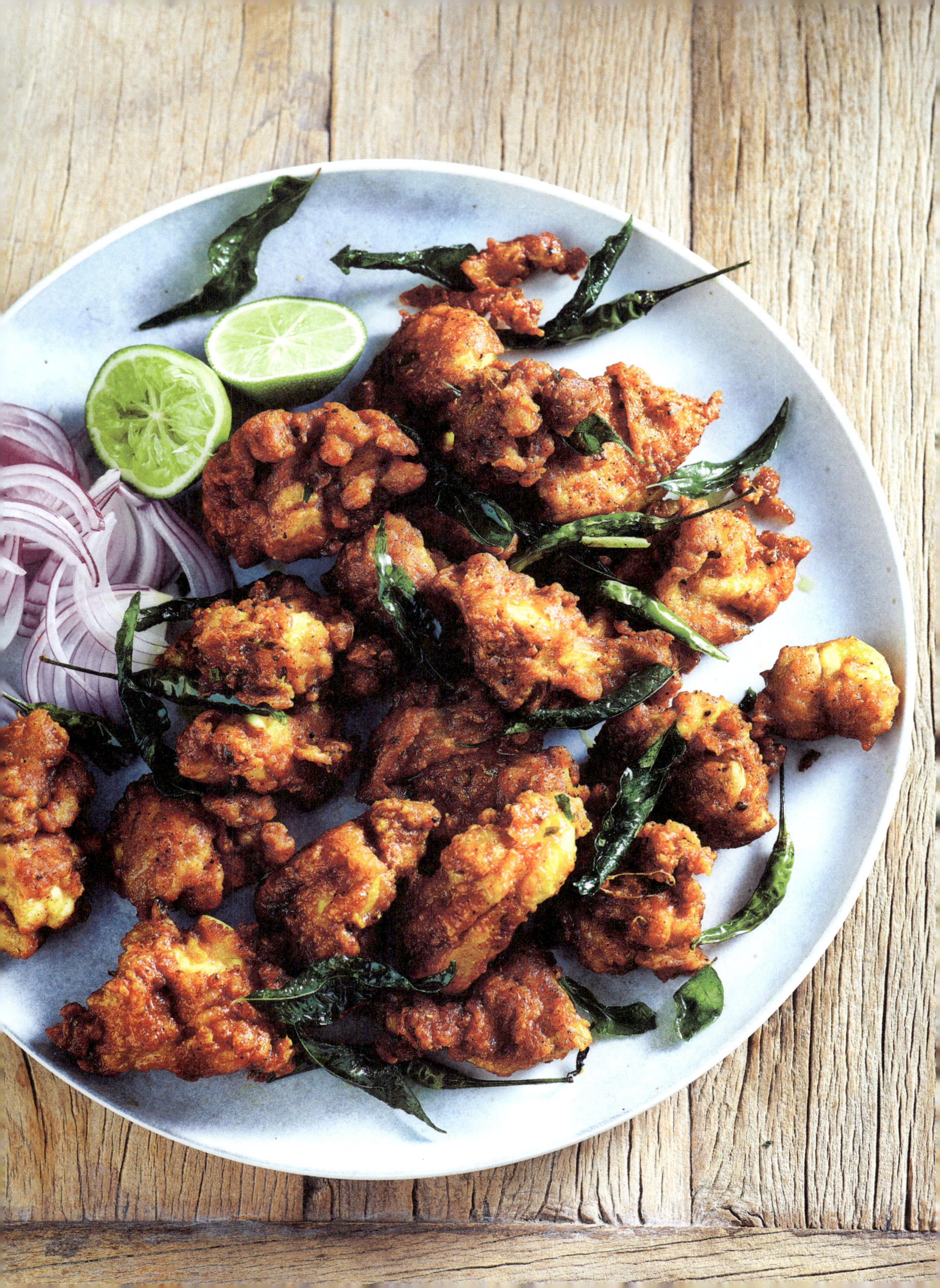

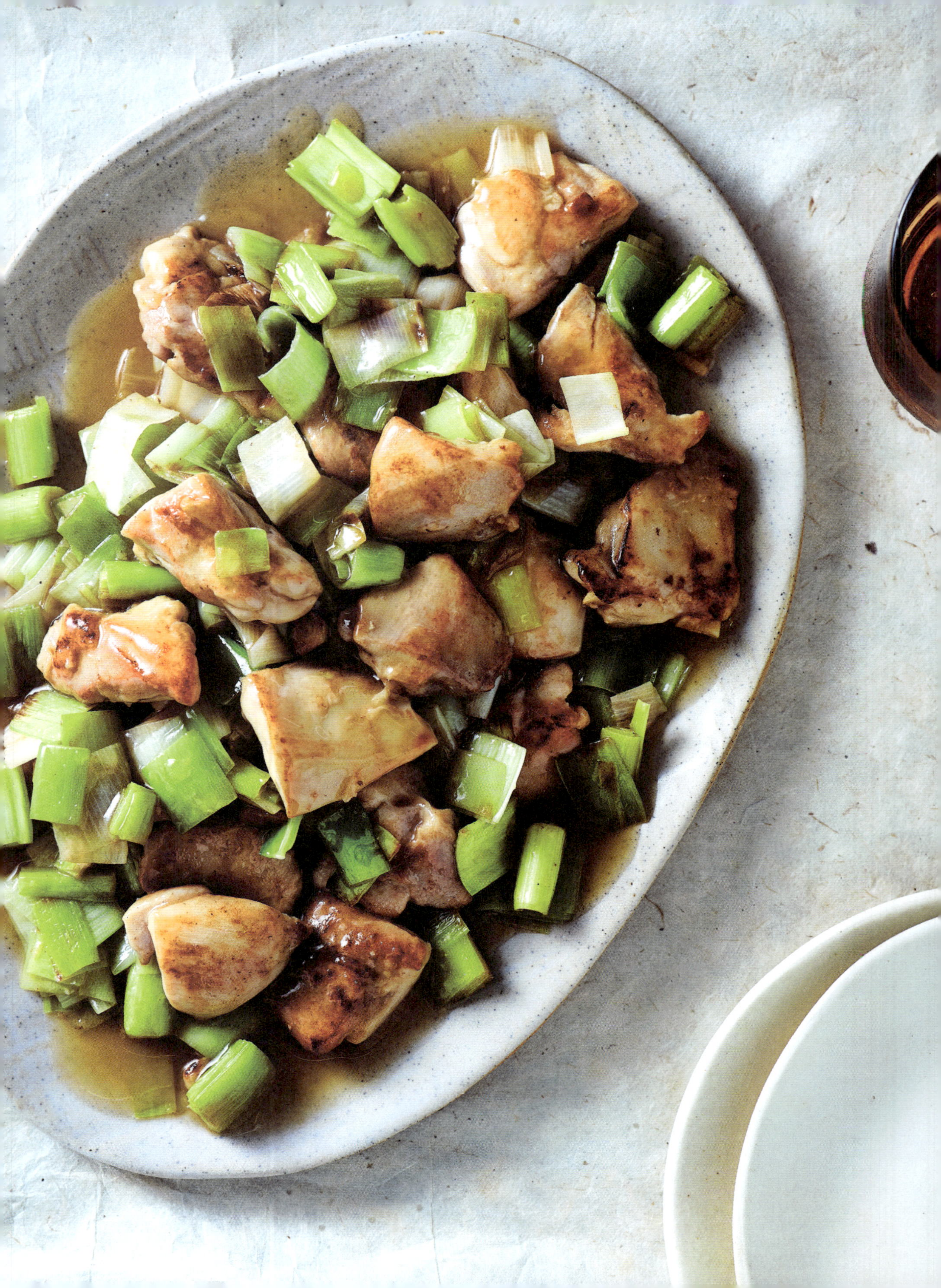

Chicken and leek

Serves 4
Prep 10 minutes
Marinate 5 minutes
Cook 10 minutes

Let me pass on to you my wife's best piece of advice for wok cooking — add more oil than you think you'll need. I think I do this intuitively, as I've grown up with cooking in woks my whole life, but my wife hasn't, and she says making this change has revolutionised her wok cooking.

400 g (14 oz) boneless, skinless chicken thighs, cut into 3–4 cm (1¼–1½ in) pieces

3 tablespoons vegetable oil, plus extra if needed

2 slices fresh ginger, bruised

3 garlic cloves, chopped

2 large leeks, white and light green bits only, halved lengthways, then cut into 2 cm (¾ in) lengths

1 tablespoon concentrated chicken stock, or soy sauce

salt, to season

pinch of sugar

1 tablespoon Shaoxing wine

1 teaspoon cornflour (cornstarch), mixed with ¼ cup (60 ml/2 fl oz) cold water

CHICKEN MARINADE

1 tablespoon cornflour (cornstarch)

1 teaspoon soy sauce

1 teaspoon Shaoxing wine

½ teaspoon sugar

Combine the chicken with the marinade ingredients and set aside for 5 minutes.

Heat a wok over a high heat until very hot, then add the oil. Fry the chicken in two batches until browned on the outside. When you first add the chicken to the wok, let it sit without stirring for about 3 minutes to brown at least one side, then toss the wok and cook for a further minute until the chicken is nearly cooked through; the chicken doesn't need to be browned all over. Remove from the wok and set aside.

Return the wok to the heat and add a little more oil if needed. Fry the ginger and garlic for a minute or two until fragrant. Add the leek and toss until it starts to soften. Return the chicken to the wok with any of the juices collected and toss.

Add the stock, salt, sugar and Shaoxing wine and toss again. Thicken the sauce with a little cornflour slurry and serve.

TIPS Many of us have a fear of using oil because we're concerned about fat. But woks (and frying pans for that matter) need oil to function properly. You're adding it for the wok, not the dish. Most of the oil will stay in the wok and on the plate anyway.

Any stir-fry will usually have at least one good source of umami (savoury taste) added. It may be in the form of soy sauce, oyster sauce, fish sauce, chicken stock, Shaoxing wine, salted black beans, yellow beans, fermented bean pastes, vinegar, pickles — or any combination of these.

Pork with black vinegar & green peppers

Compare this dish with the Fireworks on page 159. Both use similar ingredients, but apply slightly different seasonings and a slightly different technique. These small differences mean that the result is completely different.

Serves 4
Prep 15 minutes
Marinate 10 minutes
Cook 20 minutes

500 g (1 lb 2 oz) pork belly, skin and bones removed, cut into 3 cm (1¼ in) pieces

1 egg

1 tablespoon soy sauce

1 tablespoon Shaoxing wine

¼ teaspoon bicarbonate of soda (baking soda)

1 cup (125 g/4½ oz) cornflour (cornstarch)

2–3 cups (500–750 ml/17–25½ fl oz) vegetable oil, for deep-frying

2 green bullhorn peppers, or 1 large green capsicum (bell pepper), cut into 3 cm (1¼ in) chunks

1 onion, cut into large chunks

1 teaspoon cornflour (cornstarch), mixed with ¼ cup (60 ml/2 fl oz) cold water

BLACK VINEGAR SAUCE

4 tablespoons black vinegar

4 tablespoons rice vinegar

2 tablespoons soy sauce

2 tablespoons Shaoxing wine

4 tablespoons sugar

Combine the pork in a bowl with the egg, soy sauce, Shaoxing wine, bicarbonate of soda and 1 tablespoon of the cornflour. Mix well and set aside for 10 minutes. Dredge in the remaining cornflour and set aside.

Heat the oil in your wok to 175°C (345°F). Fry the peppers and onion for about 3 minutes until blistered, then remove from the oil. Fry the pork in two or three batches for about 5 minutes until browned and cooked through. Remove to a plate.

Pour the oil out of the wok. Add the black vinegar sauce ingredients to the wok (see Tips) and cook for a minute or two over a high heat until bubbling and reduced.

Return the pork belly, peppers and onion to the wok, toss to coat in the sauce and serve.

TIPS I often mix the liquid ingredients for sauces together first so that I'm not wasting time measuring while I'm standing at the wok. I add the sugar directly into the wok, though, so it doesn't settle at the bottom of a bowl.

The way you cut ingredients is very important for wok cooking, because traditionally most wok-fried dishes are made for eating with chopsticks, with no knife or fork to cut things smaller. But that actually makes things simple. When cutting ingredients, just think about how you might be eating them with chopsticks and you'll end up cutting intuitively.

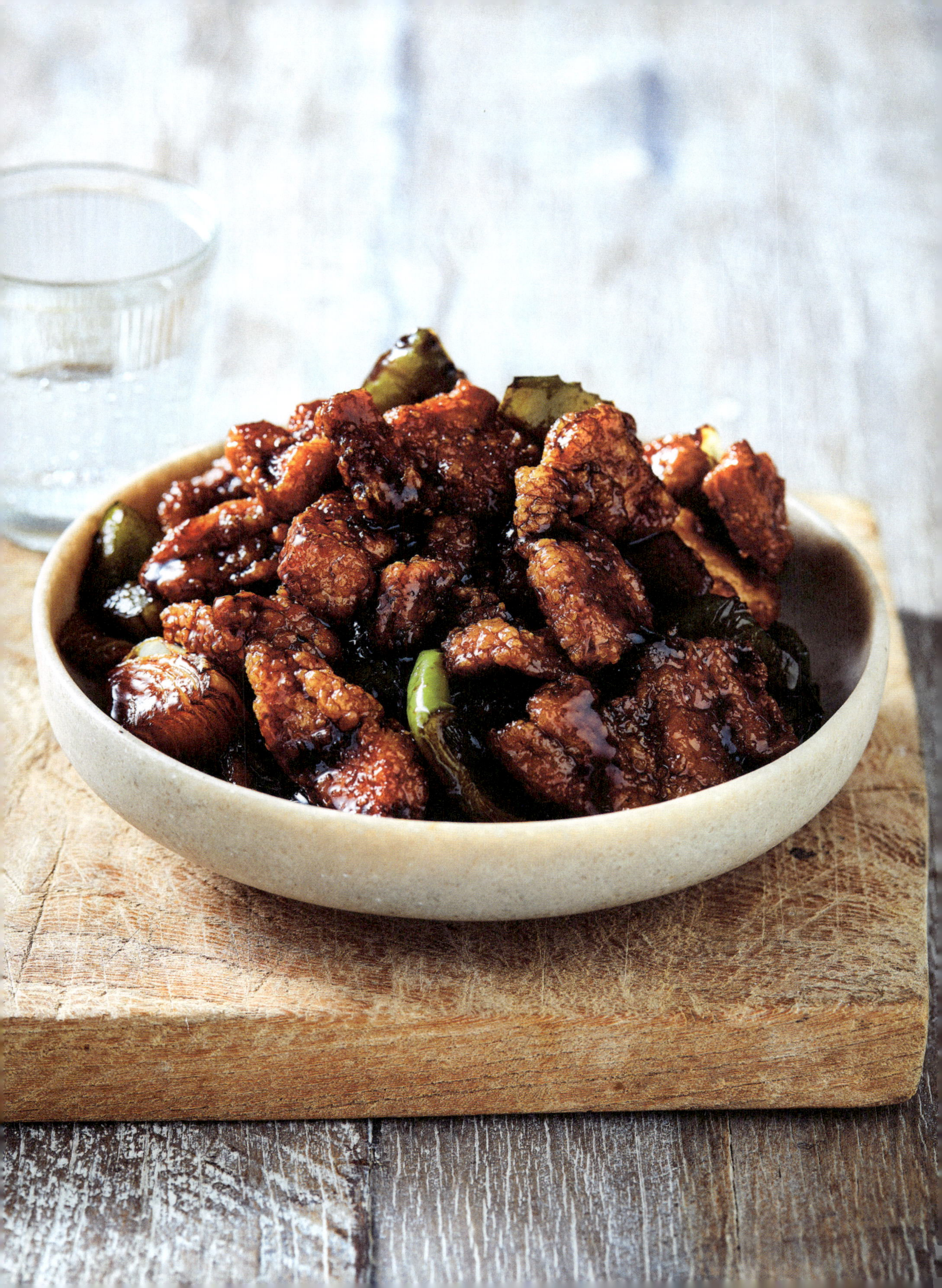

Noodles marinara

Serves 4
Prep 20 minutes
Stand 30 minutes
Chill 20 minutes

Be very gentle with the seafood here. You don't want to overcook it, and you don't want to smash it apart when you toss it through the noodles.

1 kg (2 lb 3 oz) hokkien noodles

4 tablespoons vegetable oil

600 g (1 lb 5 oz) good-quality seafood marinara mix

5 garlic cloves, roughly chopped

2 cm (¾ in) piece fresh ginger, peeled and sliced

1 small brown onion, thinly sliced

4 spring onions (scallions), cut into 5 cm (2 in) lengths

1 celery stalk, peeled and thinly sliced on a diagonal

1 carrot, halved lengthways and thinly sliced on a diagonal

½ cup roughly chopped coriander (cilantro)

SEASONED SWEET SOY SAUCE (MAKES EXTRA)

1 tablespoon vegetable oil

2 spring onions (scallions), roughly chopped

2 garlic cloves, bruised

2 cm (¾ in) piece fresh ginger, peeled and sliced

½ cup (125 ml/4 fl oz) soy sauce

2 tablespoons dark soy sauce

3 tablespoons sugar

For the sweet soy sauce, heat a small saucepan over a medium heat, add the oil, spring onion, garlic and ginger and fry for about 2 minutes until fragrant. Stir in the soy sauces, sugar and 2 tablespoons water, then simmer for 5 minutes. Remove from the heat and leave to infuse for 30 minutes, then strain.

Poke a few holes in the bag of noodles with a sharp knife and microwave for 4 minutes. Allow to cool slightly, then massage the bag to loosen the noodles without breaking them. Set aside.

Heat a wok over a high heat and add the oil. Fry the seafood for about 3 minutes until just barely cooked, then remove from the wok, leaving the oil in the wok. Add a little extra oil if needed and fry the garlic, ginger, onion, spring onion, celery and carrot for about 3 minutes until softened but not browned.

Add the noodles to the wok with about 5–6 tablespoons of your sweet soy sauce and toss for a minute or two to coat. You can add a little water or extra sauce if needed to moisten the wok while frying.

Very gently toss the seafood through — or even just scatter it on top of the noodles. Drizzle with a little extra sweet soy sauce, scatter with the chopped coriander and serve.

TIP This sweet soy sauce is one of my children's favourite things. The recipe makes more than you need, so keep the rest for drizzling over grilled or steamed fish or chicken, over rice or noodles, or even just over some char siu and siu yuk (roast pork belly) from a Cantonese barbecue shop.

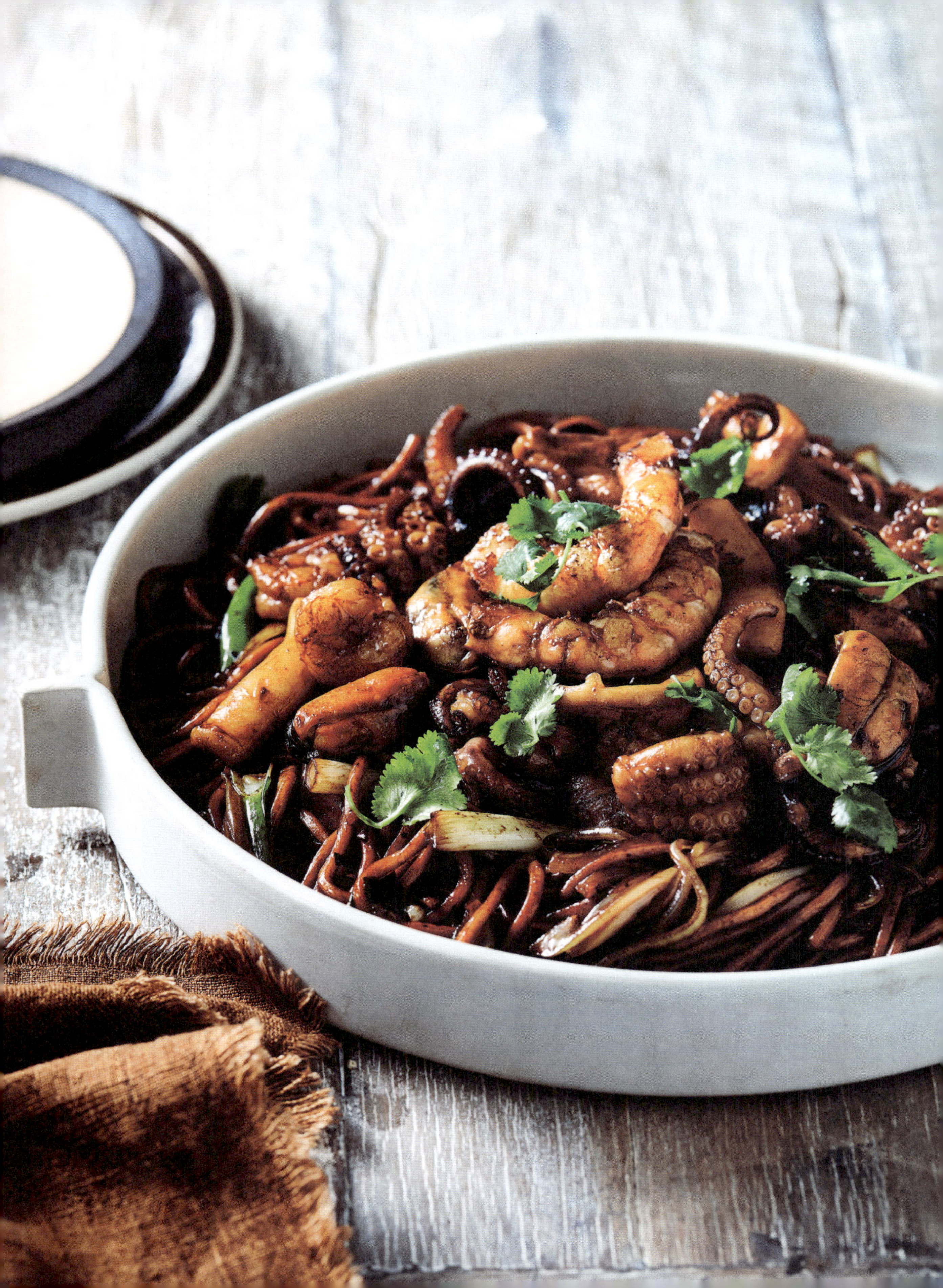

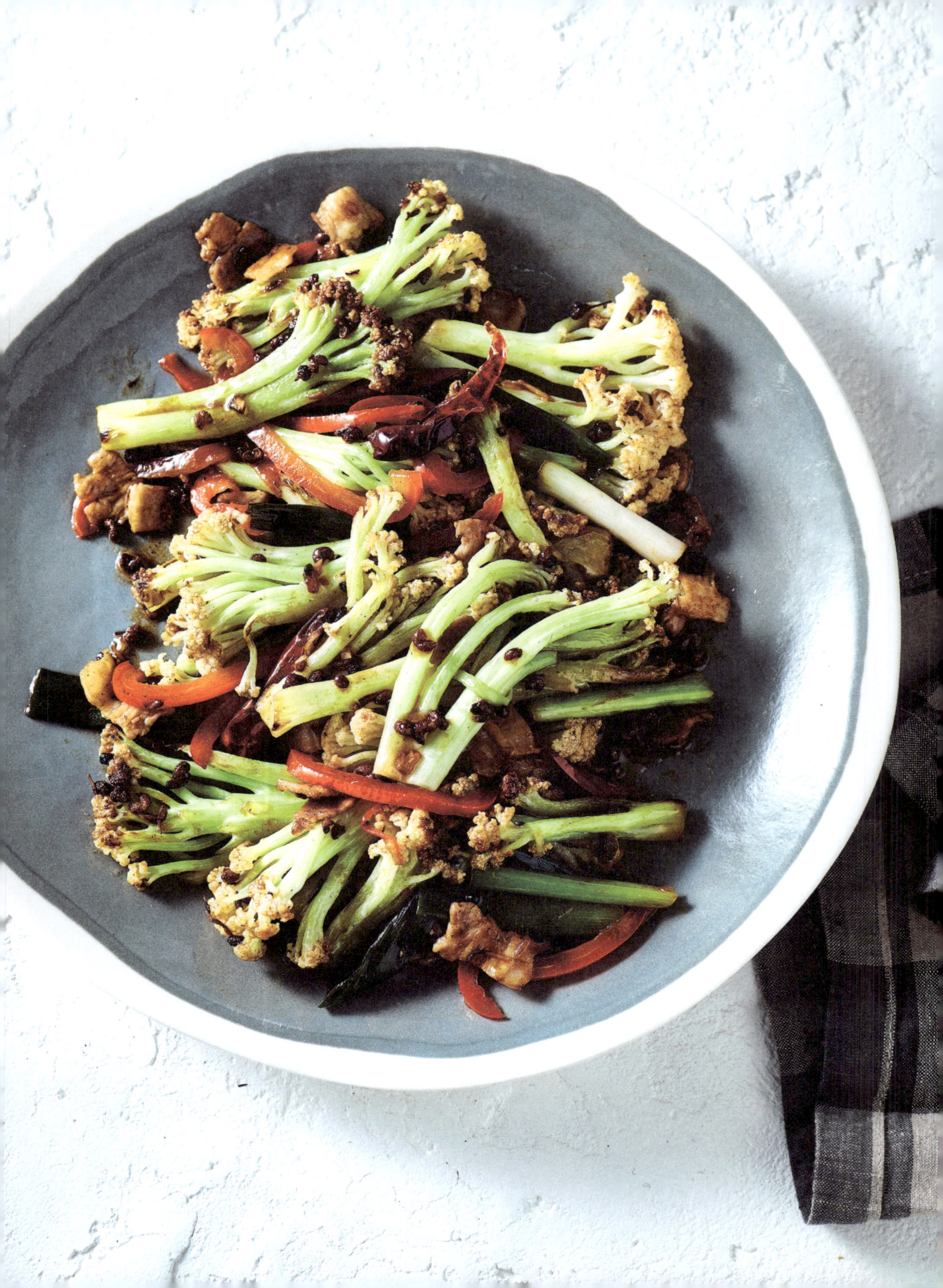

Dry-pot cauliflower

—

Serves 4, as part of a shared meal
Prep 5 minutes
Cook 10 minutes

One of the most interesting things in the modern evolution of wok cooking is how homestyle Sichuanese dishes like this (and the Fireworks on page 159) are growing in popularity around the world. It makes sense. They're easy to make, full-flavoured, cheap and completely delicious. This one is often made with cured pork or sliced pork belly, but you can leave it out for a vegetarian meal.

1 bunch longer-stemmed cauliflower, fioretto or regular cauliflower (see Tip)

1 cup (250 ml/8½ fl oz) vegetable oil

salt, to season

4 garlic cloves, roughly chopped

3 thin slices fresh ginger, peeled and julienned

1 tablespoon whole Sichuan peppercorns

80 g (2¾ oz) thinly sliced pork belly (optional)

4 dried red chillies

1 small red capsicum (bell pepper), thinly sliced

4 spring onions (scallions), cut into 5 cm (2 in) lengths

1 tablespoon soy sauce

1 tablespoon Shaoxing wine

a good pinch of sugar

½ teaspoon cornflour (cornstarch), mixed with ¼ cup (60 ml/2 fl oz) water

Cut or break the cauliflower into large florets. Heat the oil in a wok over a high heat and add the cauliflower. Season with salt and fry for about 6 minutes, stirring occasionally, until the cauliflower is well browned. Remove to a bowl.

Pour off all but about 2 tablespoons of oil from the wok. Add the garlic, ginger and Sichuan peppercorns. Season with salt and toss for a minute until the garlic starts to brown. Add the pork, if using, and fry for about a minute. Add the chillies, capsicum and spring onion and toss for a few minutes until the capsicum has softened.

Return the cauliflower to the wok and add the soy sauce, Shaoxing wine and sugar. Adjust the seasoning to taste.

Drizzle in a little of the cornflour slurry while shaking the wok to thicken any liquid in the wok. Serve immediately.

TIP Chinese cauliflower has longer stems than ordinary cauliflower and is more suited to this kind of dish. It's quite similar to fioretto if you can find it, but you could certainly use regular cauliflower here — or even broccolini.

/swi:t/
adjective

1. the pleasant taste characteristic of sugars
2. pleasing in general; delightful

SWEET

The thing I love most about sweets is that they are almost always purely for pleasure.

The pleasure we derive from food is valuable and worthwhile, and it's not something we should feel guilty about. It is of course important to look after our health, but enjoying what we eat is a huge part of that health.

These days I eat sweets mainly on their own rather than as dessert at the end of a meal — a slice of Honey crackle cake (page 187) with coffee for morning tea, a batch of beavertails (page 188) made for a special treat, or Birthday traycake (page 195) to celebrate an important milestone.

We're not machines, calculating our every calorie for optimal performance or to meet some magazine ideal of beauty. We eat for nutrition, but we also eat for joy, because it's all a part of life.

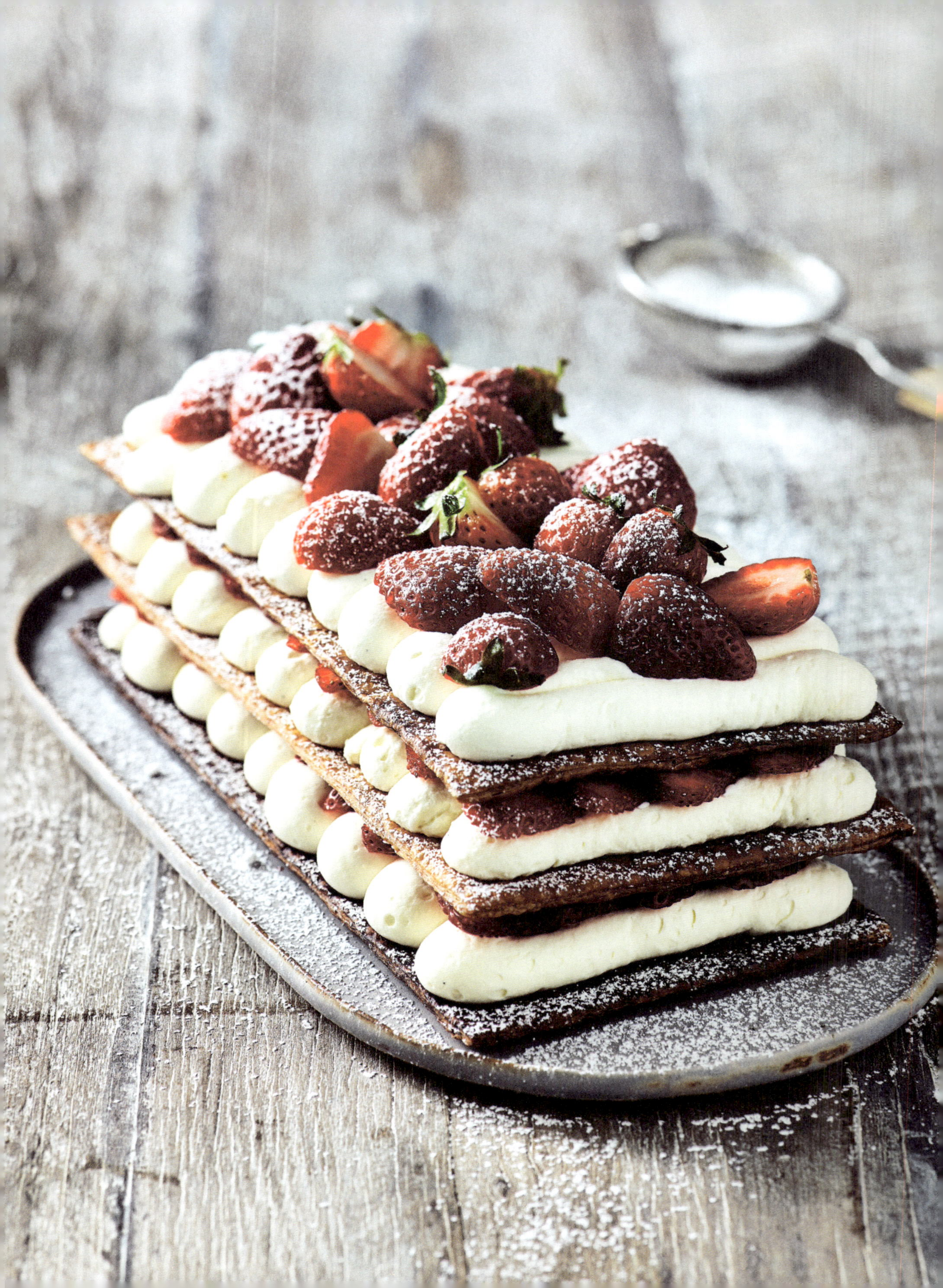

Strawberry & cream millefeuille

—

Serves 8
Prep 10 minutes
Cook 25 minutes
Cool 30 minutes

Impressive looking, deceptively easy and with endless possibilities, this is one sweet recipe that you'll want to keep in your pocket to come back to again and again. Change the fruits and cream flavour depending on your taste and the season.

1½ sheets of frozen puff pastry

2 tablespoons icing (confectioners') sugar, plus extra to serve

500 g (1 lb 2 oz) strawberries, halved

MASCARPONE CREAM

300 ml (10 fl oz) thickened (whipping) cream

¾ cup (90 g/3 oz) icing (confectioners') sugar

1 teaspoon vanilla bean paste

250 g (9 oz) mascarpone

Heat your oven to 200°C (400°F) fan-forced. Cut the whole puff pastry sheet in half, so you end up with three rectangles of puff pastry the same size. Place them on a baking tray lined with baking paper and dust with the icing sugar. Place another sheet of baking paper on top, and then another baking tray to sandwich the pastry.

Bake for 20–25 minutes until the pastry is dark brown and caramelised. Remove from the oven and leave to cool completely for 30 minutes. You can trim the edges with a bread knife if you want very clean pastry edges, or just leave them natural if you don't mind.

For the mascarpone cream, whip the cream, icing sugar and vanilla together to soft peaks, then whisk the mascarpone through; do not overwhip.

Transfer to a piping (icing) bag if you like. Pipe or use a spatula to spread one-third of the cream over one piece of the pastry. Top with one-third of the strawberries, then another pastry sheet.

Repeat with another one-third of the cream and strawberry. Top with the remaining pastry sheet, cream and strawberries. Dust with more icing sugar and serve.

TIP Try a mango and coconut version, substituting mango for the strawberries and coconut yoghurt for the mascarpone, and also adding a dash of coconut essence to the mixture.

Double-chocolate skillet cookie

Serves 4–6
Prep 10 minutes
Cook 30 minutes

Part cookie and part brownie, this is a fabulous family dessert that could work just as well at the end of a dinner party. The fun of bringing a giant warm cookie to the table for everyone to share is something nobody wants to miss out on.

250 g (9 oz) butter, softened

100 g (3½ oz) caster (superfine) sugar

100 g (3½ oz) dark brown sugar

3 eggs

1 teaspoon vanilla extract

3 cups (450 g/1 lb) plain (all-purpose) flour

1 tablespoon baking powder

180 g (6½ oz) milk chocolate, roughly chopped

180 g (6½ oz) white chocolate, roughly chopped

½ cup (50 g/1¾ oz) pecans, roughly chopped

1 teaspoon salt flakes

vanilla ice cream, to serve

Heat your oven to 160°C (320°F) fan-forced.

Using an electric mixer, cream the butter and sugars together. Beat in the eggs, one a time. Add the vanilla. Sift in the flour and baking powder a little at a time, folding it into the liquid. Fold in the chocolate, pecans and salt, without overmixing, reserving a few pieces for the top.

Spoon the batter into a 24 cm (9½ in) ovenproof frying pan (you don't need to line the pan). Press the reserved chocolate and pecans into the top. Transfer to the oven and bake for 30 minutes until browned around the edges but still slightly soft in the centre.

Serve warm, with vanilla ice cream.

TIP I like to let the cookie rest for about 10 minutes before serving, so it firms a little and is more warm than hot, but that's up to you. If you like it a little gooey and piping hot, you can go straight from the oven to the table.

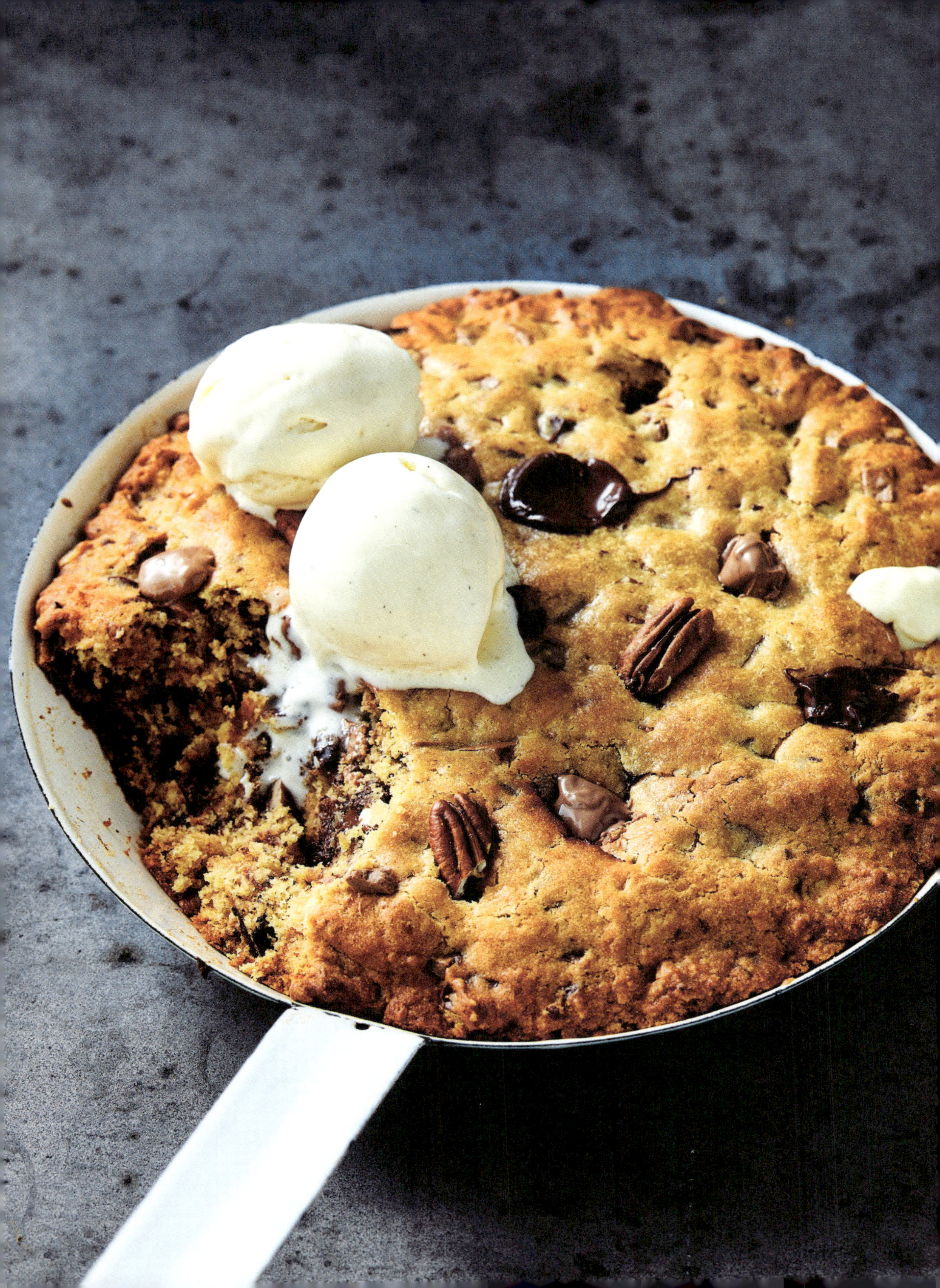

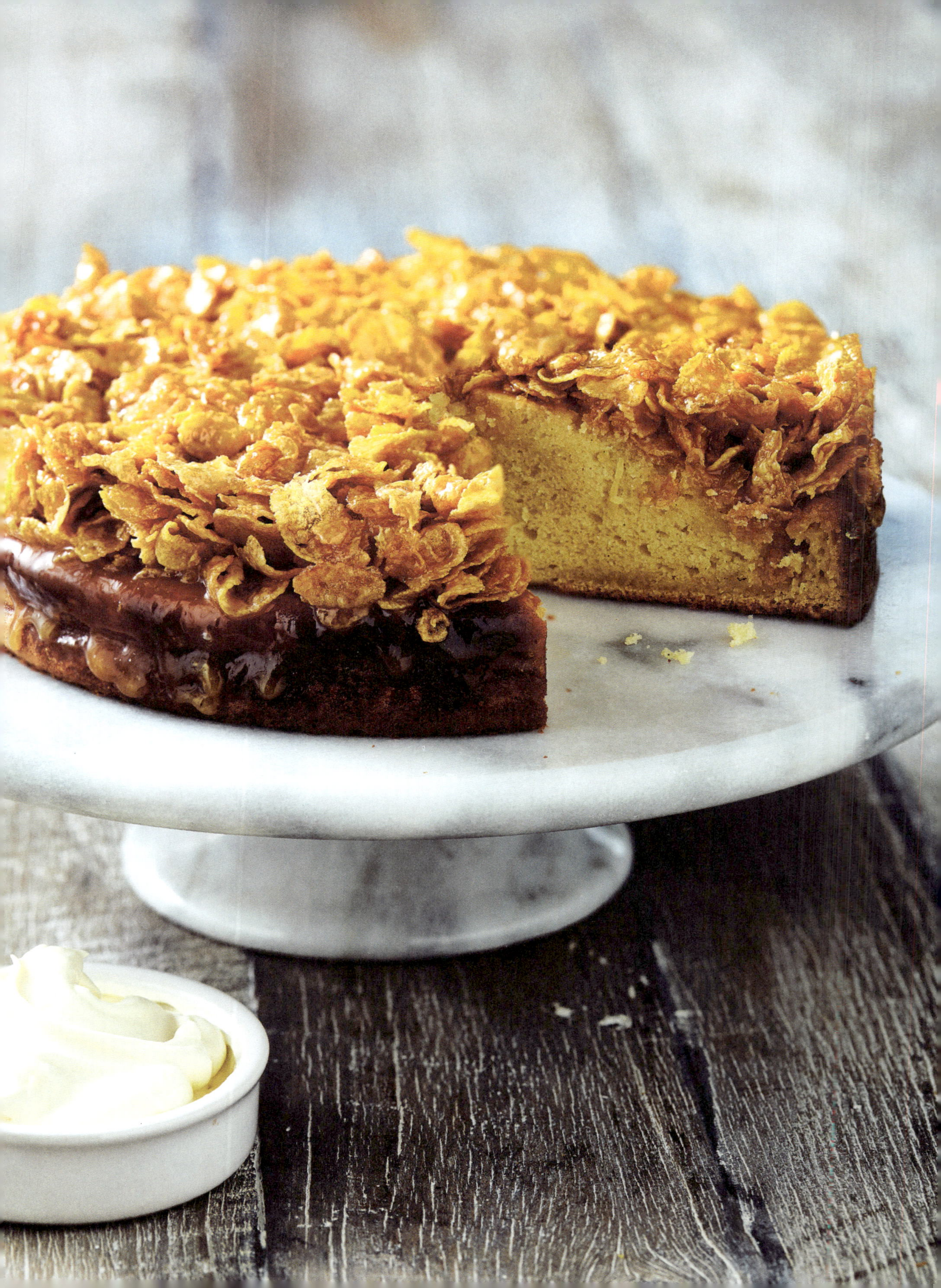

Honey crackle cake

—

Serves 4
Prep 15 minutes
Cook 40 minutes
Cool 1 hour

If you grew up eating honey crackles (or honey joys, if that's what you called them where you're from), this cake is a slightly more grown-up way to enjoy them. It tastes like a birthday party you went to when you were eight.

100 g (3½ oz) butter, plus extra for greasing

¾ cup (190 ml/6½ fl oz) milk

3 eggs

¾ cup (165 g/6 oz) sugar

1 teaspoon vanilla extract

1½ cups (225 g/8 oz) plain (all-purpose) flour, plus extra for dusting

2 teaspoons baking powder

whipped cream, to serve

HONEY CRACKLE TOPPING

100 g (3½ oz) butter

4 tablespoons honey

2 tablespoons sugar

3 cups (90 g/3 oz) cornflakes

Heat your oven to 190°C (375°F) conventional. Grease and flour a 24 cm (9½ in) round springform cake tin.

Warm the butter and milk in a saucepan until the butter has melted. Remove from the heat and set aside to cool slightly.

In the bowl of a stand mixer, combine the eggs, sugar and vanilla. Beat well for about 6 minutes until the mixture is thick and pale. Sift the flour and baking powder together, then fold the dry ingredients into the batter, alternating with the milk mixture.

Pour the batter into the cake tin, place on a lined baking tray and bake for 20–25 minutes.

Meanwhile, make the topping. Combine the butter, honey and sugar in a small saucepan over a medium heat. Stir until the mixture comes to the boil, then stir the cornflakes through.

Reduce the oven temperature to 150°C (300°F). Remove the cake from the oven; it will not be completely cooked at this point. Pour the cornflake mixture over the cake and spread it out evenly.

Bake for a further 10 minutes until the topping crisps and a skewer inserted into the centre comes out clean. If the skewer isn't clean, bake for a further 5 minutes and test again.

Remove the cake from the oven and leave to cool in the tin for at least 1 hour. Slice and serve with whipped cream.

TIP Usually, cream with cakes, pancakes or sweets in general works because the rich cream acts as a foil to the sweetness of the sweet itself. I don't like to sweeten whipped cream as a rule. It really doesn't need it.

Maple butter & cinnamon beavertails

—

Makes 10
Prep 15 minutes
Prove 1 hour 30 minutes
Cook 20 minutes

Beavertails are a Canadian twist on doughnuts, and, as with doughnuts, I prefer them warm and dusted with cinnamon sugar rather than topped with icings, syrups and sweets. Brushing them with maple butter, though, is highly recommended.

vegetable oil, for deep-frying

cinnamon sugar, for dusting (see Tips)

DOUGH

1 cup (250 ml/8½ fl oz) warm milk

50 g (1¾ oz) butter, melted

2 eggs

1½ cups (225 g/8 oz) plain (all-purpose) flour, plus extra for dusting

2 cups (300 g/10½ oz) wholemeal (whole-wheat) flour

½ cup (115 g/4 oz) caster (superfine) sugar

1 sachet (7 g/¼ oz) dried yeast

1 teaspoon salt

MAPLE BUTTER

50 g (1¾ oz) butter, melted

¼ cup (60 ml/2 fl oz) maple syrup

Combine the dough ingredients in the bowl of a stand mixer fitted with the dough hook. Knead for about 10 minutes until you have a smooth dough; if the mixture is too sticky, add a little extra plain flour. Transfer to an oiled bowl, cover with a tea towel (dish towel) and leave to prove for 1 hour.

Punch down the dough on a floured surface and roll into a cylinder. Divide into 10 pieces, and roll out each piece to an oval about 15 cm (6 in) long. Place on a lined baking tray and leave to prove for another 30 minutes.

Combine the maple butter ingredients and keep warm.

Pour the oil into a large saucepan to a depth of about 5 cm (2 in) and heat to 170°C (340°F). If you like, use a sharp knife to score a crosshatch pattern into the top of each beavertail, then fry for about 1–2 minutes on each side until golden brown and puffed.

Drain on a wire rack, then brush liberally with the maple butter and sprinkle with cinnamon sugar.

TIPS This basic yeasted doughnut dough can be made into doughnuts, too. Instead of rolling into ovals, make balls of the dough, poke a hole in the centre and tease them out into a ring before dropping into hot oil.

Make your own cinnamon sugar by mixing caster (superfine) sugar and ground cinnamon. You can decide your own mix, but I like a ratio of 3:1 — so, 3 teaspoons sugar to 1 teaspoon cinnamon, for instance.

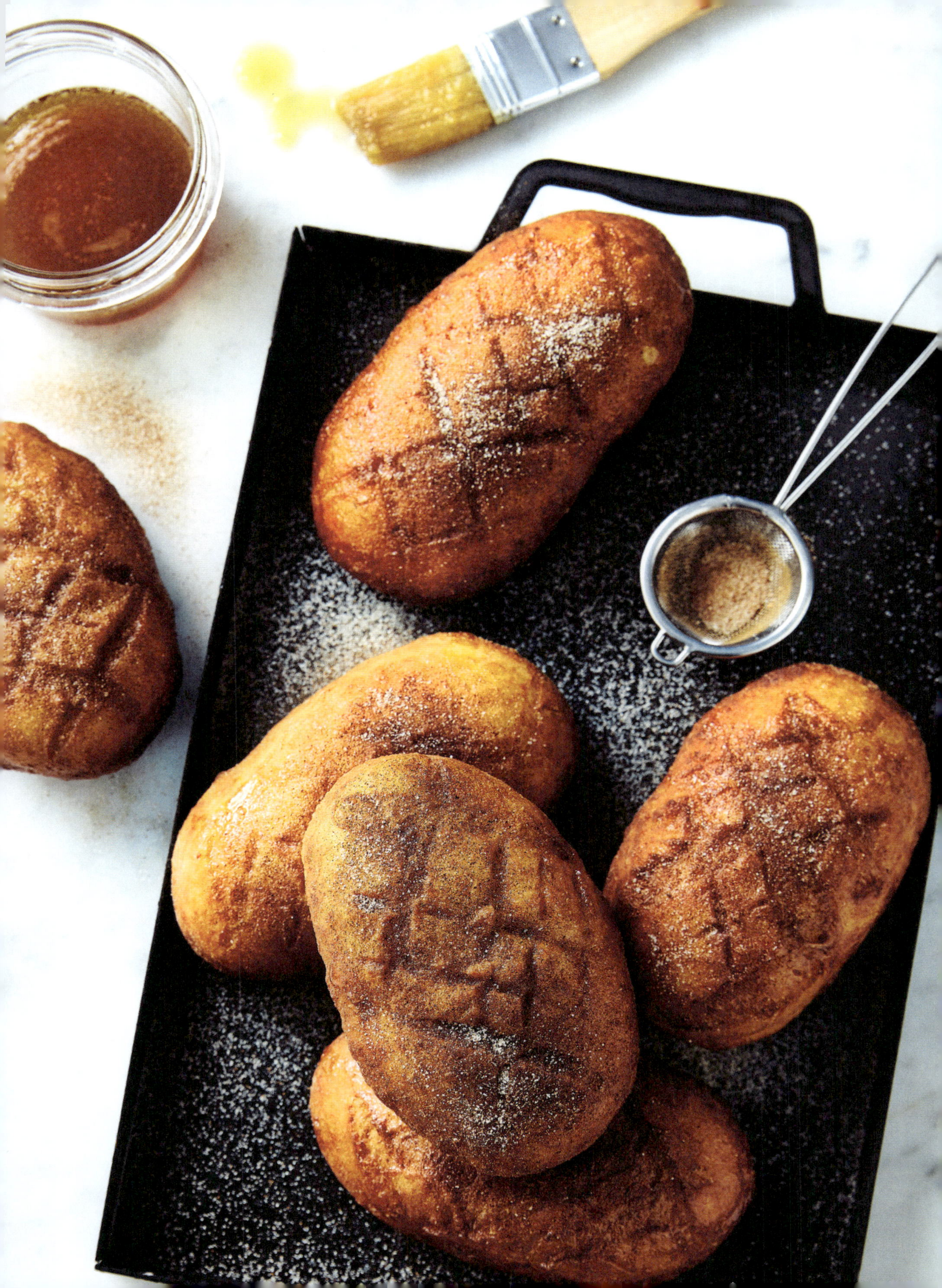

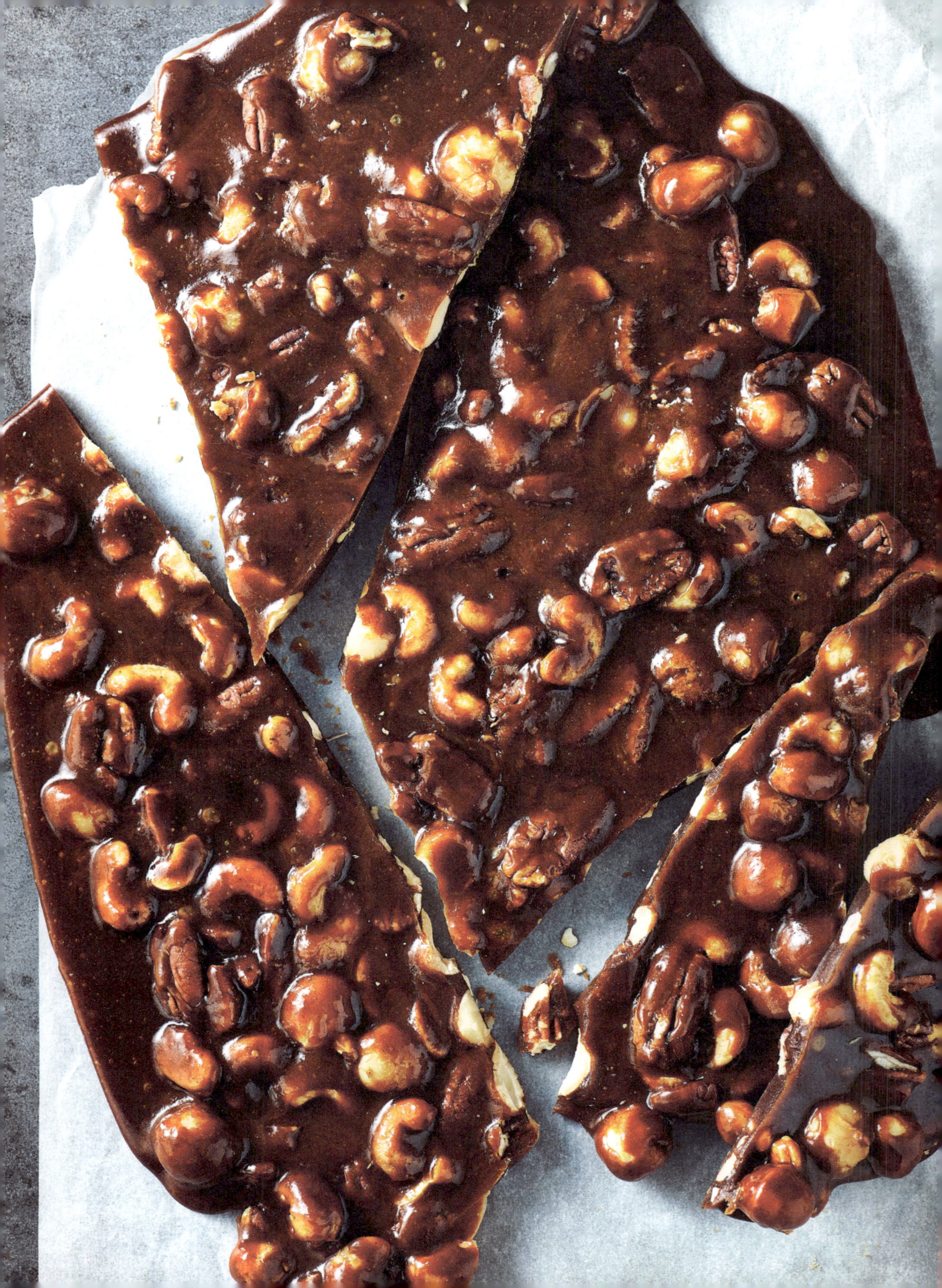

Roasted nut & caramel praline

—

Makes about 700 g (1 lb 9 oz)
Prep 10 minutes
Cook 20 minutes

This is the kind of sweet you can have just a little of if you want to. I love having a jar of something like this for just a tiny morsel of sweetness to go with a coffee or a cup of tea. In an airtight container, the praline will keep for about 3 weeks.

100 g (3½ oz) macadamia nuts

100 g (3½ oz) pecans

100 g (3½ oz) cashew nuts

300 g (10½ oz) caster (superfine) sugar

250 g (9 oz) dark brown sugar

100 ml (3½ fl oz) thickened (whipping) cream

1 teaspoon vanilla extract

100 g (3½ oz) butter

1 teaspoon salt flakes

Heat your oven to 200°C (400°F) conventional. Spread the nuts in a roasting pan and roast for about 15 minutes.

Place the sugars, cream, vanilla and butter in a saucepan and heat to 150°C (300°F) — see Tips.

Stir the nuts and salt through the sugar mixture and carefully pour out onto a sheet of baking paper.

Allow to cool completely, then crack into shards to serve.

TIPS Thermometers are very useful in cooking. I have a few that I use regularly — a meat probe for checking the internal temperature of meats, an infrared thermometer for checking the temperature of oil (and sometimes sugar), and a sugar thermometer for dishes like this. They're all quite inexpensive, and I promise they'll improve your cooking immediately.

If you don't have a sugar thermometer, drop a little of the molten syrup into a bowl of cold water. At 150°C (300°F), it will form brittle threads that break when bent. This is known as the 'hard crack' stage of sugar.

Panettone con gelato

—

Serves 2–4
Prep 10 minutes
Freeze 4 hours

Pavlova is the most popular Australian Christmas dessert, but I think something like this should give it a run for its money. It's incredibly easy, delicious, cool for the Australian summer, and the panettone helps insulate the ice cream from melting.

1 large panettone, about 1 kg (2 lb 3 oz)

6 cups (1.5 litres/51 fl oz) gelato or ice cream, in a variety of colours and flavours, slightly softened

300 g (10½ oz) white chocolate

glacé fruits or fresh fruits, to serve

Using a bread knife, cut the domed top off the panettone and, without removing the paper wrapping, cut a cylinder from the centre of the loaf, leaving about 2.5 cm (1 in) of panettone around the sides and on the base. Reserve the centre of the loaf for another purpose (see Tip).

Spoon the different colours of ice cream into the panettone in layers or in a random fashion to create a mottled effect.

Put the cap back on the panettone, and place the whole thing in a plastic bag. Seal the top with a clip, then freeze for 4 hours.

Place a glass or metal bowl over a medium saucepan of hot water, simmering over a low heat. Add the chocolate to the bowl and stir with a spatula to melt.

Place the frozen panettone on a serving plate and pour the melted chocolate over. Decorate the top with fruits of your choice and serve.

TIP Try to cut the centre out of the panettone cleanly, as it makes great French toast for Boxing Day. Whisk 3 eggs with 1 tablespoon sugar and 1 cup (250 ml/8 1/2 fl oz) milk and soak the bread in it overnight before frying in butter. If you can't be bothered doing that, use it to make ice cream sandwiches with any leftover ice cream.

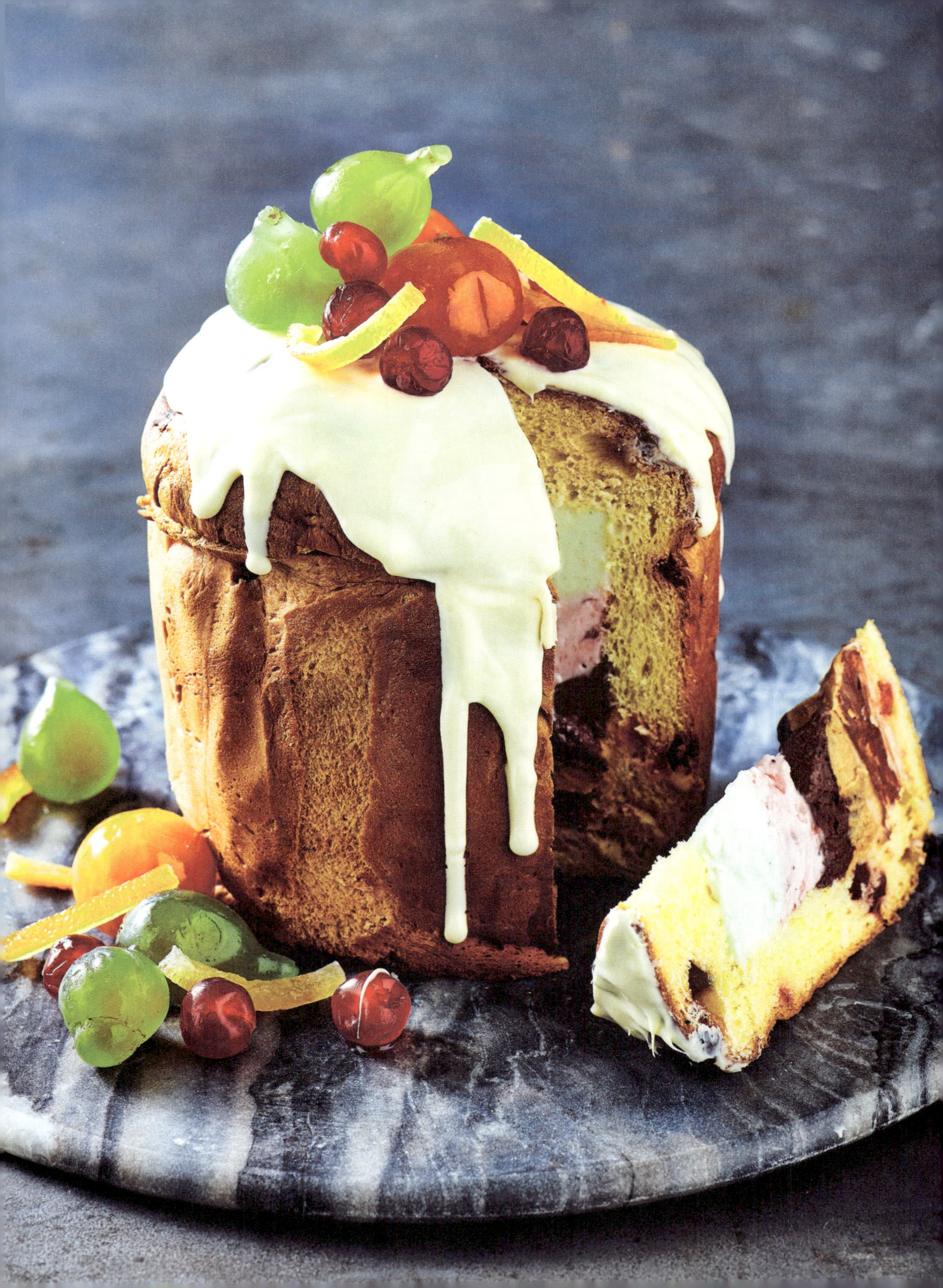

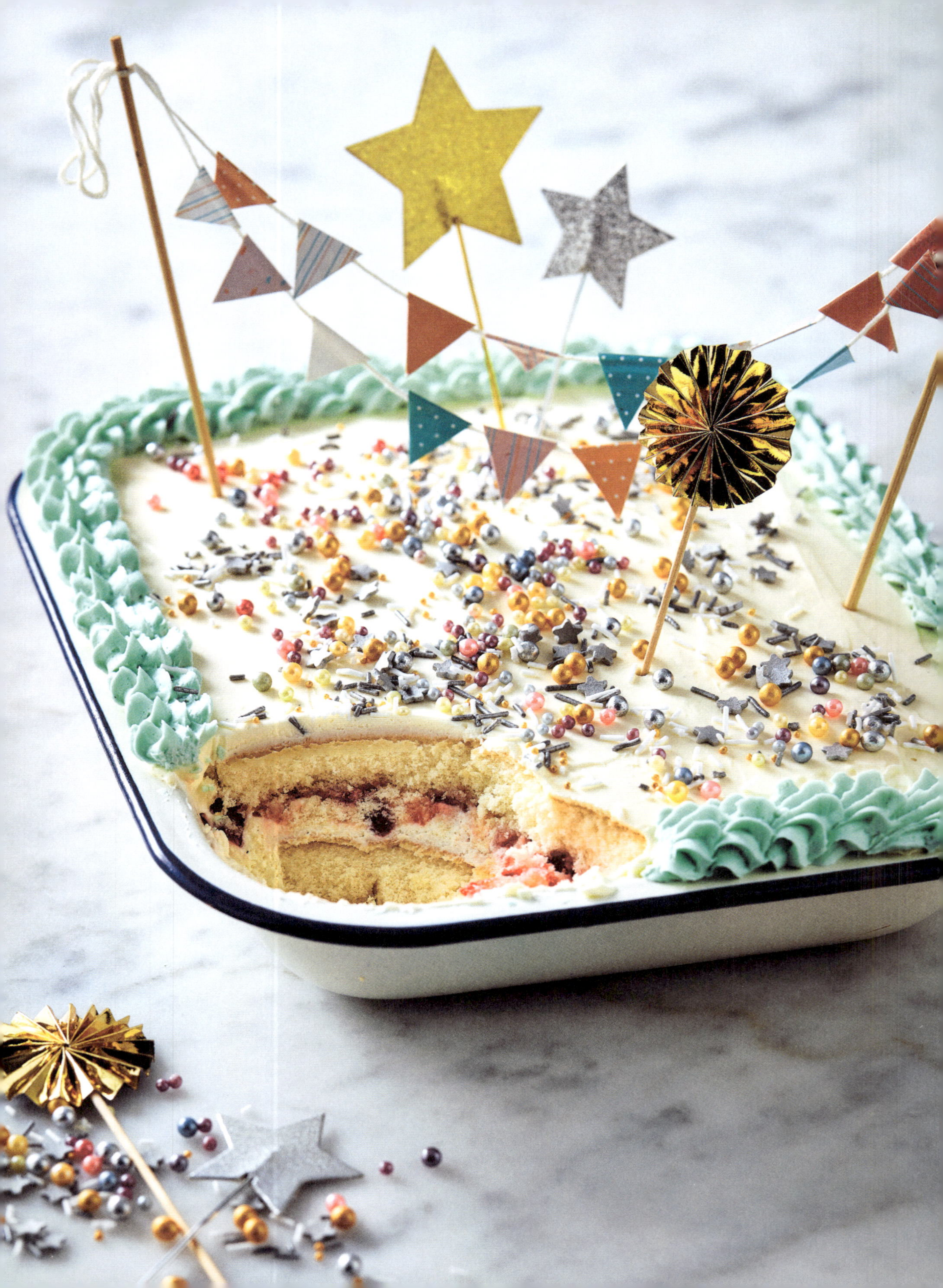

Birthday traycake

—

Serves 12
Prep 20 minutes

As a father of three, my life is now more full of birthday cakes than ever before. In search of something simple, portable and personal, but still enough of a celebration to mark a special day, I came up with this — the birthday traycake. Make it, stick it in the fridge, and transport it to the party on the floor of your car.

2 pre-made sponge cakes

2–3 cups mixed fresh fruit, diced

sprinkles and cake decorations, to decorate

CREAM CHEESE ICING

250 g (9 oz) cream cheese, softened

150 g (5½ oz) icing (confectioners') sugar

600 ml (20½ fl oz) thickened (whipping) cream

1 teaspoon vanilla bean paste

BUTTER ICING

100 g (3½ oz) butter, softened

200 g (7 oz) icing (confectioners') sugar

1 tablespoon hot water

½ teaspoon vanilla bean paste

gel food colouring, in your preferred colour(s)

For the cream cheese icing, use an electric mixer to whip the cream cheese and icing sugar together until smooth. Add the cream and whip to stiff peaks. Refrigerate until ready to use.

For the coloured butter icing, beat the butter and icing sugar together until combined, then add the hot water and vanilla and mix until smooth. Tint with your preferred food colouring and transfer to a piping (icing) bag.

Use a bread knife to cut the cakes into slices 2 cm (¾ in) thick.

Spread a thin layer of the cream cheese icing over the base of a serving dish. Cover with a layer of cake slices. You can cut smaller pieces of cake to fill any gaps. Add another layer of cream cheese icing, a layer of fruit, and then another layer of cake. Cover with cream cheese icing and smooth the top.

Scatter the top of the cake with sprinkles and decorate as desired. Finish by piping your preferred pattern of butter icing on top.

You don't need a knife to cut this cake. You just scoop out portions with a large spoon, so it's great for young kids.

TIPS This amount of butter icing makes enough to pipe the border of the cake once, with a bit left over. If you need more, or want to cover the whole cake with butter icing, make a double portion.

Cake purists frown on using non-edible decorations on a cake, but I can tell you from plenty of experience that kids are happy with a few extra toys and figurines if you want to use some to decorate the cake.

Gingerbread apple crumble

Serves 8
Prep 20 minutes
Cook 35 minutes
Rest 10 minutes

This spiced gingerbread crumble topping is a perfect match for slightly boozy baked apples. I don't mind leaving some of the peel on the apples, or even on all of them. It adds to the rough and rustic nature of this simple sweet.

2 kg (4 lb 6 oz) mixed apples, peeled (optional), cored and cut into 2 cm (¾ in) chunks

50 g (1¾ oz) soft brown sugar

50 g (1¾ oz) sugar

juice of 1 lemon

2 tablespoons brandy or dark rum (optional)

vanilla ice cream, to serve

GINGERBREAD CRUMBLE

200 g (7 oz) butter, cubed

150 g (5½ oz) soft brown sugar

2 tablespoons golden syrup, treacle or honey

2 cups (300 g/10½ oz) wholemeal (whole-wheat) flour

½ teaspoon baking powder

1 teaspoon ground ginger

½ teaspoon ground cinnamon

½ teaspoon salt flakes

¼ teaspoon ground cloves

¼ teaspoon ground cardamom

Heat your oven to 200°C (400°F) fan-forced.

Combine the crumble ingredients in a food processor and blend to a rough crumble. Alternatively, you can rub the butter through the other ingredients with your hands, or roughly mix them all together with a stand mixer.

Place the apples in a saucepan with the sugars, lemon juice and brandy, if using, over a medium heat. Gently cook for about 5 minutes until the apples are warm and slightly softened.

Tip the apple mixture into a baking dish, spreading it out evenly, then top with as much of the gingerbread crumble as you need.

Bake for 25–30 minutes until the crumble topping is well browned.

Remove from the oven and leave to rest for 10 minutes, then serve with ice cream.

TIP You can make individual crumbles if you prefer. Just reduce the cooking time to about 15–20 minutes.

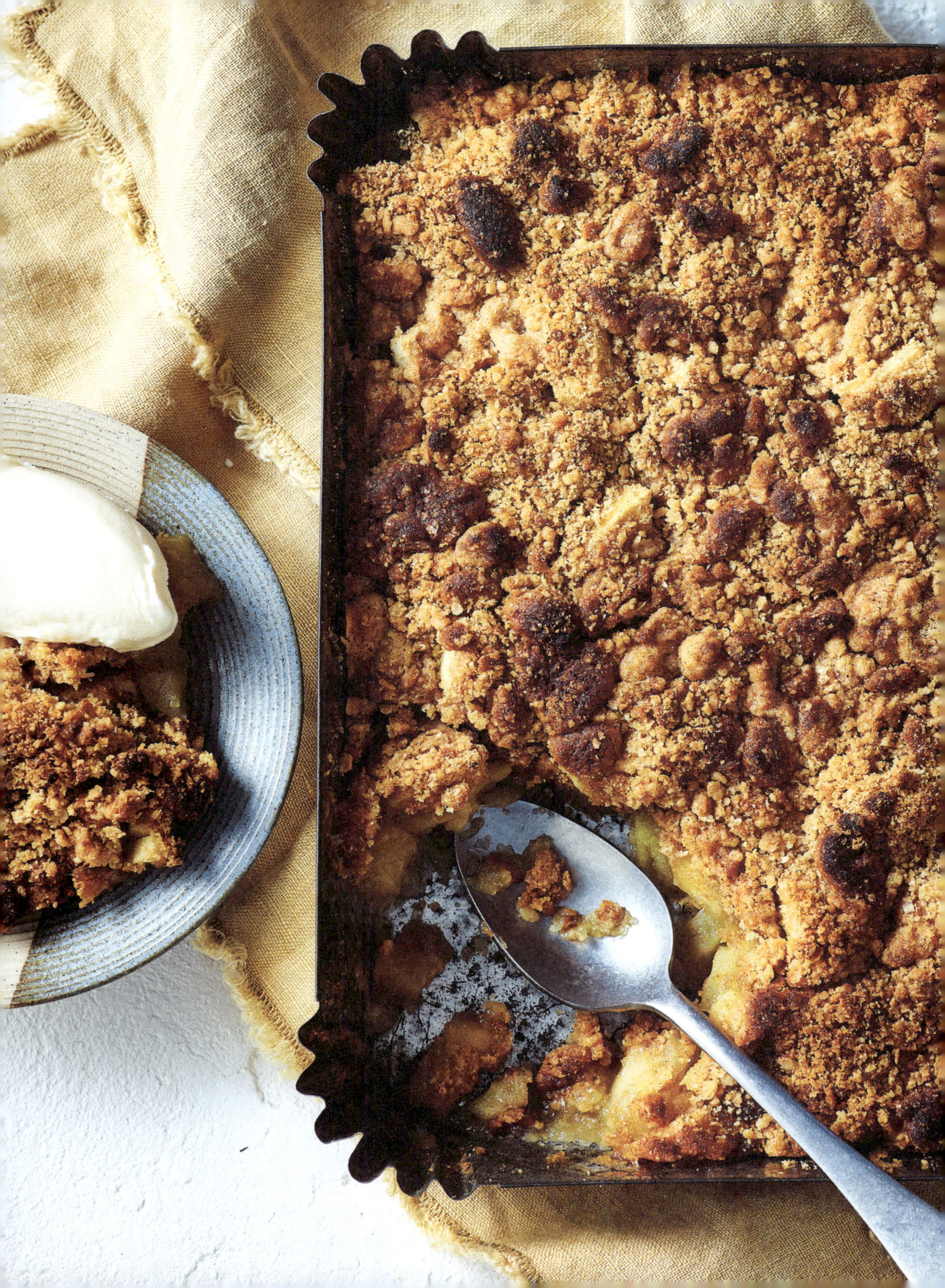

Danish butter cookie cupcakes

—

Makes 12
Prep 30 minutes
Cook 20 minutes

Those ubiquitous butter cookies packaged in blue biscuit tins were my favourites growing up. Here I've used them to create a cookie butter that we then turn into an icing for these delicious cupcakes. If you don't want to make your own cookie butter, you could use something like Biscoff's version instead.

100 g (3½ oz) unsalted butter, softened

100 g (3½ oz) caster (superfine) sugar

1 teaspoon vanilla bean paste

2 eggs

1 cup (150 g/5½ oz) self-raising flour

150 ml (5 fl oz) milk

½ teaspoon salt flakes

12 Danish butter cookies and 2 tablespoons pearl sugar, to decorate

BUTTER COOKIE BUTTER (MAKES EXTRA)

2 cups crumbled Danish butter cookies, plus extra to serve

50 g (1¾ oz) unsalted butter, softened

¼ cup (60 ml/2 fl oz) thickened (whipping) cream

½ teaspoon salt flakes

BUTTER COOKIE ICING

50 g (1¾ oz) unsalted butter, softened

150 g (5½ oz) butter cookie butter (from above)

50 g (1¾ oz) icing (confectioners') sugar

Heat your oven to 160°C (320°F) fan-forced.

For the cupcakes, cream the butter and sugar using a stand mixer fitted with the paddle attachment. Beat in the vanilla, then the eggs, one at a time. Fold in the flour and milk a little at a time until combined, then stir the salt through. Place 12 paper cupcake liners in a muffin tray and fill each about three-quarters full (see Tips). Bake for 20 minutes, or until a skewer inserted comes out clean. Cool completely on a wire rack.

For the butter cookie butter, place the cookie crumbs in a small food processor and process to a fine powder. Add the butter, cream and salt and process to a smooth butter; if necessary, add extra cream or milk to get the consistency of a thick but spreadable butter.

For the icing, whisk the butter and butter cookie butter using the whisk attachment of a stand mixer until smooth. Add the icing sugar and mix on low speed until incorporated, then increase the speed until the icing is fluffy. Transfer to a piping (icing) bag fitted with a star nozzle. Generously pipe the icing onto the cupcakes.

Top each cupcake with a butter cookie and a few pearls of sugar.

TIPS I like to use a piping (icing) bag to fill cupcake liners. The consistency of filling that a piping bag provides really does help give your cupcakes a good shape and rise.

You can use the cookie butter in lots of ways. Have it on toast, waffles or pancakes. Mix into a cheesecake. Serve with porridge or muesli. Drop scoops into the mix of a bread pudding ... and so on.

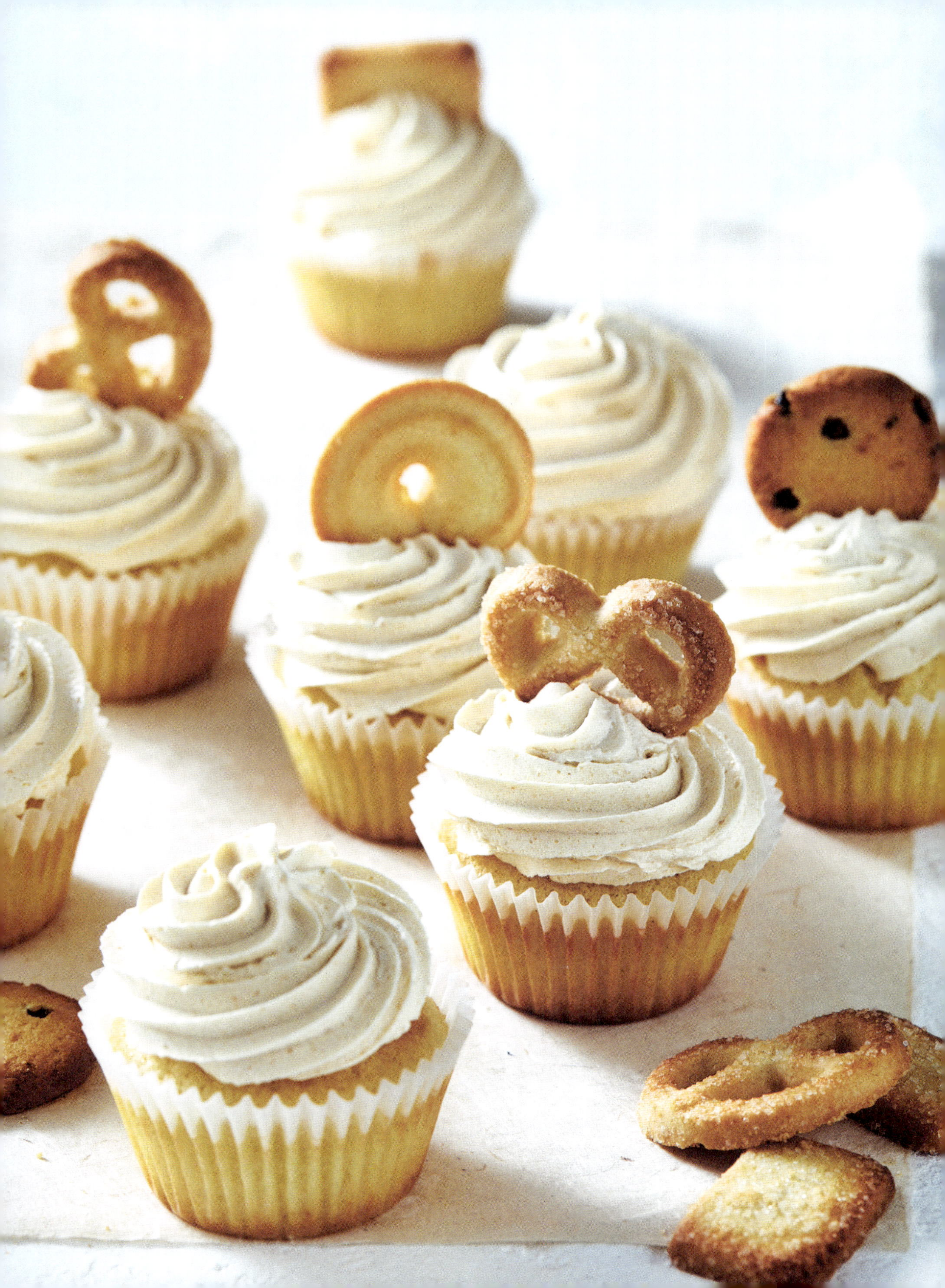

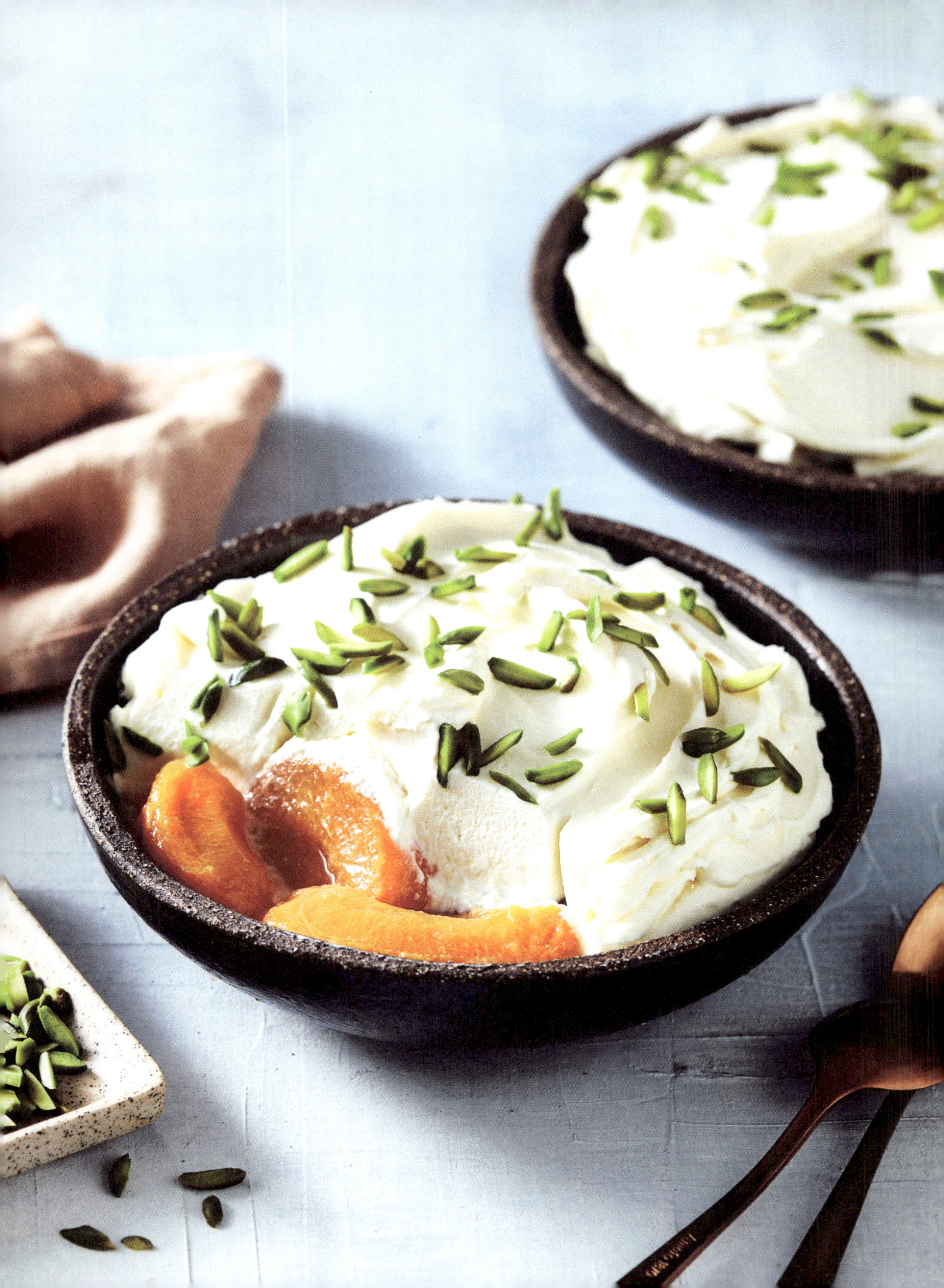

Roasted apricots with mascarpone & pistachio

—

Serves 6
Prep 20 minutes
Cook 30 minutes
Chill 2 hours

12 apricots, halved, stones removed

100 ml (3½ fl oz) white wine

2 tablespoons honey

2 star anise

300 ml (10 fl oz) thickened (whipping) cream

½ cup (60 g/2 oz) icing (confectioners') sugar

250 g (9 oz) mascarpone

75 ml (2½ fl oz) amaretto (optional)

½ cup (60 g/2 oz) crushed pistachio nuts

This is a dessert I inevitably make every stone fruit season. It's incredibly easy, very beautiful, and the combination of the slightly aniseedy apricots, almond-y amaretto and pistachio is just perfect.

Heat your oven to 200°C (400°F) fan-forced. Place the apricots in a baking dish, cut side up. Pour the wine and honey around and over the apricots. Add the star anise.

Roast the apricots for 30 minutes. Allow to cool completely, then refrigerate for about 1 hour until chilled.

Whip the cream and icing sugar together to soft peaks, then fold in the mascarpone and amaretto, if using, until well combined.

Remove the apricots to a smaller dish that will just hold them together. Spread the mascarpone mixture over them, then scatter the entire top with pistachio nuts.

Chill for at least a further hour, then serve.

TIP This recipe works fantastically well with just about any summer stone fruit, or even persimmons in autumn.

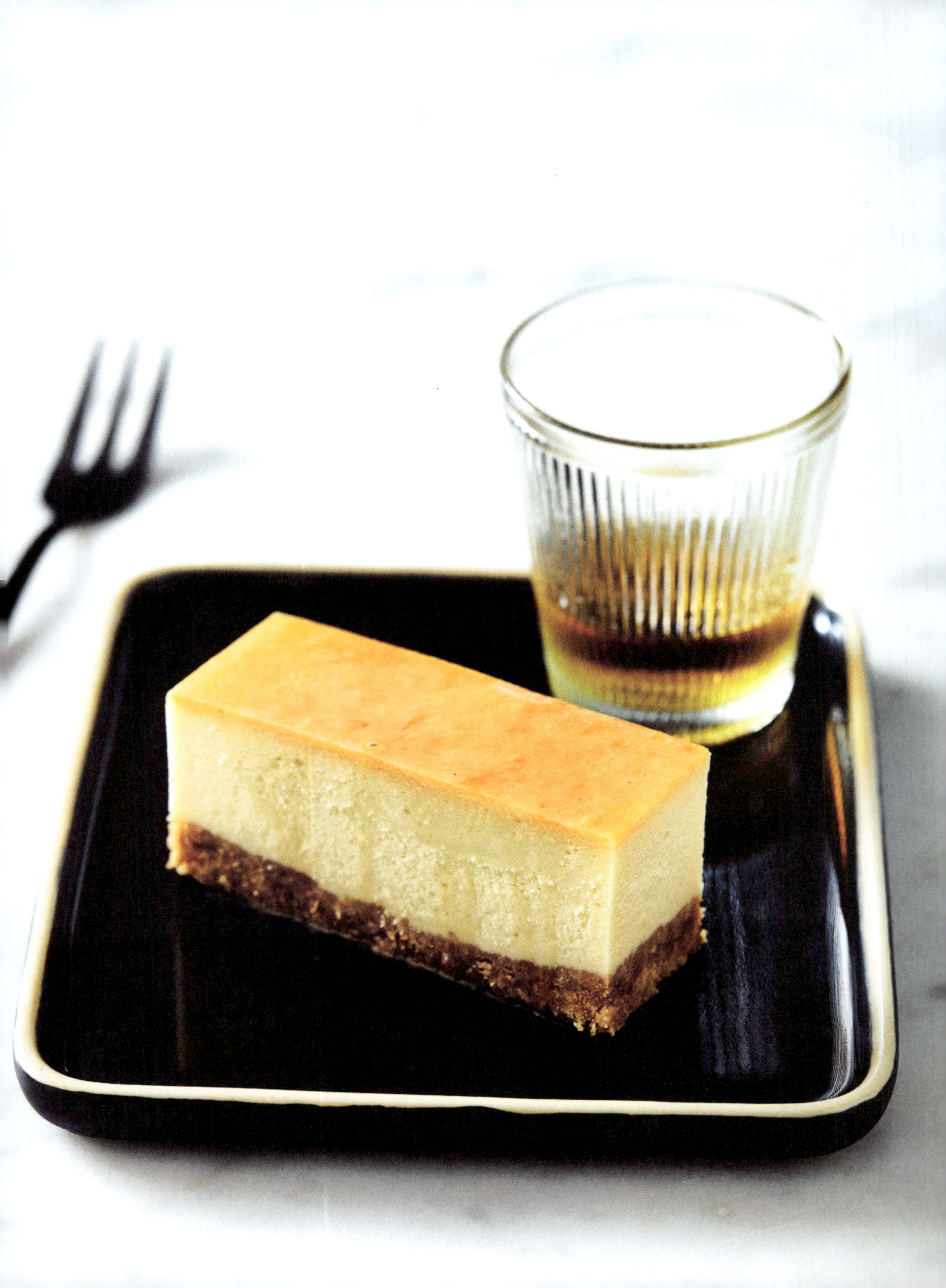

Single-malt cheesecake

—

Serves 6–8
Prep 30 minutes
Chill 30 minutes
Cook 1 hour 15 minutes
Stand at least 8 hours

There are three keys to this cheesecake: straining the thick filling through a sieve to remove any air bubbles, cooling in the oven to really develop the caramelised flavour, and then refrigerating the cheesecake for a day or so to really bring out its creamy texture.

6 wholemeal (whole-wheat) digestive biscuits

35 g (1¼ oz) unsalted butter, melted

sea salt, to taste

single-malt whisky, for drizzling

FILLING

½ cup (125 g/4½ oz) sour cream

250 g (9 oz) cream cheese

1 egg

50 g (1¾ oz) soft brown sugar

50 g (1¾ oz) caster (superfine) sugar

100 ml (3½ fl oz) thickened (whipping) cream

2 tablespoons single-malt whisky

1 teaspoon vanilla bean paste or vanilla extract

2 tablespoons cornflour (cornstarch)

Put the biscuits in a plastic bag and bash them. Tip the crumbs into a small bowl, pour the melted butter over, season with a pinch or two of sea salt and mix well. Line a 10 × 20 cm (4 × 8 in) rectangular loaf (bar) tin with baking paper and press the mixture well into the base of the tin. Chill in the fridge for 30 minutes to firm.

In a large bowl, mix the sour cream and cream cheese together using a spatula. Mix in the egg and sugars. Add the cream, whisky and vanilla and fold everything together. Stir in the cornflour, then pass the whole mixture through a fine sieve, spreading it over the biscuit base. Firmly tap the tray on the bench a few times to remove any air bubbles inside the filling.

Heat your oven to 160°C (320°F) fan-forced. Place the cheesecake tin in a larger baking tray. Pour boiling water into the baking tray, halfway up the side of the cheesecake tin.

Bake the cheesecake for 1 hour 15 minutes, or until the top is well browned. Turn off the oven, keep the door closed and leave the cheesecake undisturbed for at least 4 hours, but preferably overnight.

The next day, cover the cheesecake with foil and place in the fridge for another 4 hours (again, overnight is better) to set further.

To serve, cut the cheesecake into bars and drizzle with a tiny splash of whisky.

TIP I prefer to double the recipe and use a square 20 cm (8 in) tin. The cooking time remains the same — and if you can't eat it all, just give some to a friend.

A DAY IN THE LIFE OF THE COOK UP

I describe *The Cook Up* as being a bit like the proverbial duck swimming — on the surface everything looks effortless, but underneath we're paddling like heck to get the job done.

The 'day' starts long before the day in question, with months of pre-production needed to contact guests, write and test recipes, organise schedules and all the other things that go into making a television program.

As in any kitchen, getting the food ready starts days before, with ordering ingredients and preparing what we can to make each filming day go smoothly. Our fabulous back-of-house team — home economists, technical chefs, food producers, food assistants and dish washers — are miracle workers, putting together hundreds of completely different recipes from our hundreds of guests every season.

The studio crew day might start as early as 4am, setting up lighting and moving sets around a few hours before everyone else is in the kitchen. Then by around 6am the TV circus is in full swing, with camera operators, sound recordists, lighting, directors, producers, floor managers, runners and production assistants; everyone with a specific and essential job to do, and everyone needing to be coordinated with precision.

Then, even before the cameras start rolling, there's script reviews, ingredient checks, talking through the choreography of how an episode will flow, make-up checks, recipe edits — and after all that, when everything is checked, double-checked, confirmed and signed off, we're finally ready to welcome you to an episode of *The Cook Up*.

The Secret to Seasoning

I'm going to let you in on a secret that I think is the most important aspect of cooking, but one that is hardly ever properly explained.

The key to making food taste good is ... taste. Let me explain.

THE FIVE TASTES

We have five tastes — salt, sweet, sour, bitter and umami — and the reason for this is biological. Humans evolved these tastes to guide us towards foods that were good for us, and away from foods that are potentially harmful.

Salt is necessary for a wide variety of bodily functions.

Sweetness indicates the presence of calorie-rich sugars, and because we evolved from apes that mainly ate fruit, this balance between sweetness and sourness is fundamental to our understanding of what tastes good.

Bitterness warns us against poisons, but in an almost poetic quirk of the relationship between humans and the natural world, we are also blessed with an ability to learn to appreciate bitter foods, which is why as children we don't like brussels sprouts, but as adults many of us enjoy coffee, tea, beer, gin and any number of bitter foods.

Umami is the savoury taste that guides us towards cooked or fermented foods that are safe and nutritious.

But what does this have to do with cooking?

In cooking, we tend to confuse the terms 'taste', 'aroma' and 'flavour', which makes cooking seem a lot more complicated than it is. Aroma is our sense of smell — and you can smell literally millions of different things. Flavour is the word we give to the combination of different experiences including aroma, texture, and taste.

But taste itself has just five elements, and it is adjusting these five tastes that is the key to making great-tasting food.

SEASONING

In cooking, we call the adjustment of taste 'seasoning'. Our approach to seasoning varies a lot from culture to culture and family to family.

In the West, salt and pepper are the traditional seasonings found on many dining tables. In North Africa, you might find salt and cumin on a table instead. In South-East Asia, there might be fish sauce, sugar and vinegar to adjust the saltiness, umami, sweetness and sourness of dishes.

It's important, however, to draw the distinction between taste and aroma. The seasonings we commonly use don't have a strong aroma because they are focused on taste. You can't smell salt or sugar, for instance.

The contents of your spice rack, however, are more a matter of aroma. Add too much or too little cinnamon and a dish will just smell more or less like cinnamon, but it won't necessarily taste bad. Add too much or too little salt or sugar, and that's the difference between something tasting good or perhaps being completely inedible.

Next to your stove you'll usually find the seasonings you use most. Next to mine you'll find salt, pepper, sugar, vinegars, soy sauce and various wines. I use these to adjust the saltiness, bitterness, sweetness, sourness and umami-ness of the foods I cook.

TRAIN YOUR TASTE

When my grandmother taught me to cook, one of the most important lessons was teaching me how to taste. When she made something like spaghetti bolognese she'd invite me to taste it and ask me specifically — does it need more salt? Does it need sugar? Does it have 'enough taste'?

The key here is that she wasn't asking about the aromas. It was always about the five tastes. I wasn't tasting the bolognese to see if it needed more garlic or tomato, it was whether it needed salt, sugar or something else.

If it wasn't salty enough, she'd add salt. If it was too sour from the natural sourness of the tomatoes, a pinch of sugar could round it out. If it was too sweet, a bit more salt or a grind of bitter pepper could help. If it was too bitter she could add a pinch of salt or dash of vinegar for balance. If it didn't have 'enough taste', that would mean it was low in umami, and would need a dash of soy sauce, fish sauce, MSG or some other umami seasoning.

When most chefs talk about seasoning, they refer to salt (and sometimes pepper), but you need to expand your idea of seasoning to encompass all five tastes, not just one.

A MATTER OF BALANCE

The balance of these tastes might seem like an art or expertise, but the good thing is it comes naturally to us. Once you know what you're tasting for, the process of adjusting it is quite easy — you just make it taste good.

Saltiness is a basic seasoning in all cooking, and when a dish doesn't have enough salt it can taste insipid or weak, or perhaps sometimes a little too bitter or sweet. Recognising what a lack of salt tastes like is important, as adding in an extra pinch can improve just about any dish.

A balance of sweet and sour tastes is found in every cuisine in the world. Vietnamese nuoc cham, Chinese sweet and sour pork and Italian agrodolce are obvious examples, but it's also key to the balance in condiments such as tomato ketchup and mayonnaise. It's also the key taste balance in carbonated soft drinks, which gives you an idea of why they are such an attractive taste profile for children.

Balancing sweetness and sourness is simple. If it's too sour, add something sweet. If it's too sweet, add a little sourness from citrus juice or vinegar.

Bitterness is found in many ingredients, and bitter taste is also associated with the spiciness of things such as mustard, pepper and chilli. Spiciness, however, is not a taste but rather a feeling more similar to touch. As such, making something more or less spicy won't make it taste good or bad — just hotter or milder.

Umami is a more subtle taste than the other four, but is key to our cooking. It's created through the cooking process and is the reason we brown meats instead of boiling them. The chemical processes that turn meat brown are called Maillard reactions, and they create umami-tasting compounds in our food. A grilled steak tastes more strongly savoury than one that is raw or boiled.

Umami taste is also created through fermentation, drying and ageing, which is why we cook with wine and not grape juice, and why dried mushrooms, meats and seafood — and fermented sauces like soy, worcestershire and fish sauce — can add so much flavour to our food.

You might say that umami is the taste of cooking itself, as the processes that create it are the ones that we use to cook or otherwise manipulate our food.

SALT

Salt is the easiest taste to understand. It's essential to cooking, but it's also a matter of personal preference. Some prefer their food salted with a heavy hand, and others prefer a lighter style of seasoning. There are lots of different kinds of salt, and the saltiness of each will vary depending on its mineral composition and shape. Larger salt flakes will often taste less salty than salt that is finely ground, so it's important to be aware of this.

SWEET

Sweetness isn't just for desserts. It plays a very important role in savoury foods, too. A pinch of sugar added to a stew or stir-fry can help balance its taste, but there are plenty of other sources of sweetness that we can add to even out savoury foods, including honey, fruits and sweet wines.

SOUR

Sourness is a part of cooking we don't pay enough attention to. The cooking process can often dull the acids in our foods, and adding them back in can give a dish qualities we sometimes describe as 'freshness'. A splash of vinegar added at the end of cooking a stew or sauce will immediately lift it. Any number of dishes can be improved by a simple squeeze of lemon, or a few tart pickles.

BITTER

Bitterness is closely associated with the pungency or spiciness of foods such as onion, garlic, pepper and chilli. Both bitterness and pungency are defence mechanisms in the plant kingdom, but we add them to our foods for interest, and to give foods a mature complexity. A good grind of pepper can turn a kid-friendly pasta into something more adult, and bitter greens are the cornerstone of any grown-up green salad.

UMAMI

Umami is the taste of cooking itself, and we have built cuisines on its foundations. Anchovies, wine, fermented sauces and dried mushrooms are excellent sources of umami, and adding one or more of these to dishes can make a world of difference.

Menu Planner

While almost all of the recipes in this book are perfectly fine as standalone meals, if you want something a little more special, you can serve a few together and turn them into an occasion.

PIZZA NIGHT

Make a batch of the All-in pizza dough and Basic pizza sauce on pages 127 and 128, and you can make all of the pizzas that follow and more. After the last pizza has come out of the oven, throw in a big cookie for everyone to share.

Classic margherita pizza (page 129)
Bolognese pizza (page 134)
White mushroom pizza (page 133)
Double-chocolate skillet cookie (page 184)

SUPER SUNDAY ROAST

A Sunday roast is still an institution in our household. With only one oven, this takes a bit of management. Bake the cheesecake a day or two ahead, then on the day, roast the cauliflower first, then bake the chicken and wedges at the same time.

Roast chicken with whole mushroom sauce (page 83)
Roast cauliflower with zucchini cheese sauce (page 108)
Oven wedges (page 72)
Single-malt cheesecake (page 203)

DINER DINNER

If you've got oil in a pot to deep-fry one thing, you may as well make good use of it. Fry the beavertails first, then the broccoli.

Ten-minute cheeseburgers (page 63)
Spicy fried broccoli (page 116)
Maple butter & cinnamon beavertails (page 188)

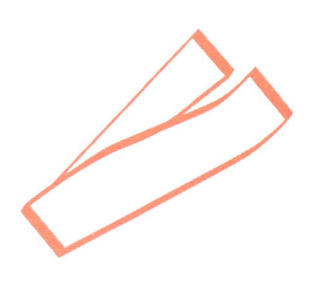

MIDWEEK MEAL

My grandmother taught me that a Chinese meal should always have an odd number of dishes. Here are three simple ones that only take minutes. Serve with steamed rice.

Tofu with sesame, garlic & chilli oil (page 119)
Chicken and leek (page 171)
Spring onion omelette (page 166)

VEGETARIAN BANQUET

This Asian banquet is full of flavour. Instead of ending with a prepared dessert, find some great fruits and put together a platter.

Dry-pot cauliflower (page 177)
Salt, pepper & seaweed tofu (page 106)
Shiitake, garlic & spring onion noodles (page 120)

A SPICY SITUATION

If you like a bit of heat, try this combination, served with steamed rice. I like to do the Vietnamese 'pizzas' on a barbecue outdoors.

Vietnamese 'pizzas' (page 52)
Prawns with chilli & basil (page 164)
Red curry roast cauliflower (page 100)
Roasted nut & caramel praline (page 191)

BRUNCH TIME

Brunch is an occasion I think we should all embrace at home. Easier than lunch, and at a more civilised hour than breakfast. Make the slice, pancake batter and apricots the day before, so all you have to do when guests arrive is fry the pancakes.

Ratatouille slice (page 103)
Falafel pancakes (page 20)
Roasted apricots with mascarpone & pistachio (page 201)

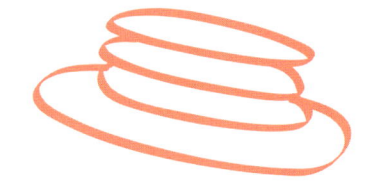

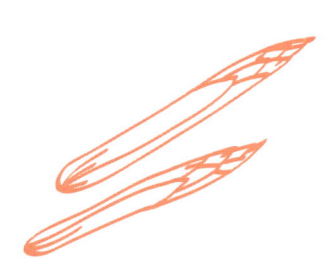

LAZY LUNCH

An open sandwich is great for a casual occasion. You don't eat it with your hands, but it's still not too fussy.

Beer-battered asparagus with curry salt (page 111)
Open steak sandwich with pickle persillade (page 54)
Strawberry & cream millefeuille (page 183)

CASUAL VEGETARIAN

I like the idea of basing a casual dinner party around a key ingredient when it's at its best. Make the salad in tomato season, and change up the dessert to use any late-season stone fruit.

Tomato & garlic bread salad (page 42)
Saffron risotto with roast tomatoes (page 104)
Roasted apricots with mascarpone & pistachio (page 201)

INDEX

A
All-in pizza dough 127
American burger sauce 63
anchovies: Midnight spaghetti 148
apples: Gingerbread apple crumble 196
apricots: Roasted apricots with mascarpone & pistachio 201
asparagus: Beer-battered asparagus with curry salt 111
avocado: Mexican noodles 151

B
baked beans, Red wine 114
Baked potato soup 37
bamboo steamers 51
bananas: Yemeni banana porridge 14
Barbecued chicken with charred greens & chimichurri 60
Basic pizza sauce 128
basil
    Classic margherita pizza 129
    Prawns with chilli & basil 164
    Ratatouille slice 103
    Rigatoni alfredo 139
    Roasted cherry tomato & olive fusilli 144
    Rosé prawn linguine 146
    rough salsa verde 139
    see also Thai basil
bean sprouts: Peanut lamb salad 48
beans
    Barbecued chicken with charred greens & chimichurri 60
    Red wine baked beans 114
beavertails, Maple butter & cinnamon 188
beef
    Black pepper beef noodles 160
    Bolognese pizza 134
    Japanese-style dry curry 68
    Lion's head meatball spaghetti 142
    lion's head meatballs 142
    Open steak sandwich with pickle persillade 54
    Potato gem shepherd's pie 81
    Rib-eye with creamy garlic prawns 77
    Spaghetti bolognese 136
    Stewed spinach & mince 78
    Ten-minute cheeseburgers 63
    Winter beef & silverbeet stew 71
beer
    Beer-battered asparagus with curry salt 111
    Welsh rarebit ham sandwich 28
Birthday traycake 195
bitter 208–10, 214
Black pepper beef noodles 160
black pepper sauce 160
black vinegar sauce 172
Bloody Mary bacon & egg sandwich 19
bloody Mary sauce 19
Bolognese pizza 134
brassicas 112

bread
    Bloody Mary bacon & egg sandwich 19
    Midnight spaghetti 148
    Mushrooms on parmesan toast 39
    Open steak sandwich with pickle persillade 54
    Spicy fried broccoli 116
    Ten-minute cheeseburgers 63
    Tomato & garlic bread salad 42
    Welsh rarebit ham sandwich 28
    Yemeni banana porridge 14
broccoli
    Spaghetti bolognese 136
    Spicy fried broccoli 116
    Tempered roast vegetables 112
broccolini: Barbecued chicken with charred greens & chimichurri 60
brussels sprouts
    Tempered roast vegetables 112
burger: Ten-minute cheeseburgers 63
butter cookie butter 198
butter cookie icing 198
butter icing 195
butters
    butter cookie butter 198
    Chocolate peanut butter 16
    maple butter 188
    mustard & parmesan butter 54
    smoked paprika butter 104

C
cabbage
    Chicken & sausage poule au pot 46
    Tempered roast vegetables 112
    Tonkatsu ribs 93
cakes
    Birthday traycake 195
    Danish butter cookie cupcakes 198
    Honey crackle cake 187
    Panettone con gelato 192
    Single-malt cheesecake 203
capers
    Chicken Marbella 66
    Midnight spaghetti 148
    Rigatoni alfredo 139
    rough salsa verde 139
capsicums
    Black pepper beef noodles 160
    Dry-pot cauliflower 177
    Fireworks 159
    Jambalaya-style sausage rice 94
    Pork with black vinegar & green peppers 172
    Ratatouille 45
    Ratatouille slice 103
caramelised onions 54
carrots
    Chicken & sausage poule au pot 46
    Japanese-style dry curry 68
    Noodles marinara 174
    Peanut lamb salad 48
    Potato gem shepherd's pie 81

Red wine baked beans 114
Spaghetti bolognese 136
turning 86
Winter beef & silverbeet stew 71
Winter lamb shank navarin 86
cauliflower
    Chinese cauliflower 177
    Dry-pot cauliflower 177
    Red curry roast cauliflower 100
    Roast cauliflower with zucchini cheese sauce 108
    Tempered roast vegetables 112
celery
    celery salt 19
    Chicken & sausage poule au pot 46
    Jambalaya-style sausage rice 94
    Japanese-style dry curry 68
    Noodles marinara 174
    Potato gem shepherd's pie 81
    Red wine baked beans 114
    Spaghetti bolognese 136
cheese
    Birthday traycake 195
    Bloody Mary bacon & egg sandwich 19
    Bolognese pizza 134
    Classic margherita pizza 129
    cream cheese icing 195
    Fried egg & chilli linguine 140
    Lion's head meatball spaghetti 142
    mascarpone cream 183
    Mexican noodles 151
    Mushrooms on parmesan toast 39
    mustard & parmesan butter 54
    Open steak sandwich with pickle persillade 54
    Ratatouille slice 103
    Rigatoni alfredo 139
    Roast cauliflower with zucchini cheese sauce 108
    Roasted apricots with mascarpone & pistachio 201
    Saffron risotto with roast tomatoes 104
    Single-malt cheesecake 203
    Strawberry & cream millefeuille 183
    Ten-minute cheeseburgers 63
    White mushroom pizza 133
    white sauce 133
cheesecake, Single-malt 203
chicken
    Barbecued chicken with charred greens & chimichurri 60
    Chicken & mushrooms 156
    Chicken & sausage poule au pot 46
    Chicken 65 168
    Chicken Marbella 66
    Chicken and leek 171
    Double coriander chicken 163
    Roast chicken with whole mushroom sauce 83
    Ssamjang chicken 74
chicken marinades 156, 171
chickpeas: Falafel pancakes 20

chillies
  bloody Mary sauce 19
  Chicken 65 168
  Double coriander chicken 163
  Dry-pot cauliflower 177
  Falafel pancakes 20
  Fried egg & chilli linguine 140
  green mustard 64
  Kansas City–style rub 93
  Kashmiri chilli powder 168
  Korean chilli powder 116, 168
  Mexican noodles 151
  Midnight spaghetti 148
  Oven wedges 72
  Peanut lamb salad 48
  Prawns with chilli & basil 164
  quick chilli oil 119
  Roast pork belly with green mustard 64
  Roasted cherry tomato & olive fusilli 144
  ssamjang 74
  Ssamjang chicken 74
  Steamed prawns with glass noodles 51
  Tempered roast vegetables 112
  Tofu with sesame, garlic & chilli oil 119
  Tomato & garlic bread salad 42
  turmeric eggs 24
chimichurri 60
Chinese cauliflower 177
chives
  Ginger pork skewers 89
  Tomato & garlic bread salad 42
chocolate
  Chocolate peanut butter 16
  Double-chocolate skillet cookie 184
  Panettone con gelato 192
choy sum: Black pepper beef noodles 160
chutney, stalk 71
cinnamon sugar 188
Classic margherita pizza 129
coconut
  Double coriander chicken 163
  Red curry roast cauliflower 100
cold-proving dough 127
cookies
  Danish butter cookie cupcakes 198
  Double-chocolate skillet cookie 184
coriander
  Double coriander chicken 163
  Falafel pancakes 20
  green mustard 64
  Mexican noodles 151
  Noodles marinara 174
  Red curry roast cauliflower 100
  Roast pork belly with green mustard 64
  Stewed spinach & mince 78
  Vietnamese 'pizzas' 52
corn: Red curry roast cauliflower 100
cream cheese icing 195
cream, mascarpone 183
crumble, Gingerbread apple 196
cucumber: Peanut lamb salad 48
cupcakes, Danish butter cookie 198

curries
  Japanese-style dry curry 68
  Red curry roast cauliflower 100
curry leaves
  Chicken 65 168
  Tempered roast vegetables 112
curry salt 111

D
Danish butter cookie cupcakes 198
dates: Yemeni banana porridge 14
dill
  Hot smoked salmon kedgeree 24
  Seafood & dill pie 90
Double coriander chicken 163
Double-chocolate skillet cookie 184
dough
  All-in pizza dough 127
  cold-proving dough 127
dressing, peanut 48
dry curry, Japanese-style 68
Dry-pot cauliflower 177
Dutch-process cocoa powder 16

E
eggplant
  Japanese-style dry curry 68
  Ratatouille 45
  Ratatouille slice 103
  Spaghetti bolognese 136
eggs
  Bloody Mary bacon & egg sandwich 19
  Japanese-style dry curry 68
  Fried egg & chilli linguine 140
  Green eggs & ham breakfast roll 22
  Hot smoked salmon kedgeree 24
  Prawns with chilli & basil 164
  Ratatouille slice 103
  scrambled eggs 22
  soy-cured egg yolks 40
  Spring onion omelette 166
  Stamina-don 40
  turmeric eggs 24
  Vietnamese 'pizzas' 52

F
Falafel pancakes 20
Fireworks 159
fish
  Noodles marinara 174
  Seafood & dill pie 90
  see also anchovies, salmon
five tastes, the 208
flour, strong 127
French toast 192
Fried egg & chilli linguine 140
fruit: Birthday traycake 195

G
Garlic butter salmon 84
ginger
  Black pepper beef noodles 160
  Chicken & mushrooms 156
  Chicken 65 168
  Chicken and leek 171
  Dry-pot cauliflower 177
  Fireworks 159

  Ginger pork skewers 89
  Gingerbread apple crumble 196
  Hot smoked salmon kedgeree 24
  Noodles marinara 174
  seasoned sweet soy sauce 174
  Stamina-don 40
  Steamed prawns with glass noodles 51
  Vietnamese 'pizzas' 52
Green eggs & ham breakfast roll 22
green mustard 64

H
honey
  Honey crackle cake 187
  Roasted apricots with mascarpone & pistachio 201
  Tomato & garlic bread salad 42
  Yemeni banana porridge 14
Hot smoked salmon kedgeree 24

I
ice cream: Panettone con gelato 192
icing
  butter cookie icing 198
  butter icing 195
  cream cheese icing 195

J
Jambalaya-style sausage rice 94
Japanese-style dry curry 68

K
kale: Winter lamb shank navarin 86
kangkung see water spinach
Kansas City–style rub 93
Kashmiri chilli powder 168
kedgeree, Hot smoked salmon 24
Korean chilli powder 116

L
lamb
  Peanut lamb salad 48
  Potato gem shepherd's pie 81
  Winter lamb shank navarin 86
leeks: Chicken and leek 171
lemongrass: Red curry roast cauliflower 100
lemons
  bloody Mary sauce 19
  Chicken 65 168
  Gingerbread apple crumble 196
  Hot smoked salmon kedgeree 24
  peanut dressing 48
  Rigatoni alfredo 139
  rough salsa verde 139
  tarator sauce 20
  Tomato & garlic bread salad 42
lettuce: Ten-minute cheeseburgers 63
lime leaves see makrut lime leaves
Lion's head meatball spaghetti 142

M
Maillard reactions 210
makrut lime leaves: Red curry roast cauliflower 100
mantecare 104
maple butter 188
Maple butter & cinnamon beavertails 188

marinades
  chicken marinade 156, 171
  meat marinade 160
  pork marinade 159
marinara mix 90
mascarpone cream 183
meatballs, lion's head 142
menu planner 216–7
Mexican noodles 151
Midnight spaghetti 148
millefeuille, Strawberry & cream 183
miso: Ssamjang chicken 74
mushrooms
  Chicken & mushrooms 156
  microwaving 39
  Mushrooms on parmesan toast 39
  Red curry roast cauliflower 100
  Roast chicken with whole mushroom sauce 83
  Shiitake, garlic & spring onion noodles 120
  Spaghetti bolognese 136
  White mushroom pizza 133
mustard & parmesan butter 54

N

noodles
  Black pepper beef noodles 160
  Mexican noodles 151
  Noodles marinara 174
  Shiitake, garlic & spring onion noodles 120
  Steamed prawns with glass noodles 51
  vermicelli noodles 51
nori
  Salt, pepper & seaweed tofu 106
  Stamina-don 40
nuts
  Chocolate peanut butter 16
  Double-chocolate skillet cookie 184
  peanut dressing 48
  Peanut lamb salad 48
  Roasted apricots with mascarpone & pistachio 201
  Roasted nut & caramel praline 191
  Stewed spinach & mince 78
  Yemeni banana porridge 14

O

oil, quick chilli 119
olives
  Chicken Marbella 66
  Roasted cherry tomato & olive fusilli 144
omelette, Spring onion 166
onion béchamel 90
onions, caramelised 54
Open steak sandwich with pickle persillade 54
Oven wedges 72

P

pancakes
  Falafel pancakes 20
  Perfect pancakes 30
Panettone con gelato 192
parsley
  chimichurri 60
  pickle persillade 54
  rough salsa verde 139
  stalk chutney 71
pasta
  Fried egg & chilli linguine 140
  Lion's head meatball spaghetti 142
  Mexican noodles 151
  Midnight spaghetti 148
  Rigatoni alfredo 139
  Roasted cherry tomato & olive fusilli 144
  Rosé prawn linguine 146
  Spaghetti bolognese 136
peanut dressing 48
Peanut lamb salad 48
peas
  Japanese-style dry curry 68
  Potato gem shepherd's pie 81
Perfect pancakes 30
pickle persillade 54
pies
  Potato gem shepherd's pie 81
  Seafood & dill pie 90
pizzas
  All-in pizza dough 127
  Basic pizza sauce 128
  Bolognese pizza 134
  Classic margherita pizza 129
  pre-made pizza bases 134
  Vietnamese 'pizzas' 52
  White mushroom pizza 133
pork
  Baked potato soup 37
  Bloody Mary bacon & egg sandwich 19
  Dry-pot cauliflower 177
  Fireworks 159
  Ginger pork skewers 89
  Green eggs & ham breakfast roll 22
  Jambalaya-style sausage rice 94
  Lion's head meatball spaghetti 142
  Pork with black vinegar & green peppers 172
  Roast pork belly with green mustard 64
  Spaghetti bolognese 136
  Stamina-don 40
  Tonkatsu ribs 93
  Vietnamese 'pizzas' 52
  Welsh rarebit ham sandwich 28
pork marinade 159
porridge, Yemeni banana 14
potatoes
  Baked potato soup 37
  Bloody Mary bacon & egg sandwich 19
  Chicken & sausage poule au pot 46
  microwaving 37
  Oven wedges 72
  Potato gem shepherd's pie 81
  Winter beef & silverbeet stew 71
praline, Roasted nut & caramel 191
prawns
  Prawns with chilli & basil 164
  Rib-eye with creamy garlic prawns 77
  Rosé prawn linguine 146
  Seafood & dill pie 90
  Steamed prawns with glass noodles 51
prunes: Chicken Marbella 66
Puftaloons 27

Q

quick chilli oil 119

R

radicchio: Open steak sandwich with pickle persillade 54
Ratatouille 45
Ratatouille slice 103
Red curry roast cauliflower 100
Red wine baked beans 114
Rib-eye with creamy garlic prawns 77
rice
  cooking basmati rice 24
  Hot smoked salmon kedgeree 24
  Jambalaya-style sausage rice 94
  Saffron risotto with roast tomatoes 104
  Stamina-don 40
Rigatoni alfredo 139
risotto, Saffron, with roast tomatoes 104
Roast cauliflower with zucchini cheese sauce 108
Roast chicken with whole mushroom sauce 83
Roast pork belly with green mustard 64
roast tomatoes 104
Roasted apricots with mascarpone & pistachio 201
Roasted cherry tomato & olive fusilli 144
Roasted nut & caramel praline 191
rocket salad 39
roll, Green eggs & ham breakfast 22
Rosé prawn linguine 146
rosemary
  Potato gem shepherd's pie 81
  Ratatouille 45
  Red wine baked beans 114
  Winter lamb shank navarin 86
rough salsa verde 139
rub, Kansas City–style 93

S

Saffron risotto with roast tomatoes 104
sake
  Ginger pork skewers 89
  sesame sauce 119
  Stamina-don 40
salads
  Peanut lamb salad 48
  rocket salad 39
  Tomato & garlic bread salad 42
salmon
  Garlic butter salmon 84
  Hot smoked salmon kedgeree 24
salsa verde, rough 139
salt 208–11
salt, curry 111
Salt, pepper & seaweed tofu 106
sandwiches
  Bloody Mary bacon & egg sandwich 19
  Green eggs & ham breakfast roll 22
  Open steak sandwich with pickle persillade 54
  Welsh rarebit ham sandwich 28
sauces
  American burger sauce 63
  Basic pizza sauce 128
  black pepper sauce 160

black vinegar sauce 172
bloody Mary sauce 19
chimichurri 60
green mustard 64
onion béchamel 90
pickle persillade 54
rough salsa verde 139
seasoned sweet soy sauce 174
sesame sauce 119
ssamjang 74
stalk chutney 71
tarator sauce 20
white sauce 133
scones: Puftaloons 27
scrambled eggs 22
seafood
    Noodles marinara 174
    Seafood & dill pie 90
    store-bought marinara mix 90
    see also fish, prawns
seasoned sweet soy sauce 174
seasoning, the secret to 208–15
seaweed *see* nori
sesame sauce 119
shepherd's pie, Potato gem 81
Shiitake, garlic & spring onion noodles 120
silverbeet
    stalk chutney 71
    Winter beef & silverbeet stew 71
Single-malt cheesecake 203
skewers, Ginger pork 89
smoked paprika butter 104
Sopa seca de fideos 151
soup, Baked potato 37
sour 208–10, 213
soy-cured egg yolks 40
Spaghetti bolognese 136
spice mixes
    curry salt 111
    Kansas City–style rub 93
    spice mix 116
Spicy fried broccoli 116
spinach
    Barbecued chicken with charred greens & chimichurri 60
    Green eggs & ham breakfast roll 22
    Peanut lamb salad 48
    Stewed spinach & mince 78
    see also water spinach
spring onions
    Barbecued chicken with charred greens & chimichurri 60
    Black pepper beef noodles 160
    Dry-pot cauliflower 177
    Jambalaya-style sausage rice 94
    Noodles marinara 174
    Peanut lamb salad 48
    Salt, pepper & seaweed tofu 106
    seasoned sweet soy sauce 174
    Shiitake, garlic & spring onion noodles 120
    Spring onion omelette 166
    ssamjang 74
    Stamina-don 40
    Steamed prawns with glass noodles 51
    Tofu with sesame, garlic & chilli oil 119
    Vietnamese 'pizzas' 52

Ssamjang chicken 74
stalk chutney 71
Stamina-don 40
Steamed prawns with glass noodles 51
Stewed spinach & mince 78
stews
    Chicken & sausage poule au pot 46
    Winter beef & silverbeet stew 71
stir-fries
    Black pepper beef noodles 160
    Chicken with leek 171
    Chicken & mushrooms 156
    cutting ingredients for 172
    Double coriander chicken 163
    Dry-pot cauliflower 177
    Fireworks 159
    Noodles marinara 174
    Pork with black vinegar & green peppers 172
    Prawns with chilli & basil 164
    Stamina-don 40
    stir-fry tips 159
Strawberry & cream millefeuille 183
strong flour 127
sweet 208–10, 212
sweet potatoes: Oven wedges 72

T
tarator sauce 20
taste, balancing 210
tasting 209
Tempered roast vegetables 112
Ten-minute cheeseburgers 63
Thai basil
    Prawns with chilli & basil 164
    Red curry roast cauliflower 100
thermometers 191
thyme
    Mushrooms on parmesan toast 39
    Ratatouille 45
    Ratatouille slice 103
    Red wine baked beans 114
    White mushroom pizza 133
    Winter beef & silverbeet stew 71
    Winter lamb shank navarin 86
toast, Mushrooms on parmesan 39
tofu 48, 106
    Lion's head meatball spaghetti 142
    Peanut lamb salad 48
    Salt, pepper & seaweed tofu 106
    Tofu with sesame, garlic & chilli oil 119
tomatoes
    Basic pizza sauce 128
    Bloody Mary bacon & egg sandwich 19
    bloody Mary sauce 19
    Bolognese pizza 134
    Classic margherita pizza 129
    Hot smoked salmon kedgeree 24
    Jambalaya-style sausage rice 94
    Japanese-style dry curry 68
    Lion's head meatball spaghetti 142
    Mexican noodles 151
    Midnight spaghetti 148
    peeling 151
    Potato gem shepherd's pie 81
    Ratatouille 45

Ratatouille slice 103
Red curry roast cauliflower 100
Red wine baked beans 114
roast tomatoes 104
Roasted cherry tomato & olive fusilli 144
Rosé prawn linguine 146
Saffron risotto with roast tomatoes 104
Spaghetti bolognese 136
Ten-minute cheeseburgers 63
Tomato & garlic bread salad 42
Winter beef & silverbeet stew 71
Winter lamb shank navarin 86
Tonkatsu ribs 93
turmeric eggs 24
turnips: Winter lamb shank navarin 86

U
umami 208–10, 215
    for stir-fries 171

V
Vietnamese 'pizzas' 52

W
water spinach: Red curry roast cauliflower 100
wedges, Oven 72
Welsh rarebit ham sandwich 28
White mushroom pizza 133
white sauce 133
wine
    Chicken & sausage poule au pot 46
    Chicken Marbella 66
    Lion's head meatball spaghetti 142
    Potato gem shepherd's pie 81
    Red wine baked beans 114
    Rib-eye with creamy garlic prawns 77
    Roast chicken with whole mushroom sauce 83
    Roasted apricots with mascarpone & pistachio 201
    Saffron risotto with roast tomatoes 104
    Seafood & dill pie 90
    Winter beef & silverbeet stew 71
    Winter lamb shank navarin 86
Winter beef & silverbeet stew 71
Winter lamb shank navarin 86
wok cooking tips 159

Y
Yemeni banana porridge 14

Z
zucchini
    Lion's head meatball spaghetti 142
    Potato gem shepherd's pie 81
    Ratatouille 45
    Ratatouille slice 103
    Roast cauliflower with zucchini cheese sauce 108
    Spaghetti bolognese 136

About Adam

Adam Liaw is a writer, cook, television presenter and former lawyer. He is host of the SBS series *The Cook Up* and the award-winning *Destination Flavour*. Adam is the author of seven cookbooks and is UNICEF Australia's National Ambassador for Nutrition. He cooks dinner for his family every night.

Thank You

The most heartening part of making *The Cook Up* is watching how it has grown into a community, and the credit for that must go to you, the viewers. Without you tuning in every night to watch us on screen, we wouldn't be able to do what we do, so first and foremost I'd like to thank you all for embracing *The Cook Up* so completely. We're truly humbled by the response we get from you every night.

Hundreds of people work on *The Cook Up* – camera crew, control room, styling, hair and make-up, kitchen team, set design, production, editing, lighting, sound and photography – and we do it to hopefully make your nightly meals a little easier and a little more enjoyable. I'd like to thank all of the crew for their efforts, and for being fantastic to work with. It makes such a difference knowing that you can turn up to the kitchen every day and be surrounded by friends.

Thank you also to our guests, who bring us new food, new perspectives and new personalities that make every one of the hundreds of episodes we have made a unique and exciting proposition. I learn so much from you, about cooking and life.

Thank you to *The Cook Up's* management team of Emily Griggs, Damien McDermott, Bruce Walters, Sophie Johnston, Samantha De Alwis, Suresh Devadas, Kate Nicholls and Vanessa Miles for the constant dedication to making what I think is the best cooking show I've ever been involved in.

When it comes to putting together this book, it's fabulous to work with a team that just gets it. From the food to the message to the art, you just get it all. Many thanks to Michael Harry, Roxy Ryan, Anna Collett, George Saad, Katri Hilden and the whole team at Hardie Grant, and to the magnificent team of Steve Brown, Bernadette Smithies, Kay Wijaya and Chui Lee Luk, who make every dish look (and taste) incredible.

And last but certainly not least, the hugest of thanks must also go to my manager, Melita Hodge, for guiding the ship through all of this. I'm constantly in awe of what we're able to achieve.

Published in 2022 by Hardie Grant Books,
an imprint of Hardie Grant Publishing

Hardie Grant Books (Melbourne)
Wurundjeri Country
Building 1, 658 Church Street
Richmond, Victoria 3121

Hardie Grant Books (London)
5th & 6th Floors
52–54 Southwark Street
London SE1 1UN

hardiegrantbooks.com

Hardie Grant acknowledges the Traditional Owners of the country on which we work, the Wurundjeri people of the Kulin nation and the Gadigal people of the Eora nation, and recognises their continuing connection to the land, waters and culture. We pay our respects to their Elders past and present.

All rights reserved. No part of this publication may be reproduced, stored in a retrieval system or transmitted in any form by any means, electronic, mechanical, photocopying, recording or otherwise, without the prior written permission of the publishers and copyright holders.

The moral rights of the author have been asserted.

Copyright text © Adam Liaw 2022
Copyright photography © Steve Brown, Kitti Gould 2022
Copyright illustrations © George Saad 2022
Copyright design © Hardie Grant Publishing 2022

A catalogue record for this book is available from the National Library of Australia

Tonight's Dinner 2
ISBN 9781 74379 904 8

10 9 8 7 6 5 4 3 2 1

Publisher: Michael Harry
Project Editor: Anna Collett
Editor: Katri Hilden
Designer: George Saad
Photographer: Steve Brown
Set photography: Kitti Gould
Stylist: Bernadette Smithies
Home economists: Kay Wijaya & Chui Lee Luk
Production Manager: Todd Rechner

Colour reproduction by Splitting Image Colour Studio
Printed in China by Leo Paper Products LTD.

MIX
Paper from responsible sources
FSC™ C020056

The paper this book is printed on is from FSC™-certified forests and other sources. FSC™ promotes environmentally responsible, socially beneficial and economically viable management of the world's forests.